THE CALL OF ENGLAND

IN CARLISLE CATHEDRAL

THE
CALL OF ENGLAND

BY

H. V. MORTON

'An island like a little book
Full of a hundred tales. . . .'
—G. K. CHESTERTON

WITH EIGHT PLATES IN COLOUR, EIGHT OTHER
ILLUSTRATIONS AND A MAP

SIXTH EDITION

METHUEN & CO. LTD.
36 ESSEX STREET W.C.
LONDON

First Published	. . . . . .	June 7th 1928
Second Edition	. . . . .	November 1928
Third Edition	. . . . .	March 1929
Fourth Edition	. . . . .	August 1929
Fifth Edition	. . . . .	February 1930
Sixth Edition	. . . . .	1930

PRINTED IN GREAT BRITAIN

TO
F. Y. D.

INTRODUCTION

THIS book, like its companion *In Search of England*, is the record of a rather haphazard motor-car holiday in spring. It is a queer mixture. In the earlier book I deliberately shirked realities. I made wide and inconvenient circles to avoid modern towns and cities. I went through Lancashire without one word about Manchester and Liverpool. I devoted myself entirely to ancient towns and cathedral cities, to green fields and pretty things.

This book is an attempt to give a more general view of England, town and country. You will find in it the past and the present, cathedrals and factories, town walls and rag markets—the wandering of St. Columba's dead body through Anglo-Saxon England is separated by only a few pages from an account of a golf-ball factory in Birmingham !

This may displease the tourist, but the traveller may see in it an attempt to present a fair and accurate picture of Old and New England. England is an incredible jumble of romance and reality.

In the other book I dwelt mainly in the south and the west, rushing, rather wildly, through the north. In this book I linger in the north. I hope that many London motorists may be encouraged to go north instead of south and west, which, at the present moment, they do instinctively. No man who wishes to understand the country in which he lives can neglect the north of England. Almost within our time we have seen a great re-grouping in the distribution of human energy, comparable only perhaps with the switchover of our ports in medieval times from the east to the west coast. The Industrial Revolution, while it has planted an enormous population in the north, has at the same time distorted our ideas of that part of the country. We are inclined to think of the north as an extended Sheffield. The symbol of the north is the chimney-stack. It is only when we go there that we realize how very slightly the age of coal and steel has deformed the green beauty of England. Our manufacturing districts, vast as they are, form merely a scratch on the map in comparison with those miles of wild and romantic country, whose history and beauty rival anything the south can boast.

The intelligent traveller will find it stimulating to talk to the men of Manchester, Liverpool, Birmingham and Sheffield and he will also discover, with perpetual pleasure and, I think, astonishment, that the north of England offers wider solitudes, more rugged beauty, more old castles and abbeys than the south. He will discover in the Peak District of Derbyshire a marvellous wilderness as desolate as Dartmoor; in Yorkshire he will find little market towns in whose corners lurk the last vestige of the eighteenth century; in Lancashire he will find shepherds and their lambs within sound of the cotton looms; along the Northumbrian coast he will enter a district whose romantic wildness cannot be surpassed in any part of England.

H. V. M.

May 1928

CONTENTS

LIST OF ILLUSTRATIONS

       * *From water-colour drawings by Frank Southgate, R.B.A.*
       † *From water-colour drawings by Walter Dexter, R.B.A.*

THE
CALL OF ENGLAND

CHAPTER ONE

I HEAR THE CALL OF ENGLAND AND SET OUT ON NEW ADVEN-
TURES. DESCRIBES HOW I ESCAPE FROM LONDON, GO
TO THE CONFESSOR'S CHURCH NEAR HAVERING-ATTE-
BOWER, EAT EGGS AND APPLE-TART IN AN ESSEX COTTAGE,
AND COME AT LENGTH, AND BY NIGHT, TO COLCHESTER

§ I

ON one of those gold mornings which April borrows from June, I set out alone in search of new adventures. And as I steered my slow and careful way out of London the joy of the road and the freedom of the days ahead sang wildly in my blood, so that I looked back on the myself of yesterday as a prison visitor regards a man who is serving a life sentence. It is easier to go to Lisbon on business than to go to Lincoln on pleasure, at least so it seems to me. In foreign countries one's daily life is out of sight and out of mind ; but a busy man who—let me whisper it—has no right to leave London in a whimsical hurry, is, while in England, still within the awful radius of his responsibilities. He can, in an emergency, reach home within a few hours, from any part of this country, and every morning, until the marks of his harness fade from his hide and he starts to prance and curvet like a colt let loose, he turns anxiously to his news-papers with the feeling that something may have happened to drag him back to duty.

What a joy, though, is the silly schoolboy humour which creeps over a man on his second day out of London ! What splendid loneliness ! What amusing, and even startling, conversations with himself in churchyards, meadows, woods, and other solitary places ! How much of Hamlet, how much of Quixote, how much of Robin Goodfellow is in him never appears until a man finds himself alone in the country.

One grave error of civilization is that we are seldom allowed to be alone. We react like steel filings to the magnetism of a multitude. Our thoughts and our expressions are never quite our own. We know so many people better than we know ourselves. Rarely indeed can we achieve that amused detachment from life which permits us to sit in the stalls and at the same time to take a leading part in the play ! More generally we see ourselves against a background of our making. We the architects ; we the mighty ones ! I remember years ago meeting in the hop-fields of Kent, near Faversham, a slum-bred boy ; and he was frightened of the stars ! At home, among the street-lamps of Whitechapel, however, he was, I have no doubt, the leader of some Arab gang.

As I was passing through Forest Gate and Ilford it occurred to me that the art of travel is lost in these days. What matters so enormously in all real journeys is not the arrival, because the beginning and the middle of all journeys are far more important than the end. The trouble with modern travel is that there is no beginning or middle. A man says suddenly :

' I'll go to Rome ! '

He turns into an office in Piccadilly, buys a little book full of coupons, one for his bed, one for his dinner, his breakfast, his luncheon ; then he catches a train at Victoria and in a few hours finds himself in Rome wearing the same mind. This sort of thing is as useless to the soul as a funicular railway. Our great-grandfathers knew more about travel when they took coach from London to Bath than we when we go to Shanghai or Cape Town. Nothing happens on most long journeys except deck quoits and indigestion.

The other day I bought three brown and tattered travel books from a stall in the Charing Cross Road. They were published between the years A.D. 1600–1700. They deal with quite simple journeys such as that to Egypt and the Ægean, but all three authors begin their travels more or less after the manner of one of them, a certain Martin Baumgarten, who says :

' In the year of Christ 1507 in the month of April, I, Martin Baumgarten, having Invok'd the Divine Assistance

and Conduct, set out from home accompanied by Vincentius
a priest, and one servant named George.   We took our
way to Venice.'

I like the idea of invoking the Divine Assistance in a journey
to Venice !   How large and wonderful the world was in the
sixteenth century.

Some dim perception that journeys should be adventurous
seems to be creeping into the minds of tourist agents.   It will
hardly be believed, but it is a tragic fact, that a man who is
interested in taking rich men and women into the Sahara said
to me not long ago :

' I feel,' he said, nibbling his cigar thoughtfully, ' that there
is great scope for some new stunt in desert travel.   I've
thought about getting a party lost for a few days.   I might
even arrange for a few tame Touregs to attack the motor-
cars—using blank cartridge, of course !   Can't you imagine
how people would talk about that when they got home ?
What an advertisement ! '

Then he looked offended and asked why the devil I was
laughing !

But there was nothing to laugh at !   It would not surprise
me to know that a new profession was born at that moment :
the young sheik—' University man essential '—who will
disappear with American heiresses for 5,000 francs per
elopement.

All the time the real adventures are on the way to anywhere, they are in our heads and hearts, they lurk at the
edges of little English woods and lie in wait on those straight
roads of England which, beginning with the tramp of legions,
have borne the weight of history for two thousand crowded
years.

I think too that any man has done well if, on his return
from a journey, he can truthfully say :

' I have had an exciting time : I have met—myself ! '

§ 2

All roads out of London look the same.   Once you have
shaken off the city, comes the inner slum belt, then the outer
suburbs, then the post-war ' model estates ' and lastly the
ancient towns and villages which have surrendered to London
and have been assimilated by it.   These also, on their own

responsibility, fling out satellite ' model estates ', but to what ' model ' they owe allegiance is, like themselves, a speculation. They are redeemed, however, by the newly married and by the glimpse they afford of mothers and first-born.

Between Ilford and Romford the London atmosphere becomes thin. You begin to feel the country ahead. Between Romford and Brentwood you touch real fields ; and here, just beyond the new community of Gidea Park, you strike that well-worn Roman road which led from London to the great city, Colonia Camulodunum, called by us Colchester.

Now at Romford I turned to the right and soon found myself in the ancient village of Hornchurch. In olden times the spire of the church served as a landmark for the Thames pilots. It is the only church in the country which bears over its east window not a cross but the pagan symbol of a bull's head and horns.

Learned men have fought about this decoration for centuries. Some say that it is the symbol of Jupiter, others that it commemorates the village's ancient tanneries (the High Street was formerly called Pelt Street), others, less imaginative, say that it merely perpetuates the name of an ancient lord named Horn.

' All I can tell you,' said an old man in the churchyard, ' is that we had the head down in 1921 for cleaning and we found that it was made of stone but the horns are made of copper and they are hollow. . . .'

I thanked him.

Some day I mean to collect all the legends within a twenty-miles' radius of Charing Cross. Among them will be the legend of Hornchurch. They say that not long after that time when a man could walk through London and see black-berries growing over the ruins of Roman houses, Edward the Confessor, that monkish King, built himself a retreat—or bower—at Havering-atte-Bower, which lies near Hornchurch but on the north side of the Roman road.

Now, until the time of Henry II the church at Hornchurch was known as Havering Church ; and the story is as follows : When this church was being consecrated by the Confessor an old beggar-man of princely bearing approached the King and prayed for alms in the name of God and St. John the Evangelist. The King had no money in his pouch, which is usual with kings and millionaires, but he removed the ring from his finger with the words : ' Have a ring ! ' The old man accepted the gift and was seen no more in those parts. He had, however, been the means of christening them—Havering.

Some years afterwards a party of English pilgrims on their way to Jerusalem were lost at nightfall, and as they huddled together in the desert place they saw approaching them, far off, a procession clothed in white, moving with lit tapers and followed by an ancient and princely man. They set off towards the procession and overtook it. The ancient man inquired from what country they had come. When he learned that they were from England he asked them to follow him. He led them to a shining city in which they were lodged in great comfort and given strange and delicious foods. In the morning the ancient man saw them on their way. He told them that he was St. John the Evangelist, saying :

' Say ye, untoe Edwarde your King, that I grete hym well by the token that he gaaf to me this ryng with hys own handes, at the hallowyng of my chirche ; which rynge ye shall deliver hym agayn, and say ye to hym that wythin six monethes he shall be in the joye of heven wyth me, where he shall have his rewarde for his chastite and for his good lyvinge.'

When the pilgrims reached the shores of England they sought out the King and found him in his bower at Havering. They gave the ring to him and the message. The story goes that soon afterwards Edward the Confessor fell sick and died on January 5, 1066 and was buried in Westminster Abbey, where he lies to this day.

The ring of Edward the Confessor is that placed to-day on the finger of the Kings of England at their coronation. Edward must have had more than one ring, however, because tradition insists that the fine sapphire set clear in the cross-paté on top of the King's State Crown was once set in a ring belonging to Edward and in later years taken from his tomb in the abbey. It is supposed to possess magic power, and among its accomplishments is the strange but useful one of curing the cramp !

I sat in the quiet church recalling all this story, so sweet from the early morning of our history ; I walked round the churchyard which until 1410 was the burial ground of Romford and until 1718 that also of Havering ; then I walked up High Street—which is really Pelt Street—hating, as I hate the men who say that her ladyship never rode naked through

Coventry and that Alfred never burnt the cakes, those nosey, confounded, restless, archaeological busybodies who say that Havering has nothing to do with rings but is derived from the Saxon ' haefer ', a goat, and ' ing ', a meadow.

Well—they can have their goat, while I, well on the Chelmsford Road, take joy in the other story.

§ 3

The sun passed behind a cloud, the rain fell and birds sang loudly as if to drown the patter on the young green leaves. The sunlight suddenly returned and the rain, now falling thinly and without enthusiasm, ended as sharply as it had started. I looked to the west and saw a rainbow spring out of the flat lands from the direction, as near as I could guess, of Bishop's Stortford, and, striding the sky to the east, lose itself probably in the North Sea.

What a miraculous freshness there is in the air after these quick spring showers, such a good smell of earth like newly pulled mushrooms, such a busy-ness of insects, such a renewed brightness of grass, and everywhere, small, sparkling globes of rain running greasily, like quicksilver, down the broad leaves in hedge and garden.

I stopped at a cottage on the Colchester road and asked for food. The woman who came to the door said, with a broad Essex accent, that she could not feed me. I pointed with a betrayed expression to a windy sign which creaked and flapped on rusty hinges bearing the word ' Refreshments '. Many cottagers seem to think that motorists require a Mansion House state luncheon, every day of their lives. Cyclists, on the other hand, are credited with a taste for eggs ; grubby young men with loam on their boots and books of verse in their pockets and arguments in their eyes, who lean their knapsacks on the fence when they talk, are known to consider bread and cheese the romantic meal it is ; but because a man goes hooting along the roads in a petrol machine, doing nothing physically to earn a square meal for his body, such simple people are frequently abashed in his presence and even when he says, with sincere emphasis, that he loves nothing on this earth better than a great fat hunk of bread with a thick slab of yellow cheese sitting on top they profess embarrassment and blushing, say: 'Oh well, if you dont *mind* ', or ' Oh, if you *mean* that. . . .'

The end of it was that her good natured, pleasant face broke into a smile and she said that well—let her think, a minute now ! Yes ; her might have eggs maybe, and bread and butter maybe, and cheese maybe, and maybe a slice of cold apple-tart left over from Sunday ! All the time she was talking I was thinking that no country on earth contains so many fine ordinary people. Give me the English country people for honesty, fine manners and sheer goodness before any race on earth !

I entered the cottage and she led me to a door on the right which resented her attempt to open it. I knew that it was that sacred mausoleum called the ' parlour '. There is no greater contrast in a dwelling than that brink between the comfortable, warm, food-smelling, human kitchen-living-room in an English cottage and the harsh, austere apartment, remote, museum-like, cold, uncomfortable, which only opens its door with alacrity to a funeral or a wedding party. Parlours are enormously interesting rooms containing, as they do, all that seems precious, sacred or beautiful in humble lives.

This room was true to type. It smelt of carpet and funeral bake meats, black gloves and old men. The stand-offish horse-hair chairs grouped themselves self-consciously as if their arms held ghosts. The mahogany table was covered with a maroon cloth picked out at the corners with coloured wool, and a queer religious-looking piano was packed away in a corner. It had an open-work front and behind this it wore a faded green satin shirt. All it knew of music, I think, was : ' O God, our help in ages past ' with one finger.

Such rooms give away much in their pictures. There were the usual family groups taken on emotional occasions. I noticed the pleasant woman, much younger and wearing a large black hat, sitting beside an incredibly stupid-looking young man whose hair because it was parted in the middle and plastered down only accentuated the fact that on normal occasions it was not parted or plastered but just rose like a bush from his skull. He looked in his high collar like a horse peering over a gate. His broad, capable hands were set one on each knee and he gazed into the eye of the camera just as a cow looks with a sort of dull interest if you stop and say a few words to it over a hedge. Both of them, then, had entered the dangerous state of matrimony in bovine magnificence. Behind them, painted on a back-cloth by a photographer who must have been a bit of a comedian, rose the towers and gables of a ducal mansion.

There were older photographs than this, faded old records of bearded men with guns under their arms and cloth caps on their heads ; women in tight, high-necked gowns of black. Above the little door was the glaring enlargement of a young man in khaki and near it the official card sent out by the War Office to notify parents that their boys had died for England. The little cottage had played its part in history.

The pictures were all morbidly devout. One showed a young girl with streaming hair, dressed in what appeared to be a nightdress, flying through the air over a sleeping city towards a rift in the sky which was obviously the door of heaven. The only books in the room were a dictionary, a book on the South African War, a novel by Marion Crawford and another entitled *Straight Paths and Crooked Ways*, by Mrs. H. B. Paull. This novel seemed to deal intimately with high life :

‘ After tearful farewells ’, I read, opening the book at random, ‘ which Hugh took care should finish with a laugh, Ralph and his bride entered the carriage, and the pair of greys pranced and curvetted as they moved off amidst a shower of old shoes. Ralph and Florence rode in silence for some minutes listening for the chime of the bells. At last Ralph drew Florence nearer to him as he said : “ There’s a silver lining to every cloud, darling. I should not have been brought up in England, nor have been acquainted with my precious Florence, but for my mother’s mistake. . . .” ’

What this mistake was I shall, probably, never know because the door opened and in came the good woman with a tray.

As I ate this meal I looked through the small window to the main road. A geranium leaf tapped the glass and the wind blew in violent gusts, driving the flowers in the window-box to a sudden swaying. Was London really only a few hours away down the road ? I asked myself. I had made the break. I was free ! Outside the magnetic field ! I was bound for open country. . . .

‘ How incredible,’ I thought, as I tapped an egg, ‘ that in Ludgate Circus now the crowds are swarming, the policemen holding back the traffic, the eager, anxious men and women looking for their chance to cross the road in safety, the newsboys rushing up the street with the latest unimportance ! '

I lit a pipe and strolled out into the hall. Through an open door I saw the woman crossing a yard carrying a heavy pail. She allowed me to take it from her, unwillingly she did it because she was not used to being helped. We crossed the yard and came to a magnificent accouchement. Lying in a patch of sun in a sty was a Burne-Jones sow with ten fleshy piglets attached to her, small pink things no larger than kittens, but legged and snouted for the great battle of life. When the mother sow heard the sound of the bucket against her sty she rolled her small eyes under their white lashes and, grunting a warning, rose flinging her hungry ones from her, scattering them pell-mell as a dinner party would be scattered if the table rose suddenly on end and left the room.

' The pear-tree will be out soon,' said the woman.

' It will,' I said. ' Another week of sunlight.'

' It's always first out about here,' she said.

I looked round me. The ' bread and cheese ' was out on the hawthorn ; new rushes sprang from a tiny streamlet that ran gurgling past the garden fence, a hen and her chickens stood in the little yard, the mother with wings trembling, ready to give all her young people shelter, making an experienced clucking all the time which they, running here, there and everywhere, stumbling over on their thin, long indiarubber legs, answered with shrill cheep-cheeps in which one could read confidence, surprise, pain and alarm. The sun was just warm on the back of my hand.

I looked down into the sty and smiled. The babies, after a moment of confused indignation, had massed again and advanced on motherhood with that undeniable instinct for self-preservation which is in other nurseries mistaken for love. The woman was smiling too. It was a day for smiling with the sun warm and such an eager pressing of youth in the world, such an irresistible feel of life in the air, of sticky green sap rising in the trees and millions of tight buds uncurling, millions of leaves. . . .

§ 4

Colchester is a busy town set on a hill and surrounded by a pinkish wall erected about eighteen hundred years ago by the ex-soldiers of Rome. Its ancient churches are built of Roman tiles ; its Norman castle is built of the debris of the Roman citadel ; its streets are not winding and medieval but run north and south after the plan of a Roman camp. And if you take a spade and dig in Colchester you find, below innocent-looking cabbage patches and beneath ordinary simple gardens, that Rome still sleeps only a few feet deep in a white powder of decayed oyster shells. Those oysters must have compensated many a miserable exile !

It was during the war, when stationed at Colchester for some time and moved by a mighty ennui, that I started digging at the end of a tennis lawn and came, at the close of a hot afternoon, to a beautiful Roman pavement of red and white terrerae. How the sun shone again on the bright cubes which had known the tread of sandals !

What a thrill exists in uncovering the everyday things of the past, of handling them fresh from the earth, of feeling the link that binds the present to the past, of saying : ' When this was made Nero was Emperor and men still lived who had seen the Crucifixion. . . .'

In another garden I found slim bronze pins with which the Roman ladies dressed their hair. I found a bronze mirror in which some unknown Roman wife examined the effect of British winds upon her complexion. I found Samian pottery marked with the maker's name and notably the work of one Flavius Germanus, previously unknown to Colchester, which was deemed worthy of inclusion in the Castle Museum. Those were great days. I shall never be so thrilled again ! It was good to sit on the edge of the excavation all alone—for who, in an army mess, believed that these discoveries were genuine ! —and surrounded by old iron keys, bits of chain, bronze ear picks, scraps of iridescent bottles, to build up pictures of their day, lovingly to replace them in life and to draw from them, it seemed, some part of their life, so that there were long hours in which I ceased to exist and had almost projected myself into the ancient world.

To climb out of that trench after a day's digging was always like awakening from a dream.

*   *   *

I arrived in Colchester as the sun was setting and decided to stay the night there. In the morning, after visiting the

Castle and the Siege House, I took the field-path to Lexden which overlooks the Colne Valley. We used to morse with flags across this valley during the war. I suppose the Romans also signalled from these heights.

Weeks of rain followed by warm spring days had caused the soft earth in the hedge banks to crumble, with the result that large stones were pushed from the soil by their own weight and lay at the foot of the hedge. I always treat broken earth in Colchester with respect. I remembered the American who once said that you had ' only to tickle Colchester with a spade and it coughed up bits of Rome.' My comment is that you do not always need a spade : a walking-stick is often as effective.

As I walked along, prodding the earth here and there with my stick, I was delighted and not too surprised to see a touch of bright red in the brown soil. I placed my stick in the earth slightly above this red streak and flicked out upon the narrow path the base of a Samian bowl with the potter's name neatly inscribed in Roman capitals upon it. The letters I read when I had wiped the caked clay and soil from the potsherd were SEVERUS. F. The F. stands for *fecit*, so the inscription reads : ' Severus made it.'

The well-known Roman potters—and hundreds of them are known with the localities of their factories, the dates they exported their various specialities to the most remote corners of the Roman Empire—invariably signed their plates, bowls and vases in this way, or their names in the nominative followed by F. for *fecit,* or their names in the genitive preceded by OF. (*officina*, or workshop), or followed by the letter M. (for *manus*, or ' by the hand of ').

And so I stood polishing the little chip of ancient Rome with a handkerchief, marvelling that through the hazards of eighteen centuries it should yet exist to fall out of a hedge with its message : ' Severus made it.' What a message to receive from an English hedge on a windy April morning !

Severus was one of the famous East Gaulish potters of the time of Nero. Galley-loads of his bright red wares were shipped to Britain. The shops stocked it in Colonia, which is Colchester ; in Londinium ; in Verulamium, which is St. Albans ; in Deva, which is Chester ; in Eboracum, which is York. Traders carried it by pack-horse up to the great Wall of Hadrian where we may imagine it decorating the tables of the better sort. Most of this ware was made in Gaul. Severus had his workshop on the Rhine at Neuss, which was then Novaesium, one of the oldest towns in Germany.

When I held this relic in my hand I saw again so clearly the Britain with which it was linked, the misty island mentioned so casually by Suetonius, Dion Cassius and Tacitus, three writers whose business-like sentences seem to blow aside the fog of history for a second to show us legions marching through Kent and Essex, heavy war galleys creeping like water beetles up wide river estuaries, cavalry scouts picking their way gingerly through marsh and forest, coming to hill-top villages fenced with wattle and desolate, for the tribes had fled to the forests, there to hide themselves from the Eagles and to bide their time.

In this fog the war horns of the legions low like bulls and grow fainter to the north, while behind them on hills beside rivers, sound the carpenter's hammer, the wood-cutter's axe, the stone-mason's chisel, the song of galley-slaves at the anchorages and, at last, the voice of a merchant praising his goods . . . London.

So England emerges from the mist.

In those days Colonia Camulodunum, or Colchester, was more important that the jerry-built trading post on the Thames. I like the story of the foundation of Colchester.

The Emperor Claudius who, if the court gossip reported so eagerly by Suetonius may be believed, was a stupid old man, desired in a moment of ambition to take his place beside the conquerors. No one had invaded Britain since Julius Caesar, nearly a century since. Why not ? Strange how great events sometimes hang on feeble pegs !

So Claudius issued orders to the admirable old general and senator, Aulus Plautius, to prepare three legions on the Rhine and one in Pannonia for service in Britain. When the news was broken to the troops they grumbled. Eventually they mutinied. Historians state that they cried out that they would not make war out of the compass of the world. No doubt they did. Memories die hard in crack regiments and perhaps some lingering recollection persisted of Julius Caesar's inconclusive invasions a century earlier. We must remember also that after Augustus settled the encampments of legions they no doubt regarded a settled home as a birthright. Tiberius moved only one legion during his long reign ! The

THE OLD SIEGE HOUSE, COLCHESTER

legionaries, their wives and families formed a great town round which was clustered the allotments of the ex-soldiers, the fathers and grandfathers of the legion. To ask such a community with years of settled habit to its credit to uproot itself and invade Britain was rather like asking a comfortable market-town of to-day to ship itself suddenly to Alaska! So the troops murmured and downed spears. Even the popular old general, Aulus Plautius, could do nothing with them.

At this moment the Master of the World in Rome made one of those brilliant mistakes which justify stupidity. He dispatched his favourite freed-man, the powerful Narcissus, to recall the legions to a sense of duty. The soldiers took one look at him and hated him on three scores : he was a Greek, he was a promoted servant, he was a civilian! No sooner had he mounted the general's tribunal and stretched forth a white hand for silence than a great roar of derision went up from the troops and the cry ' Io Saturnalia ! ' That surely must have pierced his soul ! As if to make the insult more effective the legions formed ranks at once without hearing his address and placed themselves under their general. So the British Expeditionary Force was ready. Such were the men who planted the seeds of London and Colchester, whose feet trod out the roads we use to-day, whose hands mapped out England.

What an important sight it was which met the eyes of watchers on the cliffs at Boulogne one morning in August eighteen hundred and eighty-five years ago as the Roman Fleet set out for Britain with auxiliaries, horse and foot, and the four legions : the IInd, the Augusta ; the XXth, the Valeria Victrix ; the XIVth, the Gemina Martia, and the IXth, the ill-fated Hispania which was cut up and destroyed in Britain in the reign of Hadrian. Two of these legions, the IInd and the XXth, were destined to remain in England for four hundred years. They were going—though they knew it not—home. We still find in English meadows the bricks and tiles they made, the altars which they erected to propitiate local deities stood for centuries in groves and valleys and at the edge of woods and beside the little brown trout-streams of the north. How little they knew as they eased their chin-straps, and made the same mordant jokes about a soldier's life which all expeditionary forces make, that they were setting out to dig the foundations of a country which men would some day compare to their own magnificent and omnipotent Rome.

They landed without opposition, and, moving up through Kent, fought two actions, one on the Medway, the other on the Thames, somewhere near the Celtic trading post of Lyn-dyn, a lake fort of no importance. Now Claudius—and this is the part I enjoy—told his general that when victory was within sight he was to hold his hand and send back to Rome for his Imperial master who would at once hasten to Britain and take all the credit ! (Perhaps he did not put it so frankly !) This was the moment chosen by Plautius to dispatch messengers for Claudius. Some say that he had suffered badly from the British attacks and needed the rein-forcement of the Praetorian Guard. How amazing to think of the Praetorian Guard marching through Kent !

Then in Rome was prepared one of the most astonishing pageants which ever trod an English meadow. The Emperor set out from Ostia with an immense retinue. He took with him the Praetorian Guard and a phalanx of elephants. Accompanying him were many senators. How grimly Julius Caesar would have smiled !

The royal entourage sailed to Marseilles and then made its way through France partly by land and partly on the rivers. This took them nearly three months. They embarked at Boulogne, landed in Britain and joining the main legions marched, with the Caesar at the head, on Colchester. Can we imagine a more remarkable sight than that which terrified the Britons as the Roman army advanced in order of battle against the little town on the hill ? We know how the elephants of Pyrrhus frightened the hard-bitten Roman troops when they saw these beasts—' Lucanian oxen ', they called them—for the first time. How much greater must have been the terror of the poor Britons as they watched the elephant corps advance, swaying their painted flanks, whip-ping the air with their raddled trunks, which, in British eyes, must have appeared to writhe like scarlet serpents, trumpeting and bellowing with rage, maddened by drink, tossing trees from their path over their vast backs, lowering tusks encased in long sheaths of spiked metal red with the blood of men and horses, twining their trunks round some speechless victim and lifting him up for dispatch to the Indian mahouts who crouched between the great ears in a nest of ostrich feathers.

Behind the phalanx tossed the plumes of the cohorts

with the high dust of cavalry above them ; and then with linked shields, the legions, the eagles and the standards borne above the spears. Surrounded by his Praetorians rode the Emperor Claudius in unaccustomed general's uniform, and with him the grave senators and a brilliant head-quarters staff. . . .

That night, as the Roman sentries paced the ramparts of the camp which is now Colchester, lights burned in the imperial marquee ; the moon, if moon there was, shone on the massed standards before it. Inside, his armour cast aside, Caesar reclined at a contest for which he was by nature and practice better fitted than for battle. For him it was an uncomfortable and an expensive picnic. Perhaps he tasted his first British mushrooms that night. No doubt his cooks in search of their master's favourite dish had searched the Essex fields where the small white buttons grow before the mist is off the grass on autumn mornings. Certainly—for there was an R in the month—they gave him oysters from Pyfleet Creek. I imagine him lying back in the lamplight on a couch from the Palatine Hill and, turning to Aulus Plautius, as he sucked an oyster from its shell, saying :

' Delicious ! Horace was right ! Delicious . . . it was worth it. . . .'

But the sentries pacing the confines of the camp under the stars, listening to the confused noise of a camp, the trumpeting of a wounded elephant, the frightened whinnies from the horse lines, the hammering of farriers and smiths working to repair harness and breast-plate by the flame of torches, listening also for those extra noises beyond the normal sound of an army at rest, heard only the wind going out over the hill into the black darkness of swamp and forest. Now and then, perhaps, in the far woods they saw small pin-points of fire where the beaten tribes huddled together unable to sleep and telling each other once more the dreadful story of the capture of Cunobelin's hill.

Caesar spent only sixteen days in Britain and when he reached Rome with his retinue, his Praetorians, his elephant corps and his spoils, he had been absent six months. . . .

* * *

What a provoking nuisance a small piece of red pottery can be on a windy morning when it comes ' from the hand of Severus ' !

§ 5

As I took the road to Bury St. Edmunds I was filled suddenly with a desire to see York again, a city which I consider the most beautiful and least spoiled in England.

I began to eat up the miles with no thought but that of getting north. . . .

Ely, Peterborough ; and then the feel of the nearness of the sea at Spalding, the fine flat roads, the Dutch canals, the windmills slowly turning and yellow cloud-scapes moving up over the flat lands like great armadas !   Then Boston ' Stump ' lifting its Dutch tower from the fields, the vast market-square, the slow Rotterdam-like stream . . . on, on to magnificent Lincoln which lifts its towers on a great hill, and then that Roman road that runs straight as a spear due north and, at last, the Humber !

I looked across from New Holland towards Hull. The ferry boats were slowly making their way over a river which is here three miles wide. It was windy and exhilarating. I liked the look of Hull's outline. I had never seen Hull before. I embarked on the steam ferry with the feeling that my adventures had begun.

LINCOLN

CHAPTER TWO

§ I

SHIPS sail right into the heart of Hull. They saunter
casually across the main streets, their masts become
mixed up with the electric cable poles. Trawlers
steam in from the North Sea across roads and nestle their
smoke stacks against the chimneys of Hull. Barges roll in
casually, with the skipper smoking his pipe and looking up
pleasantly at the long line of taxicabs, oil-cake wagons,
cement carts, and tram-cars which wait respectfully for the
bridge to swing back.

Ships never apologize in Hull ! Never ! They have the
right of way ; and they take their time, knowing full well
that they are all that Hull was, is, and will be.

This happens in the ' Old Town '. Old Hull is a tiny island
surrounded by docks. Its streets are narrow and medieval.
New Hull is a monster that is slowly spreading out north,
south, east, and west, in great factories, in finely planned
suburbs.

And the heart of Hull is a seven-mile long line of
docks, with ships on one side and railway wagons on the
other.

The streets of Hull are full of Vikings.

The men are big, fair-haired pirates ; the women are blue-
eyed Danes. Their names are—goodness knows how—
Robinson and Brown. Occasionally you find a Karl Thorgeld,
or something like that, but it seems too good to be true.

A book is yet to be written about the people of the east
coast of England. I am thinking of Hull and of Boston,
in Lincolnshire, which looks as though it was blown over
from Holland, and of certain parts of the Norfolk sea-coast

which seem to have been enthusiastically raided by anyone who could afford a war galley. . . .

In the evening I like to stand at the ferry pier in Hull and look across the Humber, which is three miles wide here, to the thin green line of the Lincolnshire coast. This small pierhead is, to me, amazingly attractive. It is built on great wooden piles, and there is a strong Georgian flavour about the buildings at the back. They all look as though they remember topsail gallants and brass guns. Men, in blue jerseys smoking the traditional clay pipes, lean over the rails and gaze towards New Holland, Lincolnshire, like Vikings contemplating a raid !

Hull is packed with character. ‘ This busy port,’ says a guide book, ‘ has little to offer the ordinary tourist.’

I am glad that I am not an ordinary tourist.

*　　　*　　　*

It is perhaps not remarkable that Hull is one of England’s misunderstood cities. There are many reasons for this. She lies, like Norwich, in a big geographical bulge, rather off the track from the ordinary travellers’ point of view, so that few people arrive there by mistake and discover her. Her name is short, sharp and snappy. It sounds modern and cocksure. It is a name with a cigar in the corner of its mouth and a Stetson on its head. Worst of all, the most famous remark about Hull compares her to Hell !

All this is most unfair !

The first thing you learn in Hull is that this monosyllable is not her real name, it is merely her telegraphic address. Her real name is the King’s Town upon the Hull, or, as they write it on tram-cars and other official documents, Kingston-upon-Hull. That gives, to me at least, an entirely new conception of the place. The king whose town this is was Edward I— ‘ Longshanks ’—who must have had a good eye as well as a good leg, because he made Hull a seaport in the thirteenth century. No other port in England was deliberately selected as such by an English king.

It is a pity that Kingston-upon-Hull has amputated a most distinguished name, but that again is a sign that she is alive and moving.

And ‘ Hull ’, of course, is unforgettable. It is, in short, the ideal address.

The connection between Hull and Hell is interesting. I

HULL TRAWLERS

suppose every one has heard, ' From Hell, Hull and Halifax, Good Lord deliver us ! ' I always thought it was composed by a commercial traveller. But after taking a shrewd and careful look at Hull, and seeing no point in this quotation, I went to a distinguished local antiquary and asked him the why and wherefore of this adhesive slogan.

' Thousands of people believe it to be a modern commentary on Hull,' he said, ' but, as a matter of fact, it goes back to the sixteenth century. In those days Hull and Halifax contained more debasers of the coinage than any other two towns in England. They used to clip round the edge of the unmilled shillings and then boil down the shavings.

' Hull and Halifax had to put down this crime with the greatest severity. We used to punish them here with death. So they did in Halifax, where they erected a guillotine worked by a horse. The horse was harnessed to a rope attached to a sharp knife. When he walked away from the guillotine the knife slowly mounted to the top of the scaffolding. The coiners and coin cutters then placed their heads on the block, some one cut the rope, and down came the knife. . . . So you see, " From Hell, Hull and Halifax, Good Lord deliver us ! " became a very earnest line in the beggars' litany.'

I thanked him and went out into Kingston-upon-Hull feeling that I was now competent to understand her a little better.

§ 2

' I can remember,' said an old man, ' when the *Diana* set out alone in 1865. She was the last whaler to leave Hull. And I remember how the people cheered and shouted as she got away from the dock with her tops and her topmasts and her look-out tubs all dressed with evergreens. It was a grand sight . . . sixty-two years ago. I don't look my age, do I ? But the wives didn't cheer, poor things ! The whalers used to go out to Greenland or to Baffin's Bay, and stay away, sometimes for a year or more. . . .

' It was two years before the *Diana* came home. The captain was dead. They had his coffin tied to the bridge. Eleven of her crew were dead, and the rest half dead. She had been locked in the ice for six months. There wasn't any cheering when she came back to Hull. . . .'

The tragic voyage of the *Diana*, which few Hull men can

still remember now, was the end of as daring and thrilling an epic of trade as any English town can boast. From the reign of Elizabeth to the middle of the last century the whalers of Hull faced the perils of the Arctic seas in order to corset the women of England and to uphold the dignity of the crinoline.

The Dutch captured the trade from them in Stuart times, but with true Yorkshire tenacity the Humber seamen won it back. Then competition set in, and the whales began to object. They became more difficult to catch. Aberdeen joined in ; so did Dundee. There were not enough he-whales to go round. Then the whalers started to harpoon the mothers and children ; and the end of the adventure drew near ! The *Diana* in 1865 was the last of a gallant company.

But on the ruins of the whaling trade Hull has built up two of her greatest industries—fishing and oil extraction. When the whaling ceased the whalers turned their attention to cod and mackerel ; and the whale-oil factories discovered the linseed.

* * *

I have spent an exciting hour among the relics of Hull's whaling days. How lucky is Hull in her museums ! The Museum of Fisheries and Shipping—which sounds as dull as the Ministry of Agriculture—is packed with the thrilling relics of these times : the harpoons, the walrus skulls, the tusks, the queer curios which the whalers brought back with them ; the carved ships and the rude paintings made by them during their long vigil in the polar seas.

The industry was underlaid with anxiety, as many old broadsheets prove. These ships literally disappeared into the blue. There was the *Swan*. She was frozen up in the Arctic ice-floes in 1836, and after a year or so was given up as lost. In the middle of a memorial service on Dock Green news was received that the ' missing ' ship had made the mouth of the Humber. A news-sheet tells the story :

' ARRIVAL OF THE *SWAN*

' FROM DAVIS STRAITS. 25 LIVES LOST

' Yesterday, Monday, July 3, in consequence of intelligence of the *Swan* having made the Humber, many thousands assembled at Southend, and were gratified with the sight of the long lost vessel, whose reappearance was regarded as a sort of resurrection. . . . The survivors of her crew, including Captain Dring and his two sons, are all in tolerable health ; the mate and one or two others look remarkably well, but the majority are still rather thin.'

The news-sheet goes on to describe the hardships and the number of whales caught, then it ends up with the most interesting piece of news in a manner which would not be tolerated in modern journalism :

' The wife of one of the men belonging to the *Swan*,' it concludes, ' who anticipated that her beloved husband would not again present himself before her, was on Sunday last united in the bonds of holy matrimony to her love-stricken swain. On Monday, on hearing of the arrival of the vessel, and the safety of her first husband, she made a precipitate retreat into the country, where, for aught we know, she yet remains.'

It was a backward age : no one interviewed the husband ! I am not surprised that the industry died out. Whales would seem to be so much easier to catch than smaller fish, and there cannot be so many of them. Thirty-one Hull whalers caught two hundred and four whales in 1821. Another fleet of twenty-one sail that went at the same time to Davis Straits caught two hundred and ninety-four. The whalebone and oil from these four hundred and ninety-eight whales realized £150,000.

Although the whaler's pay was good he earned it. Now and then a whale would not tamely surrender to the corset trade. The *Baffin*, in 1821, struck a whale that ran out fifteen lines each two hundred and forty yards long and dragged two boats and fifteen men for a long voyage. When eventually they killed the monster they discovered that in addition to them it had been carrying under water six similar lines and a boat belonging to the *Trafalgar* of Hull !

The most dramatic relic of the whale trade is to be seen not in this museum, but in Trinity House. It is an Eskimo's canoe containing an effigy of its dead owner sitting upright with his paddle across his knees and strapped to his seat.

He was found like this, dead, drifting on the Atlantic Ocean in 1613.

*   *   *

You respect the Humber fishermen when you remember that it is from the old whaling stock that he comes. When you see him in the fish market landing his catch you think of the bigger fish his fathers caught. You remember the queer old prints in the museum which show him iced up in the Arctic, great bergs towering above the ships. He amused himself at such moments by cruising through the broken ice in small boats, taking a pot shot at a walrus or trying to catch a diffident polar bear.

Now the men of the Humber, living in a world which fortunately needs no corsets, go out after the haddock.

They are a fine and distinct type. They are, like jockeys, the result of specialization. Generations ago they caught whales, twelve years ago they caught German mines, to-day they catch the breakfasts of England.

They are, like most people in intimate touch with the sea, superstitious. They believe in luck more than in the Board of Agriculture and Fisheries ! A ' lucky ' skipper can own his own motor-car and his own house. He is supposed to possess some uncanny sixth sense which leads him to the right fishing ground, and it is a fact, I am told, that ' lucky ' men seldom fail to return with a good catch. Whether this is due to a secret study of helpful official charts dealing with the movements of fish, or whether it is due to an instinctive knowledge of the fishing grounds month by month, I would not dare to say.

I met a man who had been deep-sea fishing for nine months. The ship in which he makes these long journeys to remote parts of the North Sea is something new. It looks unlike any ship that sails the sea. Upwards of thirty small rowing boats hang from davits all over it. The ship itself is simply a gigantic ice chest.

It has been designed to catch large halibut. These, the largest of all flat fishes, are sometimes from five to ten feet in length. They are caught in from fifty to one hundred and fifty fathoms. The ordinary trawl net which bumps about on the sea bed passes over these giants and the only way to land them is by hook and line. When the halibut ship reaches the fishing ground, its thirty little boats are launched and the crews angle month after month for the halibut, putting back to the parent ship with their catches each evening. Once the ice chests are full of frozen halibut the crew give three hearty cheers and the ship returns to Hull, home, and beauty.

'And the very night I landed,' said this man, 'I had to stay in dock all night to see the halibut taken off the ice—and my missus waiting to see me for nearly a twelve-month!'

Alas, a fisherman's life is not always a happy one!

*　　*　　*

In one of Hull's ubiquitous museums is an amusing collection of motor-cars. It will become more interesting and valuable as time goes on. It traces the development of the motor-car from the first incredible 'stink-cart', designed like a brougham, down to the comparatively recent but now quite comic motor-cars which our fathers drove. Few things are more calculated to fill us with reverence for the bravery of our fathers and grandfathers than these queer machines. Among the veterans is the car in which Lord Montagu of Beaulieu took King Edward for his first motor-car ride.

King Edward was a brave man and Lord Montagu a reckless one! I think they fed it with coal.

*　　*　　*

The Lord Mayor of Hull is an admiral.

An admiral's flag is thrown in with his chain of office. He is entitled to fly this flag, and His Majesty's ships must salute it with six guns.

This takes us back to the reign of Henry VI. This King instructed the Corporation of Hull to appoint an Admiral of the Humber who should be independent of any other of the King's admirals. He was to have authority over the broad waters of the Humber and to keep an eye over the river system of which it is the centre.

When you speak to the Lord Mayor of Hull you still speak also to the Admiral of the Humber.

Hull is not a showy city, but it has a fine air of solidity. It has, too, that characteristic seaport atmosphere as of something important happening every minute. The next corner may show you the high masts of a schooner from Norway coming into dock heavy with wireless aerials. This is a new industry. Little fir-trees which before the invention of the crystal set were allowed, if they survived Christmas, to live to a certain maturity are now being cut down in millions. The docks of Hull are stacked full of them.

Or you may see round any corner a grain ship, or a wool ship, or a ship setting out laden with coal or machinery, and, if you are lucky, some morning you may see the trawler fleet come in with North Sea salt caked on its high smoke-stacks, the low sturdy ships heavy with a three-day harvest.

In they come to St. Andrew's Dock, fussy, important; and you remember, as you look at them, that Humber trawlers accounted for three thousand German mines during the war, that the Humber turned out eight hundred trawlers and ten thousand men to sweep the North Sea for this strange fish, and that over one thousand officers and men lost their lives on minefields. So that when the trawlers come steaming slowly into Hull with haddock and plaice in the early morning you feel like raising your hat to them, and to all their cargoes —past, present and to come !

§ 3

I topped the rise beyond Bishop Burton. Below me in green fields lay the ancient town of Beverley.

There come moments in England when travellers pause in their journey, brought to a full stop of mind and body by a beauty so sudden, so old, so right, and so English that there is nothing for a man to do but to look gratefully before him.

A man looking down on Beverley may think that any ancestor of his who rode that way five hundred years ago saw the same bright meadows rolling to the valley, loved the same flash of silver hawthorn, saw the same twin towers of the minster lifting above the tree tops, the same glow of red roofs, the same blue hint of smoke in the quiet air of evening.

There are certain times when a man should not be ashamed to fall on his knees by the roadside ; and what a strange thought above Beverley ! This hill-top must have been the spot on which the pilgrims to the shrine of St. John of Beverley sank down in the meadow-sweet to give God thanks for their journey's end.

At this point fugitives with the blood of a murder still on

them took new heart as they raced for sanctuary. There is something strange about these sanctuaries. I noticed it at King's Beaulieu, in the New Forest ; I notice it at Beverley.

One might almost think that 'the Peace of the Church' is still over these green fields.

I dipped down through the park and passed into Beverley under the gate-house of the North Bar, remembering that St. John was one of the four famous saints of the North of England. His bones made Beverley a town of miracles. Even William the Conqueror, when he laid waste the north, rode round Beverley in order not to 'disturb the peace of St. John'.

Kings came to Beverley to ask for St. John's banner when they went to war. This banner was borne reeling above the arrows of so many battles. Stephen took it to the Battle of the Standard when he enlisted the four northern saints on his side : St. Peter of York, St. Cuthbert of Durham, St. Wilfrid of Ripon, and St. John of Beverley.

Pilgrims trooped to Beverley with their woes. Those who prayed at the shrine during the Battle of Agincourt said that the saint's tomb sweated drops of holy oil. After the battle King Henry V brought his French wife, Catherine, to Beverley, where before the shrine of St. John he gave thanks for the English victory.

And Beverley naturally became rich. It became one of the principal towns of England. Its poll-tax returns in 1377 were eleventh in point of population ; and now Beverley has only 13,500 inhabitants.

I have explored the quiet streets, admiring the cobbled squares, the saddles and the guns in the shop windows, the little homely shops full of homely things.

'No ; nothing ever happens here !' said a shopkeeper, rather surprised that I should have thought it worth while to ask him.

What a fine example is Beverley of a town built on the bones of a saint. The trade that now exists grew up before the Norman Conquest, when merchants came in to sell goods to the constant pilgrims. Once a market is established in a street it goes on for ever ; once men erect their stalls against the wall of a church you have to invoke Parliament to stop them ! It has been much the same with Beverley : the pilgrims have gone, the priests have gone, but the commerce remains : sheep, farm implements, corn.

In its death-like stillness the great Church of St. John

dominates Beverley, mentally and physically. It is as large as many a cathedral. People who do not know its history often wonder, as they dash through in motor-cars, how so great a church came to so small a town !

It has been called the most beautiful Gothic building in England. Its perfection speaks of an age when all the genius of man now squandered in a thousand professions was poured faithfully and unquestioningly into the church. Each small carved stone is full of love and belief. The Church of St. John looks as though men sang all day long as they made it.

All the energy which men now put into the floating of a company some unknown worker at Beverley put into the head of one good devil ; all the effort which men now spend on things they love has been put by a builder of Beverley into the face of a small stone saint. When the world ceases to believe even in itself men will still stand awed and rather puzzled in Beverley.

Beverley has a ghost, but it is not the kind of ghost I would have expected. They say that Sir Jocelyn Percy sometimes drives a team of headless horses through the town on windy nights, but I could find no one, even in the bar of the ' King's Head ', who had seen him ! What, I wonder, has happened to the ghosts of all the fugitives who sought sanctuary there ?

The records in Beverley prove that in sixty years one hundred and eighty-six murderers, two hundred and eight debtors, fifty-four thieves, and over five hundred other criminals came clamouring at the great sanctuary knocker as if all the devils of hell were after them, as they were, no doubt. Some of these fugitives came from London ! I wonder why ! Were they cut off from nearer sanctuary at the time of their crimes, or did they believe that St. John of Beverley would give them greater protection ?

In the church they show you a massive Saxon chair carved from one block of stone. It is called the Freedstool. On reaching this the fugitive was safe. The area of safety must have been increased in later times, for sanctuary obtained within a mile radius of the minster.

Beverley was once noted for its beavers. That is the meaning of the word : the beaver-lea, or meadow of the beavers.

I was surprised to find them still busily at work beside the river ! A little distance from the town is the most discreet shipyard in the world. It stands in fields. Four trawlers were on the stocks, and the men with hammers swarmed over them, while from a shed standing farther back glowed the light of forge fires, and the sound of rivets being shot into metal plates.

Shipbuilding is Beverley's most ambitious modern effort. It turns out excellent trawlers for the Hull fishing trade, and it launches them broadside from the slipways, as at Selby, because the stream is so narrow. But the rural secrecy of this little shipyard appealed to me. It was almost clandestine, almost as if the busy beavers of Beverley do not, like William the Conqueror, wish to disturb ' the Peace of St. John '.

§ 4

I am sitting in the great Abbey of Selby remembering a story.

About the time when William the Conqueror was sharpening his sword, with an eye on the Channel ports, a young monk, called Benedict, was praying before the High Altar of the Abbey of St. Germanus at Auxerre, in France. The holiest object in the abbey was the middle finger of the right hand of St. Germanus.

Now, as Benedict prayed, asking that God might deem him worthy to achieve some great deed, lo ! St. Germanus came to him in a vision, and he said :

' Go to England, to a place called Salebeia (Selby), and there build a church to the glory of God and dedicate it to me.'

Although Benedict revered his patron more truly than any other monk of Auxerre, he was too good a Frenchman not to view residence in England without a sinking heart. He even dared to procrastinate with the saint ; but Germanus appeared in a second vision and repeated his order. Benedict was still piously stubborn. Yet a third time the saint appeared to the young man ; and this time he instructed him to take the sacred middle finger of the right hand from the High Altar and to make a hole in his arm between the shoulder-blade and the elbow, assuring him freedom from pain or inflammation, and, by virtue of the holy thing he bore, safety in England.

Benedict then obeyed.

Now Benedict had misunderstood his instructions. We next hear of him not in Salebeia (which was Selby in Yorkshire) but in Salisberia (which was Salisbury in Wiltshire). He was preparing to settle down when St. Germanus, appearing patiently for the fourth time, corrected the young monk's geography.

He then found his way across wildest England to King's Lynn, in Norfolk, where, taking ship, he sailed up the Humber and planted his cross in Selby.

Now, while poor Benedict was working out his salvation, a Frenchman of a different type was rampaging through England with excellent cavalry. The arrow had fallen into the eye of Harold at Hastings, and the Tower of London was being built. At this time the Conqueror's baron at York happened to be sailing on the Ouse at Selby, where he saw a cross on a hill and a young man building a wooden church. He left his ship, heard his countryman's story, and promised to enlist his lord's sympathy.

In a short time Selby Abbey was founded by royal charter from William I.

*   *   *

Selby is still royal. It shares with Westminster, York, the Chapels Royal, Windsor, and Bristol the right to robe its choir in red. It still remembers the King who built it so long ago. On 17 July 1928 all that is left of the great abbey of Selby will celebrate the nine-hundredth anniversary of the birthday of William the Conqueror.

All that is left? Its power and its grandeur have gone, only its superlative beauty remains. It was once the third richest abbey in the north. Its abbot was mitred. He rode the way to Parliament. Kings came to Selby. Now its only endowment is £56 a year, and the hat is always going round to keep these lovely stones in repair.

' If only I were a younger man ! ' said the vicar to me, ' nothing on earth would keep me away from America. There I would get the money we need ! '

He looked up eloquently towards the south windows of the choir, where George Washington's arms, the stars (which are really spurs) and the stripes have been in position since 1584. Americans will go to any part of England to look at the Washington Arms.

There is another interesting piece of heraldry in the Selby

windows. One shield shows a bend sinister, the sign of illegitimacy. Who on earth, people have wondered, wished to advertise this ? The explanation is that when the window was repaired and re-leaded in 1866 this shield was placed inside out so that the ' bend ' became a ' bend sinister '.

Surely this is the only instance of a man being made illegitimate by a glazier's blunder !

The mystery of Selby Abbey is the dark room over the north porch. It is not open to the public, but I was taken up into it. Nothing has ever been written about this, and no expert who has seen it has been able to explain it.

The way up to it is by a series of dark, winding, spiral staircases on the south side of the west end of the church. You then, still climbing dark, dusty steps, enter the triforium on the north side, go down some more steps and find yourself in a room that was never intended to receive one ray of light.

It is a pitch-black dungeon. It has never had any windows. The theory that it was a punishment cell for the monks seems disproved by the remains of an altar at the east end of the room. What service was held in the dark there ?

*   *   *

I cannot leave Selby without quoting two gravestones in the south aisle. One is walked over and the other missed by most people :

> Here lyes ye body of poor Frank Row
> Parish clark and gravestone cutter,
> And ys is writ to let ye know,
> What Frank for others used to do,
> Is now for Frank done by Another.

Here is the second one :

> Next to this stone lies Archer (John)
> Late sexton (I aver)
> Who without tears, thirty-four years,
> Did carcases inter,
> But death at last, for his work past
> Unto him thus did say :
> ' Leave off thy trade, be not afraid,
> But forthwith come away.'
> Without reply, or asking why,
> The summons he obeyed,
> In seventeen hundred and sixty-eight
> Resigned his life and spade.

*   *   *

The glorious Norman nave of Selby, marked by the same masons who built Durham, stands like a mighty forest of oaks with the sun slanting through it.

' No, sir,' said the verger, ' I see no ghosts. I'm an old soldier. Served in China, India, and Egypt. Take more than ghosts to frighten me. I came here for a quiet life.'

' And you've got it.'

'Yes, sir, you're right ! '

CHAPTER THREE

APRIL SUNLIGHT ON THE WALL OF YORK, WHY THEY RING
THE CURFEW EVERY EVENING FROM ST. MICHAEL'S,
SPURRIERGATE, HOW THE MERCHANT ADVENTURERS WERE
SAVED BY A WOMAN, WITH A FEW REMARKS ON DICK
TURPIN'S RIDE TO YORK, RAILWAY ENGINES, AND THE
GIRLS WHO MAKE CHOCOLATE.

§ I

IT was early in the evening. The sun was going down over
the Vale of York and the grey towers of the Cathedral Church
of St. Peter rose over the flat lands.   There was a wind blowing at my back or I might have heard the minster bells,
whose chimes, on a still evening, go over the fields for miles.
As I went on between the hedges my spirits rose, because
York is the loveliest city in all England.   She is England's
last real anchor to the Middle Ages.   Other cities have cathedrals, one has a wall, many have castles and ancient houses,
but York is the supreme, unself-conscious queen of them all.
She does not ask you to love her : she is like London in that.
She is there : *she is York*.

As I saw the red roofs draw near, all the Catholic ancestors
in me rose and shouted, and all the Protestants leapt up
quickly and took them by the throat.   It was a marvellous
feeling.   I was not like one man going to York : I was like
the arrival of an army !

York, let me tell you, is the last city left in England which
a man should enter on horseback or on foot.   Unfortunately
few people know this !   When I came to the high, white,
machicolated wall that circles this city I looked up at the
great bastions that guard its angles, at the cross-slits for the
bowmen, at the gate-houses on whose topmost turrets little
stone men, outlined against the sky, hug boulders to their
stomachs and seem about to heave them down on you as
you pass.

Men were driving cattle through the gates of York.   There

was a smell of smoke, the last sun lay warm over red roof tiles, and from within the walls came a marvellous feeling o men and women, of life, which, although present in all cities lacks identity unless a city sits cosily behind its wall like house full of friends.

I made a circle of the walls, and walked round to Boothar Bar so that I might read this notice posted up on it :

'Entry from North through Forest of Galtres. In old times armed men were stationed here to watch and to conduct travellers through the forest and protect them against wolves.'

I entered York and so up into High Petergate and Stone gate.

Above the busy noise of crowds and the sound of shop keepers closing their shops came the tolling of one insister bell. I looked at my watch : it was eight o'clock. The were ringing the curfew from the belfry of St. Michael' Spurriergate, not only to warn men to damp their fires, bu also to guide wanderers through the long-vanished Forest Galtres—which is still officially wolf-haunted every night eight !

York is surely the loveliest fairy tale among the cities the world.

*   *   *

The walls offer you a three-mile walk, which I consider be the best before-breakfast walk in England.

It was one of those hushed, sweet, washed-clean Api mornings, the smell of grass in the air and the wind runnir round corners like a pup in search of his tail. An old ma was shaking a religious mat on the south steps of the minste the sun was washing the east window, and the great chure lay in unexpected early morning shadows.

I climbed the steps into Bootham Bar and up a secor flight to the wall an hour before the first smart little chocola maker had taken herself, her bicycle, and her pink garte to work. (York, by the way, goes to work on bicycles, ar every bicycle has its bell.)

The walls of York lift you above the chimney-pots. (one side is a six-foot fortification pierced every few yar with square, waist-high openings for boiling oil or for arche

ON THE WALL OF YORK

Through these openings you look down over the green moat to the back gardens and the homes of York outside the wall where, in the early morning, people are awakening, pulling up blinds, making tea, dressing the babies, or blowing up the inevitable bicycle tyre—a peaceful scene which would have astonished the fifteenth-century sentinels more than an army with banners !

How strange they would have thought it to hear on that spot, where in winter the wolves bayed Bootham Bar, no sound more painful than some Yorkist in the throes of teething !

On the other side of you the ground falls away from the wall to the cathedral and the deanery gardens. You see York Minster through a hedge of silver-white pear blossom. Everything is silver-white in the early sun. The wall itself is silver-white. Tadcaster stone is washed by every rain, so that the Wall of York has always looked new. And this white, enchanted ribbon twists on and round, never straight for more than twenty yards, losing itself in green bowers as the tops of the trees on either side arch themselves over the white bastions.

Rooks were cawing round the west towers. The dean's gardener was bringing the lawn mower to a smooth lawn. A blackbird with the early worm in his saffron beak flew to an apple-tree. A thrush was pouring out his heart from a high bough, the starlings, whistling, fighting, shining, and beetle-backed, flew in truculent flocks, only becoming sober to rush to the help of some enormous and ravenous fledgling whose shaking wings and open beak were the sole signs of infancy.

The minster bell chimed a half-hour. Smoke began to curl from the chimneys above the red roofs. York was awakening. Beyond the wall the bicycles went by. There were bells, bells, bells ! Did you ever hear of a medieval city without bells ? (They even sell coal with a bell in York !)

So I went on to Monk Bar, where the stone men have been holding their missiles for centuries, on to Walmgate Bar, which has a great barbican, or outwork, lying before it and a wireless aerial attached to it ! Here lives a member of the police force in the most romantic house in York. Then Victoria Bar and Micklegate, which bears on heraldic shields the lions of England quartered with the lilies of France ; and so round the bend to Tanners Moat, and right ahead that classic view of York Minster lifting its towers above the city and the white wall twisting on and on. . . .

What a walk, and what a city, for an April morning !

*   *   *

At night, after curfew, I like to walk in the streets as it grows dark.   How York clings to the swinging shop-sign ! I like to walk up High Ousegate, past the Church of All Souls, mentioned in Domesday Book, in whose open tower once hung a lamp to guide travellers through that awful Forest of Galtres.   I wonder why York does not relight this lantern ?

Then I go to Whipmawhopmagate just to smile at the way it looks on the street sign.   Surely we have here the funniest street name in England.   This was where they used to whip and whop the felons !   Then—then I am delightfully lost !

I may find myself in Jubbergate or Goodramgate or Swine-gate or Stonebow-lane or Shambles, but it does not matter because I like the names.   If, however, I strike the Shambles I discover the butchers—or fleshers—who have traded in this street for over five hundred years—in the act of washing down their shops after the day's work, so that the broad stone gutters run with water.

And the houses of the shambles thrust out their upper stories, like paunchy aldermen, and nod together over the narrow road, shutting out the sky and approaching so near that you could, I imagine, from the upper windows of at least one house, kiss the girl who lives opposite.   The butchers joke together as they swill down their slabs, the little lamps throw just the right shadows, and I go on expecting to meet Pistol or Corporal Nym round the next corner. . . .

The minster chimes strike ten.   I go to bed very conscious that I am sleeping within the white walls of York, loving her beauty, her peace, her dignity, and the calm, unhurried way she has, anxious to be up early in the morning to white walls and apple blossom.

§ 2

I suppose nine out of ten natives of York are unconscious of the most romantic sound in the city.   I, a stranger, am acutely sensitive to it.   I wait for it.   If my watch is a bit fast and I do not hear it prompt to its time I get worried, restless, open windows, and make a fuss until I assure myself that I have not missed it.

Sharp at 8 p.m. the curfew tolls from the white stone tower of St. Michael's, Spurriergate. The old tower seems to lean slightly, as well it may after so many centuries of curfewing. William the Conqueror started this bell ringing, William the Kaiser stopped it for a little while, but with the exception of the war years it has been ringing every night for over nine centuries.

It sounds when all the other bells of York are drowsy with their day's work. When the city falls into one of these chill, delicious April evenings, the sun setting, a stillness in the air, the chimney smoke going up straight, this bell, insistently tolling for two or three minutes, is like the ancient voice of York telling the children that it is time for bed.

' Oh, yes,' says young York indulgently, ' that's all very well, but you forget that we live in the twentieth century ! Who's coming to the pictures ? '

But the curfew rings on with the single-mindedness of the very old.

I have found myself wondering who rings the curfew, what he is like, and if he enjoys ringing it. Last night I thought what a great thing it would be to ring it myself. What a fine boast : ' I once rang the curfew in York ! ' Men boast about so many stupid things, but this, I thought, would be a splendid boast.

So at about 7.30 p.m. I walked down the Street of the Spur Makers, which is Spurriergate, and let myself into the Church of St. Michael known still in York as ' the Conqueror's Church ' —York has the longest memory in England. The church was empty and it was growing dark. The sound of my knocks on the vestry door boomed round it like thunder. The empty pews, when I returned to them, had a stiff, mildly outraged look. I sat down in the least unfriendly, and waited for the coming of the curfew man. The church grew darker minute by minute.

At five to eight a clang of metal reverberated through St. Michael's like a gun-shot. Some one had taken the big round handle of the oak door and had come in from the street. There was a sound of footsteps on the stone, and in walked a grey-haired, elderly man holding a cloth cap in his hand. He started as I rose out of a pew ; and we regarded each other distrustfully.

' I've come to ring the curfew for you,' I said.

' Are you a bell-ringer ? ' he asked.

' No,' I replied, crestfallen, ' but surely your union would not . . .'

' It isn't that,' he said. ' The curfew bell weighs twelve hundredweight, and if you are not used to big bells the rope will either cut your throat or pull you up to the cross-beams and stun you, or worse. I wouldn't like that to happen,' he added thoughtfully. ' There was once a man . . .'

He mounted the spiral stairs to the belfry, I after him, and as he went up he told me how a too-confident stranger once professed to be a bell-ringer and how the great bells of St. Michael took him by the throat and nearly shook the life out of him. Still, I was puffed up with the vanity of ignorance. ' Once he gets the curfew going,' I thought to myself, ' I'll persuade him to hand it over to me. . . . Perhaps, after all, it would be better for him to start it ! '

Up in the belfry it was rather eerie and ominous, with the long ropes hanging out of the darkness like dead snakes.

So we waited for the tick of eight. A clock outside began to strike. The curfew man took the rope in both hands and sharp on the last stroke of eight down he came with it, and from high above us, out of the darkness, sounded a loud, sweet :

' Ker-lang ! '

The curfew was ringing over York. . . .

Now when I saw the bell-rope in action my courage faded ! I knew then that I would never ring the curfew in York ! It came down out of the black beams like a boa-constrictor in torment, writhed a second, whipped the floor with its flying tail, and shot up into darkness faster than eye could follow. The power above it was something I had not contemplated. But John Wilson, the curfew man, had tamed the thing ; it ran sweetly and softly through his experienced hands. He could even carry on a conversation as he manipulated the flying rope. I asked him if there were any legends about the York curfew.

' You'll find nothing in books about it,' said Mr. Wilson, ' but the story has been handed down. In the Middle Ages a man left money for the curfew to be rung in York for ever and ever.'

' Ker-lang ! ' agreed the bell.

' You see, he was lost one night in the Forest of Galtres,

which in the old days used to stretch right down to Bootham
Bar. And the forest was full of wolves. Now as he was
wandering about wondering which way to go he heard——'

' Ker-lang ! ' said the curfew.

' ——the sound of a bell ringing in York. He followed
it. It led him to Bootham Bar and into the city, and the
first question he asked was : " Which bell is that I hear ? "
and they said to him, " The bell of St. Michael's, Spurriergate." '

' Ker-lang !' boomed the bell of St. Michael's, as if to say,
' All this is true ; all this happened ages before any of you
was born, and even then I was old ! '

' Now,' continued Mr. Wilson, ' this traveller, in order to
return thanks for having been guided away from the wolves,
left money for the curfew to be rung for ever so that other
travellers in the Forest of Galtres might hear it and be led
to the gates of York. And it's his ten pounds I get every
year for ringing the curfew. . . .'

' Ker-lang ! ' said the curfew ; then it ceased to ring.

The glow of the Spurriergate lights was a little disheartening.
No one seemed to have paid any attention ! And the echoes
were drifting in the still air over the neat suburban gardens
which stand now in that fearsome Forest of Galtres !

But—never mind—York had kept faith with its past.

' I've rung the curfew for thirty years,' said Mr. Wilson,
as he descended from the belfry and solemnly locked the
door. ' And I've missed it only once. That was when I was
out Tadcaster way gathering flowers for the harvest festival.
I missed the train. . . .'

I detected a world of sorrow in that admission. He had
missed the train ! I had a pathetic vision of him standing
with his arms full of autumn flowers on the station at
Tadcaster, knowing that ' the curfew shall not ring to-
night '.

' And only once did I make a bad mistake. Before the
war I used to strike the day of the month after the curfew.
Well, one night—I'm blessed if I know what I was thinking
about—I lost count. But a policeman had me as soon as I
got out. " Hullo," he said, " I've been waiting for you. So
there's thirty-two days in this month, is there ? " '

Mr. Wilson locked the oak door of St. Michael's, and we walked up through the lights of Spurriergate.

'These things,' he said, waving a hand to include the belfry, ' are very important, I think. You see, when a man leaves money for a thing to be done for ever you've got to carry it out for him properly, just as though he were alive and could come and see you do it. It's a duty, that's what it is. I might say I'm proud to do it. Good night. . . .'

His cloth cap lost itself in the crowd. The man who for thirty years has been obeying William the Conqueror and the lost traveller went off with nothing about him to tell his fellow-men that he had just warned them against wolves.

§ 3

An ancient door in Fossgate bears over it the good prayer *Dieu Nous Donne Bonne Aventure* ; and when you pass through you find yourself in a stone courtyard. Facing you is an old building approached by a flight of steps. This is the hall of the Merchant Adventurers of York. It was the head-quarters of the wealthy and powerful cloth merchants of the sixteenth century who ruled York when this city was the seat of the woollen trade. You might say, without stretching facts too far, that Leeds, Bradford, Halifax, and Huddersfield were born and cradled in this hall.

When you go up the steps and pay sixpence for a ticket, a white-haired woman will come from an inner room and conduct you round the building. Before she has spoken three words you know that she is no ordinary curator. Then what is she ? She is a puzzle. Is she, you wonder, ' a gentlewoman in reduced circumstances ' ? You notice that when she refers to the Merchant Adventurers of York she says 'we', not ' they '—always ' we ', and with considerable pride as though she were a Merchant Adventurer !

As a matter of fact *she is* ! She is the only woman Merchant Adventurer in the world, and the only woman who is a full liveried member of a city company. Her name is Miss Maud Sellers, Litt.D., known in York as ' Dr. Maud '.

How ' Dr. Maud ' became a Merchant Adventurer of York is not only a romance : it is also a monument to her scholarship and her enthusiasm.

Some years before the war ' Dr. Maud ' visited York covered in academic honours to dig out the history of the

Merchant Adventurers. She was Mary Bateson, Fellow of Newnham, and Mary Ewart, Travelling Fellow of the same college. She, as all students of medieval England are aware, had devoted herself to the history of early commerce, and her name is known all over the world.

After a while she came on the wreck of the York Merchant Adventurers. The old guild had done its work well and was dying of atrophy. There were about twenty-five members and a tumble-down hall of great but decayed beauty. In the cellar a few poor old women pensioners huddled over a fire as they had been doing since the Middle Ages. ' Dr. Maud ' ransacked big oak chests, found the records of the company, transcribed and edited them.

Things began to happen ! She fell in love with the old hall and with the dying company. She lectured all over Yorkshire. The twenty-five surviving Merchant Adventurers began to fling out their chests ! ' Dr. Maud ' and her researches made them feel proud of themselves ; they had a great inheritance ? It was like waking up and finding yourself heir to an historic title—useless but soothing to the vanities.

Through the eyes of ' Dr. Maud ' they saw the little boats of their forefathers going up the Ouse with broadcloth for Hamburg. They saw the fight these stubborn old merchants put up against the Hanseatic League. They saw red York-shire faces in foreign markets and remembered that this was the beginning of the commercial north of England : this was the north country's first trading adventure beyond the seas.

Being men of York who see past, present and future as a straight line and not a triangle, they rallied round the woman who had brought their past glory to life. They even put their hands in their pockets and gave money to the company ! Men of York became proud to be elected to the company, and the members increased from twenty-five to sixty-one.

One day they assembled in solemn conclave, and in the old hall under the oak beams made ' Dr. Maud ' the only woman Merchant Adventurer in the world.

*   *   *

It is to me remarkable that a woman of Dr. Sellers' attainments can spend her life showing schools and Americans round the old hall ; and I told her so.

' Good gracious, no ; I'm not wasted ! ' she said, ' and I've never been bored in my life. If I kept a fish shop I should find things to be excited about. Perhaps I have a balanced mind : everything matters, and nothing too much. I meet here in the course of a year people from every part of the world. I have travelled all over the world and I like to meet them. I am interested in people. This is my hobby. . . . Any success I've had here is not due to me : it's accidental. I've been well helped. The city of York has been notably generous.'

We walked through the magnificent old hall, the only medieval Merchant Adventurers' hall in England. It is rich in panelling, oak beams, and in objects illustrating the work of an ancient trade guild. It contains scales dated 1790 made by a firm of scale makers which still constructs scales for the Bank of England.

' When I was in London,' said Dr. Sellers, ' I went to this firm and complained about the scales. They were most apologetic and promised to put them right at once. " When did you buy them ? " I was asked. " In 1790," I said. They were just slightly taken aback, but, oh yes, they adjusted them. . . .'

In addition to her other resurrection work ' Dr. Maud ' has systematically and pertinaciously restored the old hall into some likeness to its medieval self. Her most sensational achievement has been the clearing away of several walls in the cellars and exposing to view a beautiful undercroft upheld by great pillars of solid oak trunks. For this work she deserves not only the thanks of York and of her company, but of all those who care for the antiquities of England.

The undercroft is now one of the sights of York.

A sudden stamping overhead, as if horses had been let loose in the hall, interrupted our conversation.

' A school ! ' cried ' Dr. Maud '. ' A school ! I must go ! I never neglect schools. Children see things so vividly if you talk the right way to them. I must go ! '

And she was gone !

* * *

I suppose there are hidden away in nooks and corners of England other scholars like ' Dr. Maud ,' who arrived on a visit and never went home again; people who have fallen in love with a place or a memory. They are to be envied.

'Dr. Maud' lives in Fossgate, now fallen from its once high estate as the abode of the mighty mercers of York. She is the last of that great company to live there. Schools know her as 'the lady that shows you round'; to Americans she is 'guide'; to her fellow Merchant Adventurers she is 'honorary warden'. But she is really none of these; she is the last genuine Merchant Adventurer of York.

When she walks down Fossgate in moonlight I expect the shades of the tough old York mercers rub their eyes. . . .

'The last Merchant Adventurer—a woman!'

I hope those men of many lucky adventures doff their bonnets to their last Adventurer as she goes by!

§ 4

Dick Turpin, after engaging the hangman in conversation on York Gallows for over half an hour and causing some impatience in the crowd, jumped into Eternity like a gentleman on 17 April, 1739.

The cell in which he was confined is not a public sight of York. It is in old York Gaol, now connected with York Barracks, which it adjoins. The cells have been derelict for many a year, and they are as gloomy as such places should be. I was preparing to enter them when a voice from the darkness cried:

'Your money or your life!'

I put up my hands immediately.

A small boy who had not brushed his hair nor washed his knees that glorious morning leapt out of the cells, making clicking noises with a toy pistol. He was, I think, so surprised that one of the large, unreal, illogical people who from time to time get in the way of Youth should have acted according to precedent that he stopped covering me and thrust his pistol into a length of string which was wound three times round his blue jersey.

'And now,' I said, 'that's a silly thing for any highwayman to do, because I've got you!' And I had, by a strand of yellow hair! 'What do they call you?'

He grinned:

'Dick Turpin!' he said.

' Well, I'm going to hang you.'

' Are you ? ' he said, interested and pleased.

Another boy leapt out of the cells and cried indignantly :

' He's not Dick Turpin—I am ! '

' You're not—you're Black Bess ! ' cried the first.

There was much violent argument and some clicking of pistols as the two Turpins fought together, but the matter was forgotten when one suggested that I might like to see the buried treasure. They tiptoed round the prison wall, with much clicking at invisible pirates every time we came to a corner, and lifting with difficulty a large flagstone exposed a deep cavity containing a small quantity of silver paper, a match-box, and many rather nice and well-selected stones.

' It's gold ! ' they whispered.

I told them I had not seen so much in bulk since I was in Panama with Sir Francis Drake, the time we burned the white town of San Diego and came home with silver candlesticks strapped to every mast.

Fortunately—for the trouble with children is that they play long after you are exhausted—a loud female voice cried : ' Willie ! '

There are many ways of crying ' Willie ', but this voice was not summoning Willie either in love or sorrow ; it was wanting to know urgently where Willie was, and with a certain bitterness in its tone which suggested that Willie was wanted for something Willie had, or had not, done ! At the sound of it the two highwaymen opened their eyes and their mouths wide, and disappeared like a couple of young rabbits.

It is a great compliment when boys of eight or ten do not condescend to you. It is a compliment to be allowed to enter, if only for a second, that lost fairyland, often bloodstained, and always melodramatic, where the world is well lost in one cabbage patch, where Spanish galleons have a habit of sailing round one corner while a tribe of Red Indians skulks round the other.

How fortunate are the boys of York Barracks with a real deserted gaol to play in, a place of mouldy cells and dank corridors, and bits of iron that go clank, clank in the darkness ! (And what a blessing Dick Turpin must be to the married quarters on washing day !)

I am glad that the two Turpins of York Gaol are not,

I imagine, likely to read this book, because it is not pleasant to kill anyone's hero.

Dick Turpin, of course, never rode from London to York, he never owned a horse called Black Bess, and he did not possess in all his make-up one spark of heroism. He was just a hit-and-run thief. I love a good highwayman as well as any eighteenth-century market woman. Claude Duval, for instance, was an artist. I imagine that many people were almost flattered after he had gone through their saddlebags. Who but a master of irony would insist, after robbing a coach on Hounslow Heath at midnight, that the wife of the man he had robbed should dance a measure with him in the nearest patch of moonlight ?

That is, of course, romance : it is lifted above the hum-drum. It is also a fine picture : can you imagine how he would bow, how he would hum one of those high, sweet tunes written for the spinet, and how they would advance, retreat, bow—her ladyship half-loving it perhaps—and he, I am sure, with a cocked pistol in one hand and his eyes on her sometimes, but mostly on the road over the heath. Such an idea would never have entered the turnip head of Turpin.

Dick Turpin owes his immortality to Harrison Ainsworth. Had it not been for this novelist no one would have heard of Black Bess, and the name of Turpin would have been lost in the criminal records.

The highwayman who rode to York was not Turpin, as Mr. Charles Harper points out in his book *The Great North Road*, but a man of the good old Robin Hood tradition who robbed the rich and helped the poor—John Nevinson. I am told that his name is still remembered in the villages round York.

Nevinson's ride to York was a longer ride than the London to York ride attributed to Dick Turpin. Nevinson rode from Chatham to York, two hundred and thirty miles in fifteen hours, which averages over fifteen miles an hour, and it happened like this :

At four o'clock on a May morning in 1676—over half a century before Turpin's alleged ride—John Nevinson robbed a man near Chatham on Gads Hill. He needed an alibi, so he wheeled his horse round and started to ride to York ! He crossed the Thames at Gravesend and rode from Tilbury to Chelmsford, where he rested his horse for half an hour.

He then rode through Cambridge to Huntingdon, where he took another half-hour's rest. From this point he rode at a gallop over the by-roads, reaching York that evening. It is obvious that he must have called several times at the houses of confederates—and many an inn stabled a mysterious horse in the eighteenth century !—to procure a fresh mount.

As soon as he reached York he rushed to his lodging, changed his clothes and strolled quietly out to the nearest bowling-green. The Lord Mayor of York was playing a game with his friends. Nevinson went up casually and asked the time. It was a quarter to eight.

When he was arrested his York witnesses readily swore that he was in York at 7.45 on the day in question, and as no one considered it possible for a man to be at Chatham on the same day, he was acquitted.

That is the true story of the ride to York from which, no doubt, Ainsworth received inspiration.

*　　　*　　　*

I discovered Turpin's cell to be a dreary, damp semi-underground room which no one but a house agent could describe as anything but a horror.

On the way out I saw the two Turpins, unnaturally clean and disarmed, walking meekly beside a woman.

§ 5

As my friend Bill, who takes the boat train down to Dover, says : ' Locos are human beings. They're just like women : you've got to nurse 'em and fuss 'em ! '

Now just outside the white walls of this city of York is a veritable abode of railway love. The amount of nursing and fussing that goes on in the running sheds of York day after day, year after year, is enough to make a driver's wife, if of a jealous nature, wish he was a guard.

The railway at York is the great employer of men, as the chocolate factories are of women. It is the grand junction to the far north. Into the great station at York are gathered all the thousand threads of travel, as through a finger ring, before they spread out, north and south, to every corner of the land. York, like Carlisle, is to hundreds of thousands merely the sound of milk-cans being bowled down a cold platform in the early hours of the morning. York Station is known to more people than York Minster.

The curved platforms of York are well worth the study of any man interested in the personalities of stations. London stations are pervaded by a radiant ' So-we-have-arrived ! ' expression. York's expression is a weary ' Hullo-it's-York ! ' and a dash at a refreshment buffet which is open all night.

York Station is a place of seedy eyes and dejected conversations. The talkative stranger who seemed so bright up to Peterborough now rouses thoughts of murder. York Station is a place where, all the stories read, people are ploughing through the advertisements. York Station is a day-long procession of tired old ladies in first-class non-smokers with their heads in plaid shawls ; of red-haired Aberdonians glaring meekly, as only Scotsmen can, from the carriages which are taking them to their granite ' hame '.

York Station welcomes the most improbable trains. They pant in like cross-country runners, some with ' Yeovil ' written on them; some with ' Dorchester ', and you wonder how they got there ! Such queer topographical salads as ' Penzance, Taunton, Bristol, Oxford, and Doncaster ' rouse no astonishment in the York official who is accustomed to welcome the rest of England under the vast glass roof.

But, come behind the scenes of York Station ! The comedy of a station is on its platforms, the drama is in the running sheds, where the big steel ' women ' are nursed and fussed before they are run out by men whose faces will soon be black, whose eyes will soon collect in each corner two small pits of coal dust. . . .

*   *   *

Trains drop and pick up locomotives at York. No. 4 shed running department is a great parade ground of green giants. A turntable occupies its centre, and round this in a circle, set regularly like the spokes of a wheel, are dozens of big engines, steam up—'just like human beings', as Bill says—waiting to run on the turntable and so out on the night's job.

Behind No. 4 shed is No. 3, full of less spectacular goods

locos, and No. 1, where the small tanks and the humdrum engines stand. Sometimes an antediluvian of no known category puffs into No. 1 shed with a brass hump like a fireman's helmet behind his tall smoke-stack. Even the natives of No. 1 shed let off a little steam at him.

'Hullo,' they hiss, 'who left the museum door open?'

'And how did you leave Mr. Stephenson, dearie?'

All the embittered 'locals' hiss with unkind laughter.

But the green Olympians of No. 4, their flanks shining, their piston-rods slightly green with new oil, the steam rising truly and gradually in their gauges, their boiler tubes clean as a whistle, their coal-tubs full, are superior to this tittle-tattle. They are removed from the ribaldry of the lesser sheds, isolated in their own magnificence like Guards officers on parade.

Their shed is dark, steamy, hot, and oil-smelling; and the Olympians wait for the clock, lean as racehorses, powerful as stallions, meek as women to the fussy touch of the man who stands in the glare of the furnace. High-speed matters such as Sheffield, London, Newcastle, and Manchester occupy their minds. They purr like tea-kettles, careless of the shrill gossip from the outer shed.

'Oh, did you see a "Pacific" with hot bearings outside? Didn't he look a fool propped up like that? If I was a "Pacific" I'd be ashamed. . . .'

'But did you hear what the Tool-van said to the Pocklington local?'

'No' (eagerly), 'what was it?'

'Well, if I wasn't a perfect lady—you know I was once on the King's Cross suburban—anyhow, it was about Seven-sixteen who took the Cup-tie special down to London. Now, don't repeat this . . .'

The horrid whisper is interrupted as a big Z type from No. 4 moves with a crash to the turntable, swings round, finds the 'road', says 'Well, good-bye all—Sheffield Ho!' and glides out into the dark where the green lights call him on over the silver metals. . . .

There is no sound in the shed but the drawing of furnaces as the clock moves on. Then, far down on the main-line track beyond the green lights is a far scream and a gathering thunder of wheels. A big green Pacific crouching over the track, a sudden meteor flash of light and a short pinkness of dining-car windows! Then deeper darkness; deeper silence.

' King's Cross,' says one of the Olympians, ' and, dash my connecting rods, six minutes late ! '

' You've never brought in the King's Cross,' comes a mild oily rebuke from the shadows ; and no one replies. A Pacific has spoken ! (No one back-chats to a Pacific except a very shabby tank.)

' Haddock—haddock—haddock . . . haddockandplaice—haddockandplaice—haddockandplaice . . .' pants a deep asthmatic voice as a high dark shape passes No. 4 shed with a grimy fireman looking for the cleaning gang.

The fish has come from Hull !

One by one the green Olympians steam out over the round table like steel knights to great adventure. Some will see the dawn come up over the blue hills of Scotland ; some will thunder south with men, women, and trade ; and in every one of them the man who nurses and fusses will stand at his gauges and levers, his face red in the fire glare, while his mate will lean from the swaying cab, gazing over the great shoulder of the flying monster to the thin line of the road ahead. . . .

' If you want a quiet life,' any running superintendent will tell you, ' and no inquiries and such-like, never part a man from his engine.'

*   *   *

There is a dead station in York.

No trains ever steam into its desolate platforms, no men and women ever walk its rough cobbles. When you stand on the wall opposite the present station the dead station of York lies below you, plainly seen, just behind Sir Edwin Lutyens' hideous railway war memorial. This was York Station when York was a terminus. Charles Dickens has stepped out on those cobbles. Our Victorian forefathers on their way to Scotland got out there and took coach northward.

I explored this ghost station ; a shy, retiring, lost little station it is, and the wind that blows round its many corners sounds like the rustle of crinolines. At midnight on George Stephenson's birthday I am sure a ghost train with a six-foot smoke-stack and a body like a barrel clanks into the dead station of York, and all the other ghosts on the platform look at it distrustfully and wonder what the world is coming to.

But for the rest of the year there is nothing more exciting

on the dead station of York than a wild scream over the way
from a train that will be in London in four hours.

§ 6

I have solved what was to me a mystery of York.

This city, which is normally medieval, is subject at certain
definite periods during the week to sudden ultra-modern
surges of small, neat girls. There is a moment when they
are not there, and there is a moment when they have arrived.
You never see it happen : you suddenly become aware that
the virginal inundation has set in as gradually and inevitably
as a tide.

Coney Street (which has nothing to do with rabbits, but is
really Conyng Street, the *via regia* or Kingsway) is their
parade ground. It is the main shopping, and the least
interesting, street in York. Frequently it has no human
interest other than a large, old, retired colonel or two in plus
fours, loud as the massed bands of the Brigade of Guards,
or perhaps a fine striding Yorkshire girl in the right
kind of tweed, with a couple of terriers at heel. Then,
generally towards evening, Coney Street is flooded by
thousands of small, smart girls.

These are the chocolate-makers of York.

When the tramcar stops on the outskirts of York a stupe-
fying smell of hot chocolate enters and gives you a crack
under the jaw. The only survivors are the children in the
tramcar, who lick their lips and look wistful. On either side
of the road are enormous red-brick factories embowered in
trees, rose gardens, recreation grounds, all constructed on
the modern principle of so much cubic air per lung.

It is a healthy sight. A Sheffield idealist said to me that
some day in the dim future Sheffield will look like this, but
it will be very dim and future.

This great factory, which absorbs the activity of about
four thousand girls and three thousand men, is one of the
sights of York. Americans dash there from the cathedral.
Forty thousand people go through it in the course of a
year. There is a reception department. You are met in the
visitors' lounge by cordial officials, who shake hands with
you and wave you towards a kind of museum where the cocoa
bean grows in oil bottles and the vanilla sprouts like a
museum specimen.

Then a pretty girl wearing a brown overall appears in the lounge, says ' Come this way, please,' and you start out to see how chocolates are made.

She leads you to a place where gigantic funnels are sucking up sawdust from the joinery departments. I forget how many tons of sawdust are collected every day, but I do remember that they are sold to make fire-lighters.

It is a logical step to the saw-mills. The world deserves all the toothache it receives : its appetite for chocolates is almost revolting. I saw men making not hundreds but thousands of crates to hold consignments of chocolate. The thin boxes were for England and the thick ones for Brisbane, Toronto, and places like Sierra Leone, where you would imagine a man would shoot to kill if you offered him a chocolate. Life is full of surprises !

She in the brown overall and I then walked a few miles down wide, white corridors hung with ferns. Men passed us riding on electric trolleys. Girls in white overalls flitted from room to room. Warm, sickly smells of all calibre, from the heavy ten-mile-range cocoa smell to the soft whispery smell of lemon jellies, assailed us every hundred yards. I believe a native, suddenly becoming blind, could tell his exact position in this factory by the smell.

We entered a long, many-windowed room, and here I solved the mystery of Coney Street. Here were the small, smart maidens of York, wearing white overalls, white caps on their heads, their busy fingers making chocolate boxes. There were hundreds of them, and beyond this great room others equally rich in small, smart girls. As they worked they sang.

The expensive gold and silver chocolate boxes which men give women before marriage are all made by hand. The strips of coloured paper are cut and deftly pasted on by girls with a special gift for this work. The plain boxes which men give their wives are made by machines, uncanny machines with horrid little steel hands that never make a mistake. There are also unnaturally perfect machines which pick up a cocoa label in terribly precise fingers, dab it gently on a tin, hour after hour. I longed to see them make a mistake, but they never do, so that you could never love them.

We went into a gymnasium.

A psychologist flitted past in consultation with a doctor in a white jacket. They were going to meet a welfare expert

4

(What a lot of remarkable people there are behind one chocolate !)

We went through so many perfect departments that I felt myself losing interest. There was nothing to quarrel with. My brain began to feel like a large lump of marzipan. I was shown a train standing in a rustic-looking siding. It steams out every day bearing consignments of chocolate to every part of the world. We strolled through a rose garden, through a large dining hall. We came to a bonded warehouse complete with Customs men. We went on to look at thousands of sacks of cocoa beans, tons of sugar and gum, the guide nipping through the labyrinth with her pretty head full of statistics.

' Yes,' I said, ' but tell me about the chocolate workers. How do they spend their money ? '

' Oh,' she said, ' some help their mothers.'

' And most buy hats and silk stockings ? '

' Well,' she said, torn by loyalty, ' some perhaps.'

So we left it at that.

One of the most impressive sights was a scientific cloak-room full of moving air with hooks placed at certain important intervals one from the other. More interesting than the science were the hundreds of little blue, red, green, fawn, and black cloche hats, the hundreds of little blue, red, green, fawn, and black velour coats all waiting to be taken for a walk in Coney Street. . . .

I don't remember when it happened, or how, but it was a thrilling moment. On looking through a glass door, quite by chance, I saw a chocolate ! It was a big one. It was sitting on a moving band travelling via twenty-six departments towards some unknown mouth.

' Look,' I cried, ' a chocolate ! '

An expression of great enthusiasm passed across the guide's face. She prepared to open more doors, but I, feeling slightly congested, and detesting the smell of warm chocolate, said good-bye.

§ 7

I climbed to the roof of the minster, as every visitor should, to say farewell to York. The way up is not difficult, and you come out at length upon a wide, windy roof protected by a stone balustrade. Far below, field lying against field, wood against wood, is the green Vale of York.

It was a sunny April morning and the Vale looked happy, prosperous and fat. The pear-trees shone and sparkled in the Deanery gardens ; when I leant over the stone wall I could see the rooks flying slowly round lower towers, blotting out with their wings half an acre of the distant earth.

On one side I looked down over the red roofs of York. There is no more medieval roof line in England. Every chimney was smoking and the lay-out of the streets was so clearly the work of the Middle Ages. But Roman York must have looked like this too, a huddled city of red-tiled houses. I looked down at this and out over the green Vale thinking of Eboracum, the Roman capital, remembering that two Caesars died at York, and that Constantine the Great was proclaimed Emperor there. Those fields had seen the legions march in to proclaim the Master of the Roman world.

I stood a long time looking at the green fields and the clouds that piled themselves up over the edge of the sunny vale.

CHAPTER FOUR

I MEET AN UNUSUAL TOWN CLERK, TAKE A MUD BATH AT HARRO-
GATE, LEARN ALL ABOUT MOTHER SHIPTON AT KNARES-
BOROUGH, AND GO TO RIPON TO HEAR A SAXON HORN
BLOWN IN THE MARKET PLACE

§ I

THERE are in Yorkshire many old country towns
waiting, it seems, in an afternoon hush for another
Jane Austen.

The curate's spectacles flash in the sunlight as he is seen,
pink and earnest, in swift transit on a bicycle. The church
bells mark off every fifteen minutes—as if they mattered !
—and the farmers lean picturesquely over a temporary sheep
market or clump heavily across the cobbles towards the tap
room of the ' Bay Horse '.

Above the frosted glass of this haven the red-headed
barmaid flashes a moment, lifting a hand in gay salute
to the good-looking auctioneer's clerk over the way. The
policeman generally has time to discuss current affairs with
the oldest inhabitant.

This ancient person leans on a stick, his sole occupation
that of spotting each stranger, and then watching him carefully with implied distrust, as though he might get away
with the town hall or the market cross. Now and then a
masterly-looking woman, who never has, and never will,
show the world her legs, cycles past on some grimly definite
mission.

Cows sometimes spread themselves over the main street,
heads down, while a boy smacks them behind with a stick,
or sheep come in a slow, grey wave, and, to a sound of little
feet clicking on the cobbles, are driven on, timid and expressionless, by a panting and enthusiastic collie.

Enormous brown-striped peppermints lie in glass jars in
the sweet-shop windows. The eyes of the post-mistress are
exceedingly wise. The saddler looks as though he owns a

motor-car; the gun-smith looks as though he might be mayor.

One is almost tempted to shatter the magnificent uneventfulness of it by sending a telegram to Buckingham Palace; and then it would be fun to rush to the extreme limits of the town and time the arrival of the news; for human nature is stronger than Post Office regulations and—nothing ever happens here except . . .

Stepping lightly, thin-legged, narrow-faced, with a white blaze on his forehead, ridden by a small groom in grey cloth gaiters, a good horse goes by, easy, pretty, his pulled tail arching out and blowing a bit in the wind like a thin waterfall. So he passes with just a faint jingle of his snaffle when he flings up his head; and the life of the town is suspended and centres for a moment in him.

I asked to see the Town Clerk. An old man who had been watching me readily directed me to a small Georgian house near the church on which was written in white paint on a black window: 'Mr. A. B. Blank, Solicitor, Commissioner for Oaths.'

In a ground-floor office a young man with red, untamed hair sat on a high stool writing painfully in a ledger.

'Upstairs!' he said shyly, pointing heavenwards with his pen and exposing five inches of bony wrist.

Every stair creaked. At the top was a half-open door.

'Come in,' said a deep voice.

An old man was sitting at a littered, sloping desk near the window. He was reading. A pair of steel-rimmed spectacles was on the bridge of his nose, a black skull-cap on his head. I coughed, but he went on reading. On the mantelpiece stood a vacuum flask, a sandwich box, and a neatly folded napkin.

While I waited for him to recognize my existence I looked through the window into the churchyard. Rooks were flying round the grey tower. A man who I am sure was the doctor came out of a house carrying a little black bag. I wondered if some one was departing from or arriving in this quiet place. There were daffodils growing in clumps among the graves, but they were finished or 'over'. I became aware that a pair of deep, humorous eyes were watching me.

'Well?' said the old man, scratching the edge of his skull-cap with a paper-knife.

' Are you, sir,' I asked, ' the Town Clerk ? '

' That is not my strict title,' he replied, ' but I perform the same onerous duties to a rural district council. And what may I do for you ? '

I had no opportunity to tell him, for swinging round in his chair, and tapping the air with his paper-knife, he said, earnestly :

' Have you ever seen an Edward VI prayer-book ? '

I said no. He handed me one. I struggled feebly with an urban district question, but it was swept aside and overwhelmed in his bibliomaniac enthusiasm as a cork is shot over a cataract.

' I picked up recently,' he said with a quiet smile of self-satisfaction, ' a first edition of *Religio Medici* for—how much do you think ? Guess ! Oh, yes ; have a guess. . . . '

' A pound ? '

A look of triumph, which cannot have come too often to the face of Caesar, lit up his eyes. He brought the paper knife crash on the desk and shouted :

' Five bob ! '

At that moment the telephone bell rang.

' Once,' he said, ' I nearly bought a black-letter Chaucer . . . '

The telephone started ringing in spurts.

' But it was not complete . . . '

The telephone continued to ring in short, urgent spasms.

A look of annoyance crossed his face, and he put the instrument on the floor under the desk. (Most of the ledgers were already there.) The telephone became tired, and he restored it to favour.

I continued to listen to him happily, glad to have found that characters as clear-cut as any drawn by Dickens still exist in quiet places. I wondered, as he dived into a discussion on the points at issue at the Council of Whitby, whether he would have behaved in the same way had I come to tell him that the town was on fire. Probably. He had a most strongly developed sense of values. I began to like him. He talked about Pope Gregory the First as if he were a cousin whom he had seen last week.

The church clock struck two. I saw him throw a quick glance towards the sandwich box, and judged that the audience was over.

' Good-bye,' he said heartily, ' and, by the way, if you really want to follow up that matter go and see Mr. Jones, our surveyor. I don't think it's worth your while, but you know best. Good-bye . . .'

I creaked downstairs.

' I say,' came his voice, and, looking up, I saw over the banisters his face, rather Elizabethan, with its straight nose and the broad forehead and the black skull-cap. ' I say,' he cried, ' you know, of course, that St. Augustine was not a bit pleased when he had orders to convert us. In fact he turned back to Rome seized with fear at the thought of journeying to so fierce and barbarous a nation. Good-bye. . . .'

* * *

The farmers were still watching cows with the same critical, screwed-up eyes expression to be seen on private view day at the Royal Academy. The little town had sunk into a cosy afternoon slumber. Two or three old women sat before baskets in which new-laid eggs and butter were exposed for sale. The church bells were mellow in the sunny streets. Dear, sleepy, uneventful . . . stay a moment !

I passed the war memorial on the outskirts, standing back in a railed-in square of turf.

What wonderful old English towns these are ; and—how swiftly they can awaken.

§ 2

I rose unhappily with the feeling that no one cared whether I live or die, so I decided to go to Harrogate.

To the introspective and to the lonely a spa is a spiritual cocktail. When sick of yourself, fly to a spa and try hard to develop a few symptoms ! You will find that every spa is full of people who ought to be sick of themselves but are not —which is most stimulating to your inferiority complex.

All spas open their arms to you. Each gazes lovingly—not into your eyes, but beyond them to your liver, and finds you more than ever worth loving. You sink right into the arms of that dear old lady of Somerset, Bath, and, in much the same way, Cheltenham, Leamington, and Buxton embrace you warmly. I concluded, and with justice, that Harrogate might have a little kindness to spare.

Harrogate is the Bath of the north of England, but unlike

Bath, which is a soporific, Harrogate is a stimulant. It is a bath-chairless spa. It is three times as large as any other English spa, and its shops, when they are not reminding you of Bond-street, recall Monte Carlo and Cannes : they are full of delightful, useless things : ivory ladies dancing on onyx stands, Japanese jade and Queen Anne tea services, which I suppose you buy as thank-offerings when delivered from myocarditis.

It is a town of flowers. As soon as I saw the thousands of tall scarlet tulips on parade in the public squares I felt a little brighter.

And the sound of Harrogate is that of a gardener pushing a lawn-mower over grass and of women discussing a white evening gown in a black velvet window.

And the smell of Harrogate—but I will come to that in a minute !

Most spas have one or two springs of healing water above which they have erected pump rooms. Harrogate, however, sits on a natural chemist's shop. No fewer than eighty-eight mineral springs discharge their waters into Harrogate. Few of these springs are chemically alike. Harrogate is a fine example of Nature's law of inequality ; here are eighty-eight spas crammed by a freak of nature into one town !

The waters of Harrogate vary from the characteristic sulphur water, by way of saline, alkaline sulphur to pure chalybeate. It seems as if Nature has said :

' Let's have a great disturbance of the strata and give Harrogate a kind of ice-cream soda fountain ; everything that the lower regions can concoct in the way of mineral water, from stuff no one can drink without a nose-bag to a pure sparkling brew like bad lemonade.'

And so it came to pass . . .

I went into the Pump Room and asked for a glass of sulphur water. This is Harrogate's speciality. No place outside a laboratory can give you so much sulphur in a glass. The air of the Pump Room reeked of sulphur : it suggested that a couple of mammoths were slowly decaying in the cellars.

But the smell of ' The Old Sulphur Water ', as they call it, was like faint music to the taste of it. Even now, after a lapse of several hours, words fail me. It seemed, as I sipped my glass, that I was drinking a queer cocktail composed of bad eggs, safety matches, and acetylene.

Nothing but acute glycosuria would induce me to ask for another glass.

So I wandered through Harrogate from Pump Room to Winter Garden, studying the patients and the doctors, meeting every now and then the queer dead mammoth smell as I approached a sulphurous spring.

I noticed the number of young men taking the cure. Bath is full of old people ! Harrogate seems to attract the young.

' Most of them suffering from rheumatic complaints contracted during the war,' said a doctor.

In the baths I saw all the things—some of them delightful, some appalling—which a modern spa can do to the internal machinery of man. I told them how sad I felt and asked them to suggest a bath for me.

' Electric peat ! ' they said.

I came out, wearing a towel, into a white, tiled room in which was a fearful and horrible thing. A large bath was waiting full of what looked like gently steaming mud. Or perhaps it was like a mixture of chocolate and porridge.

It was peat, from the Yorkshire moors near Thorpe. In the season Harrogate uses twenty-five tons of it a week. It is mixed with sulphur water and heated. As I sat on the edge, trying to pluck up enough courage to touch the horrid mess with my toe, I asked the attendant how many people preferred their arthritis to the cure.

' In all the years I've given peat baths, sir, only one young fellow couldn't bring himself to get in, and he was full of rheumatism from head to foot. He just looked at the bath and shivered. It was no good—he couldn't get into it . . .'

This nerved me. What a lot of weak fools in the world ! I thrust my foot through the soft, warm mess right to the bottom, expecting to encounter there some foul, slimy, moving thing. But it was just warm and muddy and faintly aromatic.

I sank into the bath, grasped it in big, soft, warm handfuls and examined it. There were small twigs in it. It was really a bath of putrescent vegetable matter. It was soothing.

' I suppose women make an awful fuss about taking peat baths ? ' I said, making a mud-pie on my chest.

' Not likely,' said the attendant. ' I've never heard of it.

I'm told they always put it on their faces, too. It's good for the complexion.'

As he fixed a copper plate at my head and feet, turned a switch, and filled me with a thousand million bright needles of electricity I reflected how greatly the delicacy of women is exaggerated.

One emerges from a peat path like some slimy sea monster. I once saw a man who had badly misjudged his suicide from the Thames Embankment. He jumped at low tide, and they fished him out of five feet of Thames mud. I remembered him as I walked to the needle bath, where spurts of clean water took the peaty moorlands from me.

* * *

I could tell you about the paraffin-wax treatment, about the electric baths, the hot-air cure, and dozens more, but I prefer to remember how good it was to sit in the Winter Garden listening to the orchestra, feeling beautifully clean, and wondering what was wrong with the girl in the green hat.

I suppose many a great romance has begun at a spa with a vague, speculative interest in the adored one's digestive juices. . . .

The old livery ones stood up slowly, the ancient gouty ones rose up protestingly, the young rheumatic ones limped heroically, magazines and novels were laid aside, the orchestra retired into silence—it was time for Harrogate to select its vitamins.

§ 3

An old man was leaning over Knaresborough Bridge. So was I. (So will you if you ever find this bridge !)

It is an overwhelming view. Knaresborough was created by Nature in one of her best landscape gardener moments. The little town climbs a rocky gorge among trees. Above the highest trees rise the round grey towers of a Norman castle. The river Nidd winds through the gorge, broad and slow-moving, to disappear beneath a tall, thin bridge like a section of the Roman aqueduct near Arles. The sun, slanting across the gorge, left one side in blue shadow and lit up the orchards on the other so that the apple-trees looked like spangled pantomime fairies waiting the order to dance.

A girl with long bare arms was punting in the shallows.

She wore a scarlet hat. It was an inspired spot of colour. It might have been placed on her head by the president of the Royal Academy.

The old man spat appreciatively in the river and said that the day was hot.

' Who,' I asked him, ' was Mother Shipton ? '

He removed his pipe and drew near, full of reply.

*   *   *

Towns are like people. Nothing happens to some. Others collect all manner of queer experiences. Knaresborough, so quiet except on market day, is really a museum of unusual happenings. Its greatest memories are of murders and witchcraft.

In the castle on the hill the four knights who slew Thomas à Becket locked themselves up for a year while the storm broke over their deed. They did not dare to show their faces until it was safe for them to go to the Holy Land and repent ; which was not for a long time. A cave not far away is famous as the abode of St. Robert of Knaresborough, who appears to have made money, and still to have retained his sanctity. It is, however, much more famous as the cave in which Eugene Aram hid the body of his victim, Daniel Clarke, in 1744. They still talk about this murder as if it happened last week, and you are expected to show sympathy for Eugene Aram, which is not easy.

But more famous than all these memories is Mother Shipton.

I suppose every one knows that Mother Shipton, who was born at Knaresborough in the year 1488, prophesied the telegraph, the railway, the motor-car, in addition to much political history which gained her an amazing notoriety for centuries :

> Carriages without horses shall go
> And accidents fill the world with woe . . .
> Around the world thoughts shall fly
> In the twinkling of an eye.

These are two of her famous sayings. Belief in Mother Shipton existed in every servants' hall until within comparatively recent times. She became the oracle of cooks and parlourmaids. I remember when a small boy hearing all about her from a large, superstitious, but godly, cook, whose life was one triumphant spotting in the passage of events the fulfilment of Mother Shipton's cryptograms.

Succeeding ages have spent much time and ingenuity in deciphering the Shipton predictions. *Blackwood's Magazine* for December 1846 mentioned a prophecy which puzzled all readers of Mother Shipton for centuries. It is as follows :

> Eighteen hundred and thirty-five,
> Which of us shall be alive ?
> Many a king shall end his reign,
> Many a knave his end shall gain.
> Many a statesman be in trouble,
> Many a scheme the world shall bubble ;
> Many a man shall sell his vote,
> Many a man shall turn his coat,
> Right be wrong and wrong be right,
> By Westminster's candle-light ;
> But when from the top of Bow,
> Shall the dragon stoop full low ;
> When the church of Holy Paul
> Shall come down both cross and ball
> When all men shall see them meet
> On the land yet by the fleet,
> When below the Thames' bed
> Shall be seen the furnace red,
> When its bottom shall drop out,
> Making hundreds swim about,
> Where a fish had never swum,
> Then shall doleful tidings come.
> Flood and famine, woe and tax,
> Melting England's strengthlike wax ;
> Till she fights both France and Spain
> Then shall all be well again.

' All ' says Blackwood, ' was amply verified. The repairs of St. Paul's, in the year stated, required that the Cross and Ball should be taken down, which was done accordingly. Bow Church happening to be in the same condition, the Dragon on the Spire was also taken down : Cross, Ball and Dragon were sent to a coppersmith in Ludgate Hill, beside the Fleet Prison, where they were to be seen by all the wondering population, lying together.

' The Thames Tunnel had been pushed to the middle of the river's bed, when coming to a loose portion of the clay, the roof fell in. The Thames burst through its own bottom, the Tunnel was instantly filled, and the workmen were forced to swim for their lives.'

*　　　*　　　*

' She was a great witch,' said the old man, ' and ugly, too.'

He removed his pipe and pointed over to the trees on the right bank :

' She was born in there,' he said, ' and her real name was Ursula Southeil.'

He then told me that Mother Shipton's father was none other than the devil. Her mother, it appears, met the devil in Knaresborough one evening and was immensely attracted by his air of refinement. They began ' walking out '. The devil deceived her. He then quietly declared his identity, which did not apparently come as a shock to her, and gave her the power to kill, heal, create thunderstorms, and generally to make herself a nuisance in the neighbourhood.

Her child naturally inherited these gifts. On the assumption, perhaps, that the devil looks after his own, the mother retired to a convent, leaving Ursula to shift for herself, which she quickly did by embarking on a career of rhymed couplets. She was so successful that she impressed her psychic powers on the whole country. Unlike most witches Mother Shipton became popular. There is no record, so far as I know, that anyone suggested that she should be burned or ducked. I think her death is characteristic. She decided to die on a certain day in 1561. When the time arrived she solemnly said good-bye to all her friends, went to bed, and died in a most business-like manner.

I am told that she is still revered in many parts of Yorkshire, and that thousands visit her cave every year.

I walked through a magnificent park beside the river. Near the cave in which Mother Shipton was born is a curious thin waterfall called ' the Dropping Well ', which turns any object placed in it to stone. This ' magical ' quality must have helped to establish the reputation of the prophetess in the eyes of the superstitious of all ages !

These chemical waters, which crop up everywhere in the neighbourhood of Harrogate, drip slowly over an overhanging ledge of rock. A motley collection of objects is always kept hanging where the waters will soak through them and petrify them. Visitors sometimes leave their gloves and return during the following summer to take them away in hard stone.

Among the things slowly turning to stone at that moment were a sponge, a stuffed dog, an owl, a child's Teddy bear, a hawk, gloves, a weasel, a cat, a bowler hat.

'A sponge petrifies fairly quickly,' said the man in charge, 'because the water soaks all through it and the chemicals act at once, but a dog or a cat sometimes take a year before they are hard and solid.'

There is a museum containing objects which have been turned to stone. They prove that visitors have been amusing themselves like this for a long time. There is a dainty very early Victorian parasol perfect in every flounce and hard as steel !

If you go to Knaresborough on market day, do not fail to walk through the crowded streets where the stall-holders are selling almost everything that farmers and their wives can desire—except, of course, the right kind of weather. If you know Devon farmers, contrast them with these equally robust, but entirely different, Yorkshiremen.

The street market of Knaresborough, which overflows from the market place into side roads, is a hearty medieval sight. I suppose Cheapside was like that once.

§ 4

Every night just before nine o'clock a man who looks like a dismounted highwayman walks into the market square of Ripon carrying a large silver-mounted horn. He wears a three-cornered Dick Turpin hat and a long-waisted fawn coat. No one pays any attention to him, because he has been doing this since the reign of Alfred the Great.

He stands about a moment listening. Sharp at nine p.m. the curfew sounds from the cathedral belfry, and as soon as the last note of the bell has died away the horn-blower lifts the horn to his lips and produces a wild moo of deep and dismal melancholy. His first moo is delivered in front of the town hall, a terra-cotta building with a sentence in gold letters running round the cornice : ' Unless the Lord keeps the city the Wakeman waketh in vain.'

The horn-blower then marches to the four corners of the market square, sending out a long blast of sadness at each of them.

Every night for over a thousand years the horn has been blown in Ripon. They call it ' the setting of the watch '

The custom is supposed to have been in existence long before Alfred the Great incorporated the town in 886. The note of the horn signalled the setting of a watch, or guard, over the town. The mayor, or wakeman as he was called in the old days, was responsible for any thefts committed. Each citizen of Ripon had to pay annually twopence for a house with one door and fourpence for a gate door and a back door.

Surely Ripon can claim to be the home of insurance against burglary ?

*   *   *

' It's not an easy job to be horn-blower in Ripon,' said that official. ' You've got to have good lungs and keep in training, because any fellow who can blow longer and better than you can challenge you to a contest and take your job. And they often test you to see if you are blowing as well as usual. The last horn-blower resigned. His record was a blow of forty-nine seconds. I'm some seconds under that record. . . . And the Americans ! They come here in hundreds in summer to hear me blow. I believe they know more about this custom in America than in England ! '

I can well believe that the horn of Ripon could, like Peel's view-hallo, awaken the dead, and this is said to have happened as recently as September, 1923. The mayor of that time revived a custom that had not been observed for three hundred and nineteen years : the blowing of the horn outside the Wakeman's House, an ancient building once the abode of Hugh Ripley, Mayor of Ripon in 1604.

A large crowd gathered outside on the pavement to see the ceremony. When the horn-blower touched his dreary top note and the whole evening was dripping in melancholy a startled murmur went round the crowd. The face of old Hugh Ripley was seen for a moment to look down on them from a top window !

There are still people in Ripon who believe they saw a ghost that night ; and who would dare to contradict so good a story ?

*   *   *

These Yorkshire market towns are as characteristic as anything in England.

You could drive a coach of Georgians into them at night, give them dinner at the ' Nag's Head ', and apart from the possibility that the port might not please them they would never guess that they had been dead two hundred years. Ripon is busy and enterprising, but delightfully unchanged. It is the only city in the north of England which keeps alive the memory of one of the four great northern saints, the pious St. Wilfrid of Ripon. The other three, St. Peter of York, St. Cuthbert of Durham, and St. John of Beverley, are not made the subject of a Protestant festa, which is surely a unique pageant! During the first week in August a procession goes through Ripon in the midst of which strangers must be astonished to see riding on horseback and surrounded by musicians St. Wilfrid robed and bearing his pastoral staff.

The custom goes back to the dawn of Ripon's history. It no doubt celebrates the saint's return to his monastery at Ripon after one of his frequent missionary expeditions. Just as the Lord Mayor's Show in London was once a solemn procession of armed merchant princes and their followers, so in this merry pageant at Ripon we can see the reflection of something very solemn that rejoiced the heart of Ripon in Saxon times. . . .

'You might remind London,' said an old inhabitant of Ripon, ' that she is the third city in England. York comes first, then Ripon, then London. I do not know whether the Lord Mayors of York and London and the Mayor of Ripon have ever met together on an official occasion, but I am sure it would be a big surprise to Londoners to find their Lord Mayor third in order of precedence. . . .'

In a restless world that changes often for the sake of change you feel in little places such as Ripon that you touch the sturdy roots of England firmly locked in a distant and important past.

CHAPTER FIVE

I DISCOVER THE THREE GLORIES OF THE NORTH RIDING: FOUNTAINS ABBEY, JERVAULX, AND RIEVAULX

§ 1

THERE are moments when the traveller stops and says to himself : ' My journey has ended almost before it has begun. There is no point in continuing it. I shall, if I follow the high-road for a hundred years, find nothing more lovely than this.'

Three times have I said these words in one day's wandering as I stood before the ruined altars of Fountains, Jervaulx, and Rievaulx. These abbeys are the three glories of the North Riding. There should be some charitable fund for the transportation of all spiritually diseased and all unhappy people to these abbeys. Here Peace and Beauty live hand in hand.

I have seen Glastonbury lifting its broken arch above the green grass, I have seen the Kings Beaulieu in the New Forest standing like a white spectre in the fields, I have seen Tintern and Tewkesbury and Buildwas, and dozens more in the south and west of England, but never have I seen three abbeys to compare in beauty with Fountains, Rievaulx, and Jervaulx. There are no places in England where I would rather spend a summer's day. I would visit Fountains in the early morning, Rievaulx at midday, and Jervaulx— because it is, to my mind, more melancholy than its brothers —at sunset.

I would say to any man or woman in England who is longing for a spiritual experience : ' Go to Ripon and visit these three abbeys in turn.' Their white bones are drenched in peace ; all the pride has gone out of them and they kneel in the Yorkshire meadows with white daisies about them like three saints at prayer. Strange and puzzling are the emotions of a Protestant in these abbeys. I cannot echo George Borrow and rejoice that scenes of gross superstition lie in ruins ; I cannot feel the horror of a Roman Catholic for the Reformation which brought about their fall, but where is the man who cannot feel pity for such beauty in distress, where is the man who cannot feel contempt for the rough, unfeeling hands which tore such loveliness to the earth?

It may occur to you when you stand in the silence of a ruined nave, or when you walk, instinctively on tiptoe, down aisles whose roofs are open to the sky, or when you sit a moment in the stalls of ruined chapter-houses where the ivy twines about the pillars, that these sanctuaries which shielded civilization in ancient times have drawn near to God again in their decay.

§ 2

The high altar of Fountains Abbey is covered with a stubborn green moss the colour of olives. In the late afternoon the sunlight slants over the western walls and, falling into the roofless church, prints sharp gold squares and triangles on the Norman columns of the nave. Small birds fly through the clerestory windows, and the brightest and softest patch of turf in all England lies like a soft carpet from the high altar to the great west door. When you look through the windows, in which not one inch of glass remains, you may fancy that the green leaves and the interlaced boughs beyond form themselves into sacred patterns against the gaping frames.

This grey and red-brown abbey stands in the middle of a park. You approach it over a mile-long path, ornamental waters shining through trees to your left; to your right little woody dells and curved lawns in which are colonies of spring flowers—clumps of primroses, forget-me-nots, violets, bluebells in a deep blue mist a foot above the grass.

Turning a bend you see before you the abbey, gaunt but lovely beyond words, standing beside a little stream which whispers through weeds and water plants into the valley. . . .

Fountains is one of the most beautiful sights in England. It is unforgettable. The eye passes over it in content, building up an arch here, supplying a pillar there. Such beauty does not come into the world now. While you are walking through the silent ruins an old caretaker with pale-blue eyes will come and talk to you. When you tell him that you consider Fountains Abbey to be the best-kept ruin in

FOUNTAINS ABBEY

England he looks pleased, and says the daisies are a nuisance, so thick and stubborn. If only this abbey had been spared the fury of the Reformation.

The lead on the roof, the caretaker will tell you, was bought in the fifteenth century by 'a speculating gentleman from London'!

' Henry VIII ? '

' No, Sir Richard Gresham was his name! He tore off the lead and boiled it down into ingots and carted it away. Then, of course, the church began to decay. . . .'

It is so quiet. No sound but the thrush, perched like a little brown saint on a grassy niche in the transept, singing, stopping, listening, his frog-like head on one side, then pouring his heart out into the evening. Birds fly the length of the church, rabbits come lolloping from the little coppice to the shadow of the ruins, then back at the slightest sound with a flash of white scuts . . .

I sit writing near the high altar, which stands raised above the body of the church, a large desolate slab of stone. I remember the Frenchman who said to Richard I :

' You have at home in England three daughters whom you love more than the grace of God ; they are Pride, Luxury, and Avarice.'

' My friend,' replied the King, ' they are no longer at home. I have married Pride to the Templars, Luxury to the Black Canons, and Avarice to the Cistercians.'

But there was a time before this marriage when the good monks wandered the roads of England looking for a place in which to found their abbeys. I prefer to think of them at their highest rather than at their lowest ; and at their highest they saved for us all that was left of culture and of knowledge. How did they build these incredibly beautiful abbeys ? I put this question to an architect the other day, and he made a surprising answer :

' They sang,' he said, ' and their work was done for them.' They sang ! Go to Fountains and remember that ; for this church looks, is indeed, a psalm in stone. They came from York, tramping the wild countryside, poor, humble, hungry, dreaming only of raising a temple to the glory of God, and they took stone from the local quarries and carried it to the

thorny meadow by the stream and—they sang! So the
great Abbey of Fountains rose up from the grass, a reflection
of their magnificent faith.

How many of the greatest things in the Middle Ages were
anonymous!

*   *   *

Now the lovely shell stands riddled with late sunlight
from every gaping window.

Only the birds sing vespers now . . . the shadows lengthen,
a bar of sunlight falls across the green high altar of Fountains
and the space between the pillars of the nave grows darker.
It is difficult to tear yourself away. The stones are soaked
in peace. You walk through ruined cloisters, in cold crypt-
like cellars, through grey Norman arches, and everywhere
the same sad hush.

Where the rabbits play at the edge of the grass you turn,
and, looking back at Fountains, see it, grey, almost silver
grey, like an old saint kneeling in a meadow. And you know
in your heart that no matter what came after, a dream came
true there for a little while.

§ 3

The sun was setting as I left Fountains and took the road
through Ripon and then north-west to West Tanfield and
Masham. Here the green valley fades imperceptibly into the
harder moors and fells of the Pennine Chain. Away to the
right I saw the Abbey of Jervaulx lying in a meadow some little
distance from the road. I knocked at a cottage door and
asked for the key. It was very late, said the caretaker, and
the sun was setting. Would I rather come back to-morrow?
All right, I could have the key; but I wouldn't see much in
the dusk. . . .

I tramped across a field full of sheep and loud with the
bleating of long-tailed lambs. Hidden beneath brambles I
found the wicket-gate to the once mighty Abbey of Jervaulx
and the lock turned silently, admitting me to the deserted
ruins. A thrush was singing evensong from a pillar in the
chapter-house, pouring out his sharp liquid notes into the
still dusk, listening a moment and then lifting his small head
and sending his song again towards the sky. The higher

walls were still warm with the afterglow; their bases in the dusk.

This great tangled ruin was like something on the other side of fairyland, it was like the Palace of the Sleeping Beauty, so that I walked gently under its spell, turning corners into little roofless courts, passing through tumbled cloisters and so to the long ghost of the mighty church. Not a sound but the piping of birds and from the surrounding meadows the childish bleating of the lambs.

I sat in the chapter-house in a monk's stall over which brambles and small blue rock-flowers had formed a close embroidery. Six pillars which once upheld the roof pointed to the sky, their feet in ivy. On the floor lay the grave-stones of mitred abbots. And I remembered the lovely story of this abbey, a fresh, beautiful story full of the early morning of the world, how a company of monks from the parent abbey of Byland were lost among these moors and fields and how as they slept the abbot was given a vision. A woman and her little boy appeared to him.

'Fair and tender woman,' he said to her, 'what doest thou with thy child in this barren and desert place?'

She smiled with her eyes before replying:

'I am a frequent inmate of desert places. I have come from Rievaulx and Byland and am going to the new monastery.'

Then the abbot, who was relieved to have found a guide in the wilderness, said:

'Good lady, I implore thee to lead me and my brethren to the new monastery, for we also are of Byland.'

She then said, with the same slow smile:

'Ye *were* of Byland but are now of Jervaulx.'

Turning to her little boy she said:

'Sweet son, be their leader, I am called elsewhere.'

And she disappeared.

The boy led the way, holding a branch pulled from a tree, and the monks followed him until they came to a barren, desolate place among the hills. Here the child thrust the branch into the earth and immediately it became filled with white birds. He looked at the monks, saying: 'Here shall God be adored for a short space,' and before they, having recognized Him, could fall on their knees in the grass He also vanished. . . .

'Here shall God be adored for a short space. . . .'

The birds were silent, the light was drained from the sky, and I sat on in the ruined stall watching the shadows grow deeper, watching the first star through a broken arch ; and a little wind blowing round the corners swept through Jervaulx like a prayer. There is some spell about Jervaulx that seeks to drive you down upon your knees on the mossy stones.

My hand touched something cold and smooth. I picked up a medieval tile, a blue fleur-de-lis on a yellow ground. It had once formed part of the pavement of the chapter-house, had felt the sandals of many an abbot on grave occasions, had felt the tread of many a visiting knight and squire, of many a holy man drawn from the bleak hills to the warmth and hospitality of the great abbey. The awful instinct of the collector drew it into my pocket and immediately my conscience rose up and argued with me :

' You cannot take this,' it said.

' If I do not,' I said, ' some American will. I will carry it away and keep it always in memory of Jervaulx.'

' Thou shalt not steal,' said my conscience.

' Is it stealing to preserve this relic ? '

' Look round ! You are not the first thief. Can Jervaulx afford to lose even one small tile from its chapter-house ? '

And the end of it was that I took the tile and hid it where no one, I think, will ever find it. In broad daylight I am sure I would have stolen it ; but in the dusk, with those ruins full of whispered prayers, it was, or seemed, sacrilege. . .

It was nearly dark. A pale, whitish mist had risen from the river Ure and it lay breast high over the meadow. The sheep moved in this mist like the grey ghosts of lay brothers. I turned and looked back at the shell of Jervaulx, silent under the stars, black against the pale sky.

' Here God shall be adored for a short space.'

§ 4

If you would like a glimpse of England which is almost too English to be true, go north of York to the edge of the moors at Pickering, and on to the Abbey of Rievaulx.

I stopped at Kirkdale, where wild bees have nested in the square tower of a Saxon church. The grey stones of St. Gregory's fairly hummed with their energy, the keynote to an afternoon drowsy with the sound of wings. Here the

SUNLIGHT OVER RIEVAULX

shadows of the gigantic yew-trees are almost blue. The little churchyard is as lovely as that of Corsham, in Somerset, near Bath, and over the porch of the church a Saxon sundial states that the church was rebuilt during the reign of Edward the Confessor !

In this part of the world apple-faced girls, whose hair is straight and yellow, stand knee-deep in the grass, their pinafores full of buttercups ; here the slow ploughs come with a faint jingle over the brown curved backs of the fields, the crows slowly following them with harsh but appreciative cries, the resigned horses pausing to nibble a few crisp shoots of hawthorn when they complete the furrow by the hedge and turn about in a wide circle to plod back over the chocolate-brown earth. Wood and coppice are alive with bird song ; the primroses are yellow-green in the ditches ; the lambs have had their catkin tails bobbed, and are old enough now, and wise enough to the world and its ways, to regard strangers without leaping sideways in the air and running to press themselves against their dams like shy children.

I went on into Helmsley, where a town-crier with a bell was shouting in the market square. There was no one to hear him, except the statue of Lord Feversham ; but the small grey stone houses looked extraordinarily intelligent. There was, he shouted, to be a cricket match that afternoon in a local meadow ! What a slice of old England ! The little town spread itself as if room was no matter ; it takes life calmly as if time were no matter, and down one of its streets a stream of clear water gurgles and splashes. Women sometimes dip buckets in it ; cows sometimes stand in it and appear to meditate.

The lane leads up out of Helmsley to Rievaulx. When I reached the crest of the hill I went to a house in the heart of a beech-wood and rang a bell beside a wicket gate. I paid a shilling to see one of the greatest views in all England, and they admitted me to a stretch of clipped turf, milk-white with daisies.

Below me lay Rievaulx.

*   *   *

In the year 1758, when fox-hunting squires translated Virgil in their spare time and quoted Theocritus in Parliament, when her ladyship, the world well aired, languished in the shade as Amaryllis, Sir Thomas Duncombe, who then swayed these parts, decided to build a little Greek temple on the hill above Rievaulx. It stands there now with its classic feet in daisies.

What an age it was! The English nobleman was happier then than ever he was, or will be again. Sir Thomas having built his pavilion above the moors, employed Burnici, the Italian painter, to cover the ceiling with prima donna goddesses in the manner of Guido's ' Aurora ' in the Rospigliosi Palace in Rome. They still talk about Burnici in country public-houses as far away as York! They say that he lay on his back for three years producing plump goddesses. (Some say seven years!) This story is told in a manner which suggests either that Burnici was too well paid or that he made the job last out as long as possible.

Anyhow, there stands the temple above the North Yorks moors, a memorial to the marvellous eighteenth century. From its steps an embankment of smooth turf curves round for half a mile or so, wide enough for four coaches abreast, and perched on the extreme edge of the hill.

Below is the silver-grey ruin of Rievaulx Abbey lying snugly cupped in the valley, and the moors rise up beyond it rolling to the sky, threaded with thin white roads that lose themselves in the green, yellow, and brown patchwork of the fields. The clouds sail up over the edge of them, the cloud shadows sweep across the valley, the winds come tearing over the vale with the sweetness of open country in them and something of the sea.

They keep the grass as closely cut and as smoothly rolled as ever old Sir Thomas did when the fancy took him to hold an eclogue round the little temple among the daisies.

*　　*　　*

What shall a man write of Rievaulx Abbey ? It is as beautiful as Fountains, it lacks the melancholy of Jervaulx. The daisies have made a tessellated pavement for its nave ; the wood-pigeons drone their offices in its ruined choirs, the long shadows fall across its transepts . . . lovely, lovely dream.

If there is a man in England who has a grudge against His Majesty's Office of Works he will, I think, lose it in Rievaulx. Years ago this abbey was given into its charge, and to-day it is experiencing the only tenderness it has known since the Dissolution.

It is a model in scientific excavation. Trained diggers have discovered buried buildings ; every stone, every fragment of glass found in the course of excavation has been carefully preserved in a museum on the spot ; and the work is still going on.

There are many more ruins in England waiting for the same kind and experienced hands.

CHAPTER SIX

§ I

THREE men were sitting on the edge of a precipice near Flamborough Head hauling at a rope. There seemed to be no other end to this rope ! It fell down over the cliff edge towards the distant sea ; and I stayed full of curiosity, wondering what they would bring up from the depths.

It was a grey windy day. The sea was steel colour except where, far below, it broke steaming and hissing against the jagged chalk cliffs or poured rushing with a distant roar into chalky caverns eating its way tide by tide into the land, swirling round long, thin spires of chalk which it had in course of time islanded from the mainland. It was Cornwall in the north of England. . . .

The three men hauled in foot after foot of rope, and it was clear that their burden, whatever it was, was heavy.

When about three hundred feet had been pulled up an unlikely apparition topped the cliff and clambered up on the grass. First came a military tin hat, then under it, a brick-red face and a pair of blue eyes, then a sturdy body in a suit of blue dungarees criss-crossed with leather harness, the legs in two wide straps attached to a webbing band which formed a kind of seat behind him, the fantastic equipment concentrating, as it were, at the waist, where the end of the long rope was firmly attached to a metal ring. Across his shoulders this man carried two bulging canvas bags. He looked like a compromise between a diver and a rather bedraggled marine in full marching order.

He walked stiffly to a large basket, thrust his hand into the canvas bags and produced from them about thirty large tapering eggs of a vivid blue colour marked with spots and spirals in jet black. He was, I learned, Sam Leng, the egg-gatherer of Bempton.

' Guillemots' eggs,' he said, uncovering as pretty a basket of eggs as I have ever seen. A schoolboy desire to collect them shot through me as I noted their lovely colours, their queer, attractive markings, their long tapering shape. ' What do I do with them ? ' echoed Sam Leng. ' Why, sell them to collectors who blow them, and to people who like to eat them. They're lovely eating.'

*   *   *

Few daring occupations have interested me more than that of the Bempton egg-men. These organized raids of the steep rock ledges during the breeding season—from May until the beginning of July—have been made for hundreds of years. It is, I believe, the only part of England where such an industry exists.

The cliffs here are unclimbable, which probably explains why the multitudes of sea-birds breed there. The guillemot, which is a delightful bird rather like a penguin, comes there from Iceland. The kittiwake breeds there, so do the herring gull, the cormorant, the puffin, called locally the ' sea parrot ' because of its red, hooked beak ; and many more. The cliffs are literally alive with them.

Sam Leng's method is supremely simple. He is harnessed in his equipment and let down over the cliff at the end of the rope. His descent is made through clouds of birds. They leave the rocks at his approach, some to fly wildly round him, others to swim in thousand-strong colonies on the sea. The kittiwakes show alarm and fly, circling above and below him, but the guillemots are philosophic birds. They seem to bear him no malice. They fly off with a cry like a gargle, but more care-free and gay than a gargle. They desert their bright eggs with a ' Hello, here's the birth controller ! ' air and amuse themselves on the water in a hundred pretty ways, rolling their lovely little penguin bodies over and over with a flash of white stomachs, or standing up in the water and flapping their wings rapidly, or diving suddenly, popping up yards away, but with a careless eye all the time on Sam Leng.

' A guillemot lays only one egg at a time,' explained Sam Leng to me, ' and she doesn't make a nest. She just lays

them on a rock ledge.   She'll lay a second, and sometimes a
third if I take the first two away.'

A most obliging bird is the guillemot !

' Why do you wear a tin hat ? '

' The big danger on this job is from falling rock.   A rock
hit me once and smashed my tin hat in. . . .'

I crept to the edge of the cliff, and watched him swing,
four hundred feet below, a tiny, sprawling figure poised
perilously above the angry waves, the birds screaming round
him as he worked his way from ledge to ledge gathering the
bright blue and green eggs.

*   *   *

An idiot desire to collect a guillemot's egg with my own
hands possessed me, so that in a rash moment I asked to be
allowed to go over the top.   To my surprise and horror, he
agreed.   I could not draw back !

He took off his gear and they strapped me into it, placed
the tin hat on my head, and the bags over my shoulders.
They tied the rope to the waist-ring, put the guide-rope in
my hand, and told me to ' let myself go ' over the edge of
the cliff.

I found myself on an almost perpendicular ledge of rock.
I braced myself against it with my feet as I hung passionately
with both hands to the rope, so that I was at right angles to
the rock.   I felt like a fly on a ceiling.   Above me was the
rough grass edge of the cliff against the sky and the voices
of the egg-gatherers shouting to me : ' Let yourself go ! '

My problem, which was one of gravity plus pure funk, was
solved for me when something gave way, leaving me swinging
at the end of the rope, kicking the cliff for a foothold.   Voices
from the sweet world above said that I was ' getting on
fine ! '

All might have been well had I not struck a piece of chalk
with my foot, which broke away when I was in a position
to follow its descent.   I watched it fall, down, down, down,
through a flight of gulls, through a cloud of kittiwakes, down,
down into the distant steaming sea.   That second's glimpse
collected all my nerves in the pit of my stomach.   Death
did not seem so awful as the possibility of swinging or spinning or turning turtle.   A few gulls attracted by my plight
screamed round me in the most insulting way.   The rope

seemed a live and evil thing, ready to give to me the instant I had the pluck to take a downward step. That moment never came !

Why do some people rush into rash situations ? I felt angry with myself. Why did I want to rob the gentle guillemot ? The view downward between my feet was simply appalling : a wall of chalk falling sheer beneath me for three hundred feet, and then the steel-grey sea hissing over spikes and needles of rocks. I gave a frantic pull-up signal and felt the rope tighten as they hauled. Four amused faces greeted my eggless return.

' Well,' said the chief hauler-up, ' you're not the first that's turned back by a long way ! '

' Thanks,' I said bitterly, as I unbuckled myself in an agony of self-contempt.

Then Sam Leng took the harness and slipped over the cliff nimbly, nervelessly, returning in fifteen minutes with a sack full of the loveliest blue-green and black eggs you have ever seen. At that moment I would rather have done that than receive a chest-ful of decorations !

You boil a guillemot's egg for four and a half minutes. You crack a hard, brittle shell, and taste a most delicious egg. It is not strong like a duck egg, and it does not taste of fish. The white is stiff and faintly blue in colour and the yolk is a rich red. It is a most distinguished egg to eat in an hotel. When the waiter bears it through the room, bright blue and wobbling in a tiny egg cup, the usual sulky calm of the British breakfast is shattered. Children think it is Easter and begin to feel left out ; the inquisitive whisper to the waiter, and everybody watches you swallow each mouthful wondering whether you really are liking it, whether you are just going through with it or whether you are merely showing off !

I am glad to say that something quite unusually good is not on the epicure's calendar.

§ 2

If a film producer did not wish to incur the expense of staging a scene in Algeria—which is an incredible thought—

he should wait for a sunny day and take three hundred property palm-trees to Scarborough !

Yorkshire is not a county : it is a country. The three Ridings contain large samples of every kind of English scenery. They have Dartmoor on the Yorkshire moors, Derbyshire in the dales, Cornwall round Flamborough Head and Hereford in the Vale of York. Yorkshire is an epitome of England. But Scarborough ! How did this happen ? Scarborough seems to have been created as a sort of *tour de force*, just to prove how ingenious and versatile the scenery of Yorkshire can be !

In full noon sunshine you would not be surprised to meet a sheik in a blue burnous riding a white Barbary stallion up one of the many hilly streets. The old fishing town at the back of the harbour which climbs the steep hill to the castle, its red roofs clustered thickly together and at all angles one to the other, has the look of a naturalized Kasba. The broad blue bay, edged with white foam, from which rise the hanging gardens of Scarborough and the modern houses, might be its French quarter. If only date palms would grow against the North Sea, what a boon Scarborough might be to the British film industry !

Then, when you have decided that Scarborough is like Algiers, the light changes, the wind drops, and the smoke from the Old Town hangs like a mist in the air ; and you think that it is more like the South of France ! At night, when you happen to look towards the castle hill, you see its long fortified line black against the blue of the sky, you see the little lights twinkling against the darkness ; and it occurs to you that Scarborough might be Gibraltar's younger brother !

I distrust the alleged beauty of large holiday resorts, but Scarborough is genuinely lovely : she is a glory of the English coast.

The shipbuilding trade has vanished, but they still unload North Sea fish in Scarborough harbour. They still have shops in Scarborough which smell of tar and tow and yarn and oilskins.

I got up at 6 a.m. and went down to see what they had caught. The rest of Scarborough was asleep, dreaming of June visitors, but the harbour was alive with blue jerseys and sea boots. The *Parisienne* had come in with the tide and the haddocks ; and very unparisienne she looked after her two or three days at sea ! Fishermen wearing little gold rings in their ears commented critically on the catch as basket after basket was brought up from the hold, sorted, and placed in the fish market.

There were skate and plaice, lobsters and crabs, and soles. . . .

A walk through the Old Town in the early morning is worth the climb. Scarborough is as full of old houses as Chester. There is a real smuggling, swashbuckling air about the place. Many of the streets are almost perpendicular, and you have to step aside when a seaman comes clumping down over the cobbles with his nets on his shoulder. In little dark yards old men of strong Quaker appearance cut up cods' heads for the crab pots.

* * *

The centre of Scarborough's seasonal life is the Spa. Scarborough is not, of course, a spa in the real meaning of the word, but she boasts a stream of mineral water, which rises from the rocks near the sea. It became famous as a cure for almost any complaint in 1620. Our gouty ancestors of the eighteenth century drank the Scarborough waters eagerly until an earthquake disturbed the strata, with the result that the healing waters were lost for something like two years. They were found again, and a more ambitious Pump Room was erected over them. They still exist, now, perhaps, the least important feature of a large but attractive social centre, which in Scarborough looks suspiciously like the Casino !

Every morning patients from local convalescent homes drink the waters of Scarborough. They go down a flight of steps into a room in which these streams well up into two mossy grottoes. I tried a glass. It was a mild and pleasant drink, but slightly earthy, as if some one had drowned a mushroom in it.

' Quite a lot of people drink the waters now for indigestion,' said the woman in charge.

* * *

No seaside town built on cliffs can afford to develop itself without a careful study of Scarborough.

The sea on this coast is slowly eating into the cliffs. Scarborough, instead of building a hideous promenade, has, buttressed the cliffs and created terraced rock gardens on them, which are better than anything of the kind I have seen.

The steep sides of the tall cliffs have been made into rose gardens. They have been made into the most delicious little formal gardens. They have been threaded with twisting paths, every square inch of room cunningly utilized and cultivated, and from all these gardens you look through trees to the broad, blue circle of the bay.

This explains Scarborough's fine air of reticence. There is no blatant promenade. Instead, there are hundreds of garden-paths perched on the converted cliff.

*　　*　　*

The visitor to Scarborough quickly notices the presence of miniature sailors in the town. They are about four feet high and they walk with a real salty roll. If you follow them you arrive at the Sea Training School, the only school in the country which puts to sea in its own ship. It was the gift to the town from Mr. C. C. Graham, Mayor of Scarborough during the war, and one of the most popular mayors the town has ever had.

(If only the hundreds of thousands of pounds squandered all over England in hideous cenotaphs, which our children, or their children, will pull down, had been spent for the benefit of youth or age in schools or almshouses !)

I found the Sea Cadets preparing their hundred-ton schooner, the *Maisie Graham*, for a voyage up the east coast of Scotland. The workshops hummed with varied energies. Bright, sturdy youngsters were sewing canvas, making a new cabin door, going over every inch of the mainsail. One red-faced little fellow who is going into the Navy stood to attention and said :

' We're to meet the Fleet on this voyage.'

' Where ? ' I said.

A blank service expression came into his eyes.

' In northern waters, sir,' he replied.

Lieutenant Heather, the head master, said that the boys come from Canada, London, Southend, Harrogate, Sheffield, and many other towns and cities throughout the kingdom. There are ninety-six boys at present training for either the Navy or the mercantile marine.

'We went to Norway last year,' he said. 'We carry no paid hands. The boys do all the work. We sailed to Wembley during the Exhibition two years running. We sailed quietly down to Deptford in three days. Yes, it's a fact that we have the only training ship that goes to sea, and we're very proud of her. . . .'

Visitors to Scarborough should not fail to go over this unique school, and rich men wishing to perpetuate their names in a seafaring town could have no better model. England should have a small fleet of *Maisie Grahams*.

The sun rises over the North Sea and sinks behind Scarborough. The white cliffs that curve south towards Filey are, by one of those sudden changes in light and colour so characteristic of this place, turned a delicate pink colour—the pink-brown of the west bank of the Nile at Luxor.

What an elusive, romantic place it is !

§ 3

Some day I will return to the town of Whitby to lounge about in a pair of ancient flannel trousers and the world's oldest hat. Whitby is one of the best lounging places in England. There are posts all over it for the purpose, posts smoothed and polished by centuries of lounging, posts friendly to the back, posts that invite your full weight and promise a state of full contentment.

You lean against them and you smoke. You discuss wind and weather and lobsters with fellow loungers whose jerseys are light and whose eyes are dark blue. A dog is sure to attach himself to you, also three or four delightfully untidy bare-legged children. Then the tide comes creaming in over the harbour bar and the sea-water marches up the River Esk. They run up an object like an overgrown football to the end of a mast at the harbour entrance to tell the fishing ' cobles ' that the water is now deep enough for them to return home. So they enter the harbour at Whitby, sailing or steaming, to cast anchor near the small open-air fish market on the quayside.

They land their crabs and their blue-black lobsters and their salmon. Women, with shawls over their heads and

6

baskets over their arms, bargain for the fish. Here and there is a slim sturdy blonde beauty, whose hair has never known scissors, and who, I am willing to bet, has never smoked a cigarette in her life. Beside her stand old toothless women with the kindest eyes set in a million fine wrinkles.

The crabs and lobsters are sold, the salmon goes its more expensive way, and Whitby's one mild excitement is over before the tide that brought it has begun to ebb.

The loungers return to their posts.

*   *   *

Every one in the south of England should visit Whitby if only to see how Yorkshire can imitate the best of Devon and Cornwall. Whitby is the Brixham or Polperro of the north-east coast. It also contains artists who reproduce its beauties on the walls of Burlington House, but you would never know this. They do not stand out from the landscape in sackcloth and ringlets as such colonies do in the south.

Two high green cliffs are separated by the valley of the River Esk. The Old Town of Whitby clings to the steep east cliff, its red-tiled houses are like a colony of scarlet mussels clustered on a rock. The roofs are ranged one above the other in irregular terraces, the red tiles and the tall chimneys form one of the prettiest roof-lines in England. High above the Old Town, at the summit of one hundred and ninety-nine stone steps, and almost on the edge of the cliff, is the silver-grey skeleton of the Abbey of Whitby, the abbey of the holy virgin St. Hilda, where Caedmon, the cowherd monk, received his famous vision one night as he lay among the oxen. There also, twelve hundred and sixty-three years ago, took place that first important debate between the Celtic and the Roman Churches; and at that same Synod of Whitby was fixed the still puzzling date of Easter.

On the other side of the gorge is New Whitby, a neat, respectable Kensingtonian series of terraces set about with gardens and close-cut stretches of turf. New Whitby, which is quite uninteresting to me, is, however, the land of promise. Here a little Scarborough is in process of growth. They already have on the edge of the waves, and built on the Scarborough model, a pseudo-casino called, for no earthly reason, ' The Spa ', in which you can eat and dance and see a play.

Lovely Old Whitby on the east cliff is a record of dead adventures. Its shipbuilding and its smuggling have ceased, its jet industry and its fishing industry are both declining. New Whitby, however, is going to make money from tennis players, clock golfers, and, of course, from others who will go to admire Old Whitby.

It is good to live on the west cliff and to spend your time on the east. I could never grow tired of Old Whitby. It is a fine unself-conscious muddle of old houses, narrow streets, and queer picturesque alleys called ' yards '. Fishermen put their salmon nets ' on the rope ' against sunny walls ; there is always something happening in the harbour ; the one bridge that connects old and new Whitby swings apart now and then to give some herring-boat access to the open sea, and the visitors who poke about and prowl about remarking with damnable persistence, ' Oh ; isn't it quaint ? ' create in return no curiosity.

Clovelly in Devon knows that she is being admired ; Whitby honestly does not know what people see in her.

The dialect of Whitby, especially if projected from a toothless mouth, is difficult and in patches impossible to understand. I would like to hear a conversation between an old man of Whitby and an old man of Brixham, in Devon !

And the children of Whitby ! I have not seen so many children to the square yard in any other town in England. Whitby is a great nursery ! Its children fill the streets, occupy the harbour foreshore at low tide, penetrate, as their elders do not, the chaste lawns of the west cliff, and generally permeate the place with a shrill, excited happiness. Many of them explore the one hundred and ninety-nine steps up to the abbey. You can on most evenings see a threatening fisherman ascending these steps in search of his young towards the hour of bed.

You will observe him bringing the captives down with him, giving expression at each step to his paternal emotion. I think that any man who, after three days on the North Sea, has to climb a hundred and ninety-nine steps to find the twins should be permitted a little self-expression !

The children of Whitby have a marvellous time ! The harbour affords them hours of frantic and pointless activity. The streets seem to have been designed by some remote generation of children as a standard background for the game of hide-and-seek. And there are hundreds of dogs always ready to join any expedition !

* * *

When the sun has gone down you must climb the one hundred and ninety-nine steps and stand in the gaunt shadow of St. Hilda's Abbey.

As the light goes out of the sky and the wind drops you will hear, like the voice of the sea, the steady tolling of a bell over the waters.

They say that long ago a heathen pirate beached his ship at Whitby and, scaling the cliff with his war band, raided the abbey and carried off the great bells from the tower. No sooner had he made for the open sea with his booty than a darkness came over the sky, a wind sprang up from nowhere, and the sea, hitherto calm, becoming of great violence, rose about the pirate galley in such mountainous waves that the ship sank and the bells fell to the bottom of the sea, where they still lie. They say, in addition, that if a lover will go up to the Abbey ruins at midnight on All-Hallows' Eve and, standing face to the sea, will whisper his sweetheart's name he will, should Fate be on his side, hear faint and ghostly from beneath the sea the great bells of Whitby Abbey ringing a wedding peal. . . .

Every still evening you can hear a bell tolling out at sea ; and in any other part of England I suppose you would admit that it is a bell-buoy !

§ 4

There was a time within the memory of living men when every woman in England wore Whitby jet. Not to have worn Whitby jet would have seemed like an insult to Queen Victoria.

The jet was carved into ingenious brooches, it was made into bracelets and into beads. Impressive ornaments like necklets of black diamonds rose and fell on Victorian bosoms. Gowns were heavily embroidered with jet ' bugles '.

Such garments (seen occasionally nowadays on the bodies of theatrical landladies) were like a standard work on British respectability. How our fathers dared to make love to women who bristled and tinkled forbiddingly in jet is a subject for some future historian.

Nothing could be wider poles apart than the jet gowns of the Victorians, which swept the floor with a prayerful rustle, and the flippant, knee-length tubes of cloth which do not in these days pretend to disguise the female knee. All the righteousness of the Victorian epoch blossomed darkly in Whitby jet, and the final glory descended on the fossil when a Whitby manufacturer was entitled to style himself 'Purveyor of Jet Ornaments to Her Majesty Queen Victoria'.

What is jet ? I am sure this age does not know. It is a bitumenized substance found in the sea cliffs near Whitby from Skinningrove on the north to Castle Chamber, near Robin Hood's Bay, on the south. It is also found inland on the Cleveland Hills. It is black and brittle and looks like tar. It is easy to work, and it takes a brilliant polish, so that when finished it shines like greased vulcanite.

British women wore jet before Caesar came. Jet beads have been found in burial mounds of the early Britons. Rudyard Kipling mentions Whitby jet in his poem 'Merrow Down', which describes the commerce of an ancient road:

> And here, or hereabouts, they met,
> To hold their racial talks and such,
> To barter beads for Whitby jet,
> And tin for gay shell torques and such.

But jet ornaments did not become a commercial proposition until the reign of Queen Victoria. I do not know why the sudden craze for jet began, but in 1853 the value of jet-work made in Whitby was twenty thousand pounds, and about a thousand men were employed in the industry.

Fashion has changed. To-day Whitby might be able to find fifty jet-workers. The brooches and the bangles, once treasured all over the world, and worn in the palaces of Europe, are now sold to day-trippers for a song.

Unless fashion revives jet—and it merits a revival—the working of it will become another of England's dead handi-crafts.

There are still many shops all over Whitby which sell nothing but jet. Many of them contain exceedingly fine pieces of carving executed in the old days. This work will probably never be done again when the old jet-workers die, because there are few young men taking up the art.

The most popular ornaments made to-day are brooches with girls' names carved on them. They are very cheap and are eloquent of the last generation. There are thousands of Marys, Maries, Janes, Dorothys, Doras, Rubys, Alices, but few of the Joans, Cynthias, Patricias, Paulines, and Barbaras of our time.

However, if you do not spot the lady from stock they are only too ready to have her carved to order in a few minutes !

❀　　＊　　❀

I went into a jet workshop which in the old days employed nearly twenty men. An old man and a young one were the sole inhabitants. Primitive machinery worked by foot-pedals ran the length of the shed.

' I remember the trade sixty years ago,' said the old man, ' and this shop and its machinery are just the same now as they were then. It was a rare good trade in the old times. You could work three days a week and make enough to take the rest of the week off. I shall never forget what a good time we had when Queen Victoria's husband died ! Why, we couldn't keep pace with orders ! We couldn't get enough jet ! Everybody wanted jet ! '

I suggested that this melancholy demand probably killed the industry and associated jet with mourning. But he denied this. The demand, he said, still continued.

' They say,' he said, ' that jet is going to become fashionable again.'

' Well,' remarked the young man, ' it had better be quick about it or there won't be anyone left to make it. What it really needs is for some big London firm to take an interest in jet and for some fashionable women to begin wearing it again.'

They produced for my inspection some remarkable carving done when the industry was at its height. The old jet-workers of Whitby produced astonishingly fine work, and no design was too ambitious for them.

The two workers in the old shop then, turning to their wheels, cut out oblongs of jet, carved with swift dexterous touches ' Maud ' and ' Mary ' and ' Janet ' on oblong after oblong, and tossed them into a box to be finished and polished.

' We always get rid of these brooches to the summer visitors,' said the old man.

' Yes,' said the young man, indignantly carving the word
' Isabel ', ' and to think that once queens were proud to
wear jet . . .'

He snorted with disgust.

' Ah,' said the old man as he pedalled, holding a piece of
jet to the wheel, ' Ah,' he said, gazing to me over his spectacles,
' you've got to take the rough with the smooth, you know.'

' Yes,' said the young man, ' but you've had the smooth.
I haven't. When I've had three days off a week it's been
on short time. If only the Queen and Princess Mary . . .
Oh well, what's the use of worrying ? '

He picked up another brooch and savagely carved on it an
inoffensive ' Doris '.

§ 5

When you are in this part of the world wait for a sunny
morning with a wind blowing, take a long last look at the
bay where the white horses ride, and go inland towards
Pickering. You will pass through the little village of Thorn-
ton Dale, which is said to be the prettiest village in Yorkshire.
(It is not ; there is no ' prettiest ' village in Yorkshire !)

Now at Pickering the cosy greenness of the Vale of York
piles itself up in fat fields and silver orchards, and stops.
In these lanes you meet a man and a cow going for a walk
together. Sometimes the man is taking the cow, sometimes
the cow is taking the man, in which case the man steers it
by tapping its brown posterior from time to time with a hedge
switch.

Sturdy grey church towers thrust themselves above the
trees, the stone cottages cluster round the church. You
come across village cattle markets held in a meadow, the
farmers leaning over hurdles smoking their pipes and returning the gaze of sheep with a similar non-committal expression.
Men come riding down these sun-flecked lanes on horseback ;
little boys mounted on gigantic shire geldings go whistling to
the smithy or the plough. In a field you see a litter of nigger-
brown pigs, busy with their snouts to earth, and the apple
blossom falling on their brown backs.

The newspaper contents bills in these villages seem like
an echo from another planet. I am sure that these kindly,
smiling people read their Sunday murders as children read
Hans Andersen.

All this important simplicity ceases at Pickering. North

of this little up-and-down town the moors begin. Pickering is a frontier town. Its stone houses huddle together as if banded against the wildness that lies at their very doors. And the road north out of Pickering leads up into the heart of a gold cloud.

The York moors are the Dartmoor of the north of England. Their bare ridges slope against the sky, moor folded against moor in long perspective like enormous frozen billows. The light is never constant. The moving skyscape flings new colours over the moorland as the clouds change pattern against the sun.

Experienced-looking cock pheasants who have earned their old-age pensions explode suddenly from the heather and fly low down across the road ; an occasional rabbit cocks his long ears to you ; the larks, fluttering motionless high in the air, send down their trembling song ; and the gorse flames in patches, mile after mile. The distant ridges are blue as hot-house grapes.

It is a cold, inspiring hardness that has never given food or shelter to man or beast. An infrequent tree, its boughs deformed, leans against the wind, and the brown heather, soggy with little peaty streams that well up from nowhere and trickle to nowhere, is alive with the restless breezes.

So this road takes you on from magnificent desolation to the edge of heathery crags from which you look down into scarred valleys of the dead or, quite surprisingly, into little grassy vales where a few houses stand in the grass. The only men you meet tramp the road slowly with guns beneath their arms and a black retriever sniffing the air ahead, or an old man will straighten his back and stop his peat-cutting to give you for one second his undivided attention.

*   *   *

A post at a doubtful little lane said : ' To Robin Hood's Bay '.

I took it and dipped down to a cleft in the rocks by the sea. Here I came to a Yorkshire Clovelly.

The streets of this small fishing village are erected on cobbled terraces. The little houses are built in an indescribably haphazard way, crowded together, facing each other over a few feet of cobbled street. Little archways give entrance to yards at the backs of the houses where there are more houses more cobbles, more terraces.

A MOORLAND STREAM

' In the old days,' said an inhabitant, ' we had something like two hundred sail of ships here. The men were away on long voyages and the married daughters lived for companionship with their mothers in the same houses. Most of the old houses are held on thousand-year leases. When a rising family grew too large for the old home small three-room houses were built as near it as possible in the yard or the garden. That's why the place is such a strange rabbit warren.'

They say also that these old houses could tell many a tale of brandy casks and of revenue cutters in the bay and revenue men wandering hopelessly up and down the labyrinth! There is also Robin Hood.

When Sherwood became too hot for this well-beloved outlaw, it is fairly clear, from the mass of vague legend that clings about his name in Yorkshire, that he sought safety on the wild moors and in the little fishing villages that cling like barnacles to the clefts in the east coast chalk. They say that he practised archery from Whitby Abbey; they say that he robbed the rich abbots of Yorkshire; they still remember how the friar, when ordered by Robin to take him pick-a-back over a stream at Fountains, meekly bent his back and pitched the outlaw into the water.

In Robin Hood's Bay they do not remember anything definite about him. They scratch their heads and say, ' Oh, yes, to be sure he came here! ' but they look vague as if it were a bit before their time, but—grandfather might remember!

I suggest to philologists who have not visited this part of the world that they could spend a profitable holiday at Robin Hood's Bay collecting new words. The dialect sounds like a foreign language. The people are the descendants of the Danish pirates who came over in Saxon times and never went back. They have been locked up by Nature in this rocky cleft and have retained many queer words, used, I believe, nowhere else in the north country.

I saw a fine old Viking smoking his pipe on the beach. His tawny moustaches were a tangled luxuriance, and his blue eyes were either out at sea or on the dog that reverently watched his slightest movement.

I climbed up to the line of the modern world and took the road to Durham.

CHAPTER SEVEN

§ I

I WAS sitting in the mighty nave of Durham Cathedral
wishing that some one with time and energy would
write a popular history of English cathedrals. Every
one of our great churches is built on a fine story. Take
Durham. . . .

An Irish monk was writing by rushlight in the monastery
of Moville, in Ireland, in the year A.D. 559. Over four
hundred years were to pass before a little church was to rise
on a hill at Durham, but this church was nevertheless in the
air when this young monk took pen and parchment at Moville
so long ago.

Now at this time Ireland was a Christian country and
the monasteries held the light of learning which had been
extinguished in England when the Romans went out and the
pirates came in. Irish monks, in coarse white gowns, with
manuscripts hanging from their waist-belts in little leather
pouches, wandered the world, and those who passed through
England on their way home from the Continent told a story
of a country without a Christian church, a country of slaughter
and pillage, of Roman cities lying in ruins with the corpses
rotting on the walls, a country given over to barbarism and
heathendom.

The monk who was writing secretly and by night in the
monastery of Moville was known as Columcille—'Dove of
the Church'—and was to become famous in later years as
St. Columba. He was a guest at the monastery and the
monastery was famous for a beautiful Psalter which the
Abbot Finnian kept in the church. The monk, who was a

great writer, could not rest until he had made a copy of this rare manuscript. He told no one. He took it from the church and worked at it secretly, but one night the Abbot Finnian found him at his task. He was angry. He claimed the copy as his right. Columba refused to hand it over to him and appealed to the High King of Ireland who decided against him.

'This is an unjust decision,' cried the monk to the King, ' and I will be avenged ! '

That was not the threat of a singing man. Columba was of royal blood : he belonged to the powerful Clan O'Donnell.

It seems that fate was determined on trouble, because at this time the young Prince Curnam, a kinsman of Columba, sought refuge with the High King after killing a competitor by accident in the sports at Tara. The King slew him. Columba then roused the clans to a war of revenge. In the year 561 a battle was fought near Sligo at Culdreimhne and the High King was defeated with great slaughter.

But he was still the High King. Smarting under his defeat he procured the excommunication of Columba, which was afterwards withdrawn on the intercession of St. Brendan of Birr. But Columba, no longer a soldier but a monk again, appears to have been filled with remorse. He went to a hermit, St. Laisren, who lived on a lonely island on Loch Erne, and asked his advice and help. The saint imposed this penance on him : that he must leave Ireland and never return until he had won as many souls for Christ as there were men slain in the Battle of Culdreimhne. And now events move towards England. . . .

Columba with twelve companions set sail from Ireland in the year 563 and, sailing towards the coast of Scotland, landed at Oronsay and climbed a hill from the summit of which he could still see, far off, the misty outline of the Irish coast. He went down to his ship again and continued his voyage, landing on 13 May 563, on the shore of Iona from which, on looking south, he saw only the waves.

Here thirteen Irish monks who were to become famous in the history of Christianity built themselves huts of wood and a little oratory. So was planted on Scottish soil the Church of Iona from which missionaries went out to convert Scotland and the north of England.

We are still centuries from Durham Cathedral, but the great church seems to take shape in the clouds, when one day there comes to the little hermitage of Iona a young man called Aidan, who was an Irishman of royal birth. He joined the monastery and remained there studying and teaching for forty years.

Long after Columba's death St. Aidan left Iona to found a monastery in imitation of it off the coast of Northumbria. He chose the little barren island of Lindisfarne, where in the year 635 the monastic ideals of Ireland took root in England —seventy-two years after the Irish saint was driven from his own country for defying the High King.

Is there a more wonderful chapter in the history of Christianity than this time of ascetic saintliness in desolate places, of chants rising above the booming of the sea and the cries of sea birds, of men intoxicated with holiness moving through the wild country winning souls for Christ ? Among the men drawn to Lindisfarne by the sanctity of St. Aidan was Cuthbert. He was prior of Melrose and in direct spiritual descent from such men as Columba and Aidan. He was brought up under the influence of the mother-church of Iona, a man wedded to poverty and holiness, a gentle saint who won his way into the wild hearts of a wild age by the beauty of his life and the force of his example. He retired from the monastery from time to time to more desolate islands where he meditated in solitude, his reflections broken only by the cries of the gulls and the kittiwakes and the breaking of the waves against the rocky shores. When the See of Lindisfarne fell vacant all men cried out for Cuthbert, and the rough Saxon chiefs travelled over the sea to the remote island where the saint had made a little cell in the rock ; there they knelt on the sand holding towards him the crozier, the vestments and the ring of the vacant bishopric. The saint became Bishop of Lindisfarne in the year of Our Lord 685. Two years later he died. On his death-bed he made the monks promise that if for any reason—for already the shadow of the Viking war-galleys may have moved across his mind —they were driven forth from Lindisfarne they would take his body with them on their travels and lay it in whatever church they made.

Little could he have dreamt how often and how far from his hermitage men in ages then unborn would disturb his bones and gaze upon them, century by century, as at a miracle. The legend grew that St. Cuthbert was incorruptible. It began about twelve years after his death when he was

THE NORMAN PILLARS OF DURHAM

canonized. In those days it was customary for the bodies of men elevated to the sainthood to be taken from their tombs and richly enshrined. The monks with the abbot at their head pitched a tent over the grave, chanting the Psalms of David, while the oldest members of the brotherhood opened up the earth and gathered the bones of the holy man. These were washed and then wrapped carefully in silk or fine linen and deposited in a mortuary chest.

Now Cuthbert had been buried in a stone sarcophagus in the little church at Lindisfarne. An ancient chronicler says:

' As soon as they opened the tomb they found, what is wonderful to relate, the whole body as entire as when they had first buried it eleven years before. The body was not fixed and stiff, with the skin shrunk and bearing the appearance of age and the sinews dried up, but the limbs were pliant with full vivacity in the joints. When they raised him out of the tomb they were able to bend his neck and his knees like those of a living person. All the vestments and the shoes that came in contact with his skin were undecayed. For when they took off the napkin that bound his head they found that it still contained the beauty of the original whiteness, and with the new shoes that he had worn, is to this day kept in witness thereof among the relics in our church.'

For one hundred and seventy-seven years the body of the saint rested in a wooden coffin in the church at Lindisfarne, but during this time the long-boats of the Norse pirates were directed towards the English coast ; the wild sea hordes came wading in through the sea mire grasping their long swords, pillaging the little monasteries, stealing the jewels, putting the monks to the sword and sailing off again with their booty. It was in the year 875 that the monks of Lindisfarne decided to leave their island ; and although there was no man alive at that time who had seen Cuthbert, the death-bed promise had been handed down faithfully through the years and they took with them the wooden coffin containing the bones of the saint. They crossed to the mainland, where they wandered looking for a site for a new monastery.

What an amazing picture this is ! How many fearful herdsmen must have told how at night they saw a body of

monks crossing the heath or winding their way through the
forest bearing on their shoulders a great coffin :

' What do you carry with you ? ' they would ask, and the
monks would reply :

' We carry the body of our saint, Cuthbert, to his new home.'

So the monks with their holy burden spent eight years
wandering the north of England. The number of churches
dedicated to St. Cuthbert in this part of the world is like a
map of their journeys. They rested some time at Crayke, to
settle down finally at Chester-le-Street. Here they remained
for a little over a hundred years. Once more, however, they
were forced to wander, and now a new body of monks took
up the body of the saint in the year 995 and bearing it to
Ripon came at length after many adventures ' with great
joy and gladnesse ' to Durham. They saw ' a barbarus and
rude place, replenished with nothinge but thornes and thick
woods ', and in this spot, on the crest of the great hill rising
above the River Weir, they ' first builded a little Church of
wandes and branches wherin they did lay his body (and
thence the church was afterward called bough church) til
they did build a more sumptuous church wherein they might
inshrine him. . . .'

That was the beginning of Durham Cathedral. At first it
was a little Saxon stone church completed by Bishop Aldhun
in 999 (and that was the church the Normans saw when they
rode through the north of England). But the Normans full
of big ideas and intoxicated with the wine of conquest could
not permit so great a saint to lie in so humble a tomb. In
1093 they pulled down the Saxon church and laid the foundations of the present cathedral. In 1104 Durham Cathedral
was so far completed that the body of St. Cuthbert was
removed from a small building in the cloisters into its place
behind the high altar, where you can see on a raised platform
a stone slab which to this day bears the word :

CUTHBERTVS.

So we have traced, through wild centuries, by way of
Ireland, Iona, Lindisfarne, the faith, and the men, who made
the greatest church in England.

*   *   *

Poor St. Cuthbert was not, however, fated to rest in peace.
Every age opened his coffin to gaze upon his incorruptible
body. At the time the body was translated to its present
position the monks could not resist a glance at the saint.

' When they had opened it,' says a contemporary version,
' with the aid of instruments of iron, to their astonishment
they found a chest carefully covered all over with leather
fastened to it with iron nails. This chest from its size and
weight readily showed that another coffin was inside it.
Inside they see a wooden coffin of a man's length, and
covered with a lid of the same kind, completely enclosed
within a rather coarse linen cloth, of a threefold texture.

' For some time they hesitated, not knowing for certain
whether it was, after all, the Saint's coffin, or whether it
contained another coffin having in it the holy relics. At
length recalling the words of Bede that the body of St.
Cuthbert was found uncorrupt after having been buried for
eleven years, they perceive that this is truly the Saint's
coffin.

' They fell upon the ground and prayed earnestly that the
blessed Cuthbert, by his intercession, might avert the anger
of an omnipotent God, if they had merited it, by any pre-
sumption on their part. Amongst the other brethren there
present, there was one, a man of great constancy in Christ,
who by the workings of grace, had effectually obtained that
charity which his name signified ; for he was called Leof-
wine, which in English means a dear friend ; for he was a
dear friend to God, and God to him.

' He had an infirmity, and bore it with great fortitude.
When the brethren hesitated to proceed further in tracing
the body of the Saint he stepped forward and thus addressed
them : " What are you doing, my brethren ? Why do you
fear? He who has given you the desire to search, also
gives us the hope of finding the object of our search."
These words restored confidence in the breasts of the
brethren, and they continued their search.

' They then removed the cloth that had covered the
coffin. The lid being removed, they discovered the Book
of the Gospels placed upon an under lid (*supra tabulam*)
near the head.

' When they had removed the linen cloth that covered
the remains, they inhaled an odour of the sweetest fragrance.

And lo ! they find the object of their desires, the venerable body of the blessed father.

'It was lying on its right side, wholly entire (*tota sua integritate*) and flexible in its joints, and resembling rather a person asleep than one dead. They were so full of joy and amazement that they with one voice cried, "Have mercy on us, O Lord, have mercy on us." There were also the head of St. Oswald and the bones of other saints and the Venerable Bede. It was necessary to remove the body apart from the relics, and two of them—one at the head and the other at the feet—lifted it, and it was seen to bend in the middle as if it had life ; a third person then supported the middle and thus they executed the necessary removal. This was on August 24th, A.D. 1104. To satisfy the Bishop, Ralph Flambard, of the state of the body, it was again opened on the following night as the Bishop could not believe that after four hundred and eighteen years corruption had not set in. Four days later another inspection was made to remove from the minds of persons the shadow of doubt. They thoroughly examined the body, and found it with its nerves and bones solid, and covered with soft flesh. When the devout searcher, who thoroughly tested the hands and feet, had finished, he exclaimed, "Behold, my brethren, this body lies here, lifeless indeed, but as sound and entire, as on that day on which the soul left it to wing its flight to heaven." '

Cuthbert was again disturbed in A.D. 1537 when it was reported that they found him whole and uncorrupt with his face bare and his beard as if it had only two weeks' growth. Another account states that he was 'sound, sweet, oriferous and flexible'. The grave was opened in 1542 and in 1827 and in 1899. . . .

* * *

I left the nave of Durham and walked to the tomb of St Cuthbert behind the high altar. Here I met an old verger and we began talking about the saint and his restless career

'I have seen St. Cuthbert,' he said in a matter-of-fact voice. 'I was present in 1899 when the grave was opened in the presence of Canon Fowler, Canon Greenwall and Canon Brown, a Roman Catholic.'

I looked at him with an interest which I had not felt before

NEWCASTLE-ON-TYNE

Here was a man who had seen the saint of Lindisfarne. Perhaps he had touched the bones of St. Cuthbert. I looked at his hands and wondered.

' Tell me all about it,' I said.

' Well,' he began, ' it was most interesting because there is a legend that during the religious persecutions under Mary the body was removed secretly and buried in a place of which only three monks were aware. The story goes that to this day the secret is handed down to only three monks.'

' But a body has been found since that time in the tomb ? '

' Yes, but the story is that the monks took a skeleton and dressed it in robes. Well ; the opening of the grave in 1899 was to determine whether this story was true or not. When we opened the grave we found that it was true. The remains of St. Cuthbert were there and examination of the bones by Dr. Selby Plummer supported this view. . . .'

' But what did you see ? '

' When the grave was opened we saw a number of bones, the remains of the wooden coffin and some wonderful Saxon embroidery. There were two skulls in the tomb, one of them that of an exceptionally big man. Now the legend is that when King Oswald died in battle in the year 642 his head was placed in the coffin when St. Cuthbert died and was buried by the monks in Lindisfarne. Oswald was a big man. When we looked at this skull we saw on it the marks of a battle-axe. Every one was satisfied that the bones were the bones of St. Cuthbert with the exception of Father Brown, who took the Roman Catholic view that the saint is buried elsewhere . . . you ought to go into the Cathedral Library and see the embroidery and the bits of wooden coffin. They were taken out of the grave in order that we might preserve them.'

* * *

Few people, I imagine, in proportion to those who visit Durham Cathedral, ever enter the library. I am ashamed to say that I had never done so until that moment. It is an astonishing place. No monastic establishment in England has left remains more complete than Durham, and the library forms a group of buildings second only in interest to the church.

This library is the old dormitory of the monks ; at right angles to it, and now incorporated with it, is a building

7

which in the old days formed the greater and lesser refectories in which the monks took their frugal meals. The first thing you notice are the immense beams which span the roof. The oaks from which they are formed came from the Prior's Woods at Beaurepaire (now Bearpark, about two and a half miles from Durham), and they have stood there for over five hundred years.

In a glass case you see the remains of the coffin lid made by the monks of Lindisfarne twelve hundred and forty-one years ago! It is with the exception of coffins taken from the tombs of Egypt the oldest coffin in existence. The piece of it that has survived twelve centuries is about five feet long and sixteen inches wide, and on it, crudely carved but with great spirit and sincerity, are pictures of Our Lord and symbols of the four Evangelists. On one end is a drawing of the Virgin Mary with the Infant Jesus, on the other St. Gabriel and St. Michael. There are also rude impressions of the twelve Apostles with St. Paul and probably St. Barnabas. These pictures have, it seems, been cut with a knife or a chisel.

The visitor who looks on these relics and cannot build up a picture of the early days of Christianity on windy Lindisfarne is to be pitied. These little snuff-brown fragments of wood, light and soft as tinder, were part of that coffin which the monks carried for hundreds of years during the wanderings of St. Cuthbert ; they formed part of the wooden shrine in which his body was enclosed twelve years after his death.

One great relic of Durham is missing from this library—the famous Lindisfarne Gospels. They were written after the style of the more famous *Book of Kells*, now in Trinity College, Dublin, by four different men in the monastery of Lindisfarne. After the *Book of Kells* they are the most famous written survival of this period. Symeon, writing in the twelfth century, says that the book was preserved in Durham, and right down to the Dissolution under Henry VIII ; it is mentioned in the Durham inventories as ' Liber Beati Cuthberti qui demersus erat in mare ' (which fell into the sea), a reference to the old legend that when the monks were trying to cross to Ireland with the body of their saint a storm rose which cast the book into the water from which it was recovered after unharmed, ' perfect within and without as if the sea-water had never touched it '. Nothing is known of the history of this book after the Reformation until it was bought by Robert Cotton from Robert Bowyer, Clerk of the Parliament in the reign of James I. It is now fortunately preserved in the British Museum. . . .

Durham Cathedral is the most difficult building in England to leave : it is not only a church : it is a period expressed in stone.

§ 2

Newcastle, to which I came in the evening, was going home after the day's work. What a Black Prince of a city ! It stands on its hill like a knight in sable armour. The first impression is one of strength. It looks as though it should make battleships and armour plate.

The view across the river where the immense high-level bridge flings its thin line so lightly over the Tyne is, I think, the most impressive sight of its kind in the north of England. If I were a painter I could never weary of this bridge. It has as many moods as a woman. I would like to paint it in the early morning when its stretches into a faint pearly mist from which rise up the vague silhouettes of roofs, chimney-pots and spires. It is different again in the evening when a rust-red sunset smoulders over Newcastle ; it is, perhaps, most wonderful on a night of stars with a railway train going over it and the orange light from the engine flushing the little mushrooms of white smoke which rise noiselessly from the chimney-stack.

Here, or hereabouts, stood Hadrian's Bridge which carried the legions westward along the wall. It would be good to paint it with the ghost of the Roman bridge near it, so much lower in the water ; a railway train on the modern bridge and a grey cohort of Roman cavalry crossing the old bridge, their plumes blowing in the wind. That, too, would express Newcastle-on-Tyne : it is a queer, romantic mix-up of English history. The best Wallsend coal (and nothing could be more importantly modern) preserves the name of the terminal station on the Roman Wall ; Gateshead owes its name to the bridge of Hadrian.

*   *   *

I wonder how many natives of Newcastle have been inside the Castle Keep. It is one of the most magnificent pieces of late Norman architecture in England. In its very depths is a little chapel as complete and perfect as the Norman chapel in the Tower of London.

I met an American architect there in a state of great excitement.

'What do you know about this?' he said. 'I'll say it's one of the finest things in England; and it's not advertised; it's just standing here waiting to be appreciated! If I could move this as it stands to any part of America the gate-money would make me a millionaire in five years.'

I walked round Newcastle wishing that I could spend a week exploring it. It is a stern, dull, black city, inspired by an air of tremendous energy. It is full of queer little quay-side corners. It is an ideal place to wander in. The view across the Tyne from Gateshead with the grim keep rising up above the roofs, and the cathedral with its open tower—the 'Eye' of the north—slightly to the right, is one of the most notable in the north of England.

I imagine that Newcastle possesses the most venerable horse omnibus service in the country. These vehicles drawn by a single horse suggest crinolines and side-whiskers. The omnibuses seem to have run leisurely out of the pages of Dickens. They ply across Robert Stephenson's remarkable high-level bridge. It costs a halfpenny to walk over the bridge or you can enter one of these Victorian omnibuses and ride over for the same sum!

They are much used by the beautiful typists of Newcastle.

§ 3

I ran into Berwick-on-Tweed in the evening.

Berwick has been tossed about for centuries between the Scots and the English. It now belongs officially to England, but the speech of the natives suggests that it still belongs to Scotland!

It is a hilly little stone town built where the Tweed pours itself into the sea. It has an embattled air. Parts of it look as though the Scots (or the English) had just raided it! It still has the appearance of a frontier fortress.

In Berwick I stumbled upon my first real country circus. The gay caravans and a number of weary-looking piebald horses had arrived in the morning. A big tent was erected.

BERWICK-ON-TWEED

The news spread through Berwick, and all the boys gathered on the ramparts to watch the preparations. Some of them rushed home and managed to raise the gate-money. When cowboys and beautiful girls in leather skirts and wide sombreros strolled about among the tents, many a favourite collection of glass marbles was sold at a knock-down price on the mound !

In the country towns and villages of England the circus is as great a thrill as ever. There are still little boys who creep over the bruised grass and crawl under the tent-flaps, from which they are pulled by the slack of their breeches by indignant proprietors ! And the Deadwood Coach still tears round the arena to the wild yells of the redskins and the cracking of whips and pistols, and in a blaze of blood-coloured light.

' Ladies and gentlemen,' says a cowboy, riding into the ring and making a low sweep with his sombrero, ' will those sitting in the front please move back as far as they can, because we are about to present to you that world-renowned spectacle performed before crowned heads and considered to be, by general consent, one of the greatest and most thrilling acts of our time ! Ladies and gentlemen, the attack on the Deadwood Coach ! '

The excitement of the boys and girls who sit on the grass in the front as they squeeze up and tuck their legs into safety is drowned by a series of blood-curdling shrieks and yells, the report of pistols and the neighing of horses as the lights go down and a horde of Sioux canter into the ring. The old rickety coach tears round, drawn by four horses. Pandemonium ! Red lights inside the coach ! Two or three girls in Victorian costumes clinging together as the decrepit thing swings round the corners with the Indians after it ! Then the cowboy rescue . . . cheers !

No one notices that already the circus men are stealing benches, loosening ropes, making ready to flit. What a life !

' Be ready to move at 4 a.m.,' cries the manager, as the acrobats, the cowboys, the Indians go over the grass to their caravans to snatch a few hours' sleep.

The boys of Berwick wander about through the encampment, smelling the coffee and the fat bacon. Now and then the marvellous woman who rode bareback in a shimmering dress is seen, strangely human, drinking a glass of stout.

And when all the boys of Berwick are asleep, dreaming of

a Wild West so much more convincing than the Wild West of the cinema, the long string of painted caravans creaks out of Berwick.

*   *   *

' I suppose it is a hard life,' said a Sioux chief with a strong Old Kent Road accent, ' but, bli'me, if we stick in one place for more than three days we go barmy.'

So the circus folk, always moving on, take their slow, cumbersome caravan of romance through unsophisticated England.

§ 4

The little island of Lindisfarne, called Holy Island, lies off the Northumbrian coast some three miles south of Berwick.

When the sun shines its sands light up, so that Lindisfarne, seen from the mainland, looks like a gold ship anchored at sea. At high tide the island is cut off from England, but when the tide is low you can approach it in a cart over three miles of watery and slippery sands.

I went down to the mainland to wait for the arrival of the cart. I was both glad and sorry to be going to Lindisfarne ; glad because I have always wanted to go there ; sorry because to forsake a dream for a reality is generally painful.

Even as I looked at the island of St. Cuthbert lying low in the sea, shining, golden, rather remote with the big clouds piled above it, I knew that no place could live up to such a name. Lindisfarne ! Only Tintagel, I think, in all England can match it for sheer romance. The very name goes through the heart like a song. Lin-dis-farne ! Surely in the sound of it is the crying of sea birds, the breaking of waves, and the loneliness of something over the borderland of ordinary experience.

The wide sands, pricked for miles with millions of worm moulds, reflected the gold clouds and were alive with eager, noisy, or industrious sea birds—gulls, oyster-catchers, kitti-wakes, sandpipers—flying in white clouds or standing in pools of sea-water. A line of posts marched over the sands towards Lindisfarne marking the way, and at intervals rose up strange box-like turrets, twelve feet high, in which those caught by the rising tide may seek refuge until the ebb.

LINDISFARNE

I made out, approaching across the sands, a slow black dot which I knew was the cart from Holy Island.

I sat on the dunes and wished that the black dot might take two hours to reach me. . . .

Holy Island ! It is one of the sacred places of England. Thirteen centuries ago, when the north was a heathen land, the Celtic hermits from Iona chose Lindisfarne as the place to make their cells because it looked a wild, unhappy place, in which the flesh might be utterly subdued. (It still looks like that.) They made of it a little Thebaid in cold British waters. It became not Lindisfarne, but Holy Island. As I have said at some length, a Saxon king sent his officers to kneel on the sands of Lindisfarne and hold a crozier towards St. Cuthbert, as they begged this holy man to become bishop. In this lovely April of Christianity miracles took place on Holy Island, and from that little bare rock in the sea the Love of Christ went out to conquer the north of England. . . .

The moving dot, now near, resolved itself into a Ford car ! This was worse than I had expected ! The indomitable thing, rust red, its mudguards tied with string, splashed and slithered towards me ; and at the wheel was a handsome young girl with blue eyes and a soft Scots voice.

So we splashed over the sands to Lindisfarne.

*　　*　　*

Time has done little to Holy Island. It is a lovely solitude It is ringed about with the cry of the gulls and the thunder of the sea.

A few hundred fisher-folk live in small stone houses. The men are brawny with brick-red faces, the women tall and muscular and, some of them, extraordinarily handsome and graceful. They are like members of one family. Their unusual cordiality marks them off from other isolated peoples, and there is, I am assured, no vice of any kind in Holy Island ; which is, of course, right.

'The police ? ' said my host, a fisherman innkeeper. ' We don't need police. A constable comes over from the mainland when the summer visitors arrive, but we don't see a policeman otherwise ! '

Their talk is all of fish, tides, and the lifeboat, of wet, salty journeys to the smaller Farne Islands where the sea birds breed and the seals bark. They talk, also, of St. Cuthbert. The legends that grew up round him still live on the island.

' When he got tired of the monastery,' said an old fisherman who rings the church bells on Sunday, ' he used to go out to that little island out there to pray. There used to be an underground passage from the abbey to the island, so they say, and it's true, because I heard my grandfather tell how he found it and went along it for some way until his candle went out in the bad air . . .'

They still find St. Cuthbert's beads on the shore of Holy Island. Tradition says that the saint manufactured these beads during storms, but they are the remains of small fossilized animals which are washed up by rough seas.

The only two buildings of note on Holy Island are the ruins of St. Cuthbert's priory and the castle.

The priory is a red sandstone Norman ruin, which in its day must have been a smaller Durham. It is built on the site of a rough church of wattle founded by St. Aidan in A.D. 635.

In the churchyard is an ancient stone trough called the ' petting stool '. When a girl is married the two oldest men in the village stand one on either side of the stone. A cavity in the top is filled with water and the bride is lifted over it. I believe that this stone is really the base of the ancient market cross.

The castle of Lindisfarne is one of the most romantic-looking small castles in England. It is the real fairy-tale castle. The rock on which it stands juts up suddenly from the centre of the island, and its top seems to have grown naturally into a castle. It is a private residence.

*   *   *

But if ever you go to Lindisfarne, walk out in the evening across the sand-dunes to the sea.

The mainland lies before you, blue hill after blue hill, and beyond them, higher, far away, the thin cloud-like outline of the Cheviot Hills. On the coastline the lordly castle of Bamborough rises in steep walls and turrets facing the sea, and opposite the waters are broken by small rocks which are the Farnes. The clouds fling their finest pageants over this scene. The sun sinks in incredible colours, and a stillness

BAMBOROUGH CASTLE

falls over Holy Island broken only by the clamour of the birds and the ceaseless surge of the waves.

You are as far away from that thing called civilization as any man can be in England. The solitude closes in on you, and you draw from it whatever is in yourself. I can imagine a man going mad in Lindisfarne or finding peace there. It may be that as you stand with the wind in your hair and the sea-water foaming at your feet you will find a holiness in this place ; a feeling of other worldliness which so long ago led to these lovely, wild shores men who found God there.

CHAPTER EIGHT

I CROSS THE BORDER, DIVE INTO SCOTLAND AND EMERGE IN
CARLISLE, WHERE THERE IS ONE OF THE MOST PITIFUL
STONES IN ENGLAND.   I GO THROUGH LAKELAND IN RAIN
AND MIST AND FIND MYSELF IN THE COUNTY OF LANCASTER
WHERE MEN CALL THE KING A DUKE

§ 1

I LEFT Lindisfarne in the early morning when the tide
served and bumped in the local Ford car over the wet
sands through clouds of gulls, kittiwakes, oyster-
catchers and sandpipers.   In the car was a man who had
experienced the dangerous reality of crossing the sands to
Lindisfarne at the wrong time of day.

' I was hurrying to get over in time,' he said, ' and I could
see the tide coming round the point.   When I got half-way
over I noticed a big limousine motionless away out there, its
wheels gradually settling into the soft sands.   The tide was
coming in quickly, as it always does, and was about ten
yards from its front wheels.   I thought that whoever was in
that car—and a big limousine is not the sort of car often seen
about here—was asking for trouble, for the tide comes in
ten feet deep and even if a man mounted the roof of his car
he would stand no chance . . .

' So I rushed over and saw a man fast asleep at the wheel !
I shouted at him.   He awakened, rubbed his eyes, saw the
waves coming for him, looked back over the sands to the
mainland and said : " Where am I ?   How on earth did I
get here ? "   Anyhow there was no time for explanations !
We just got that car going and out of it in time.   In fifteen
minutes it would have been under water.   The explanation
of it was this.   The driver met a few friends at Berwick
where he enjoyed an unusually jolly lunch, and when he
struck the Beal sands he thought he was on the main Newcastle road !   When his car stuck in the sands he just—under
the influence of his jolly lunch, you know—fell fast asleep.

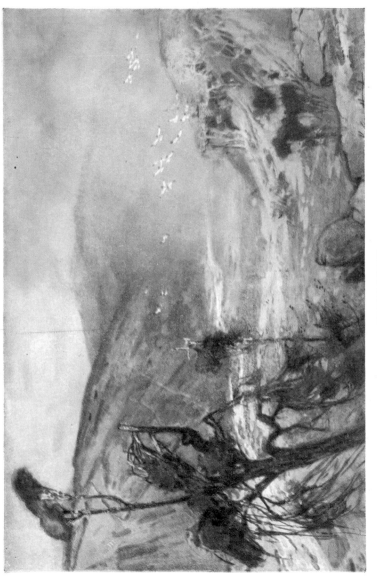

ON THE BORDER

' " Great heavens," he said when we reached Lindisfarne, " you saved my life." We looked back and the sands to the mainland were under ten feet of water. . . .'

We arrived at Beal sands where my own car was waiting, and in a few minutes I was heading for the Border.

§ 2

The road over the Border lies through Coldstream and Hawick. It is a gentle road as far as Hawick because it follows the green valley of the Teviot.

To the left ride the tall crests of the Cheviots and to the front lie the high hills and the deep gorges which separate England from Scotland. There is a difference about the Border. You dip down into little stone towns which seem lost in some dream of Border fray. They are solid little towns, sometimes with the ruin of a fortress near them, defensive little places which have the air, noticeable in Berwick, of wondering whether they are English to-day or Scottish ! It was over them that the Border warfare swayed, now this way and now that.

Suddenly the hills devour you and go on for miles through rocky land where the sheep gaze at you resentfully, where little streams bubble up and fall down through cracks in the rock, where mists suddenly steam across the crest of a hill and come rolling on in chilly dampness, blotting out a range or two for miles and, suddenly disappearing, leave you with the delightful impression of having emerged from a wet to a fine day.

So you dip down into the embattled city of Carlisle. You may turn, perhaps, and see far off the ranges of the Scottish Borders, romantically inviting, dangerously alluring.

§ 3

Carlisle is to me always the sound of milk-cans being bowled over an echoing platform at about 2 A.M.

It is one of those places at which you always awaken in a sleeping car and peer out through a misty night into the grotesque coldness of a great station in the still hours, watching, with a numb sense of unreality, porters bowling shining churns one after the other, or pitching boxes and baskets of merchandise from truck to truck.

Carlisle ! The very name seems to hold the sound of those long hammers with which men hit carriage wheels in the still hours of the morning.

This shows you how one-sided a point of view may be. There are probably more people who have this impression of Carlisle than those who know it for the quiet dignified city it is. There is little about it to-day to suggest the wild days of the Border wars. It is, to my mind, less eloquent than Berwick. That town does not seem to have quite recovered from the surprise of finding itself at peace ; Carlisle, on the other hand, has, generally speaking, forgotten that it was ever at war.

There is that strange truncated cathedral with its few surviving red sandstone Norman pillars. It is worth while to climb to the top of its tower and look down on the busy panorama of Carlisle and out over the castle to Scotland. You will then feel that Carlisle is the great west gate to the north ; you will, by closing your eyes slightly, see the moss troopers on the hills again and imagine the Lord Warden of the Marches riding out to establish the law in that district whose peculiar life placed it for centuries rather outside the normal laws of England.

Carlisle Castle was for centuries the chief bulwark in the north-west against our friend the Scot. For centuries the claymores whistled round it ; for centuries the sentries, watching through the narrow slits in the Norman keep, strained their eyes for a movement from the Cheviots and their ears for that incredibly eerie sound, a skirl of pipes over the hills.

Carlisle Castle is to-day a military store ; and a very unsatisfactory one, I imagine. It was built for a sterner purpose. It seems to be shared by the War Office and the Ancient Monuments Department.

A guide shows you over the keep. He takes you down to the dungeons and tells you of Bonnie Prince Charlie's Rising in 1745. He shows you a small semi-underground dungeon in which three hundred captured Scotsmen were packed tight so that they fought together in the foul darkness to reach the air from the narrow window slits. When the gaolers went to this ' Black Hole of Carlisle ' in the morning the dead lay trampled to death beneath the bodies of those who still lived.

More dramatic, more horrible even than this story, because you can see it and feel it, is a stone low down in the wall of another dungeon. This cell is underground and has never known daylight. The prisoners had to mount a narrow ledge some few feet above the level of the floor. There they were manacled and chained by the neck so that if they stepped from the ledge they hanged themselves ; a release which I suppose many of them welcomed. At certain times they were unchained in order that they might walk about. They discovered in this fetid dungeon a stone which was colder than the rest. They must have felt it in the dark. It is still ice-cold. No one knows the reason for this. It seems to sweat frozen moisture. And this stone—I have seen nothing more terrible in any torture chamber—is hollowed out by the fevered tongues of the men once imprisoned in this vile hole. Just above it, cut inches deep in a higher stone, is the shape of a human hand worn in the stone by the fingers of hundreds—thousands—of poor wretches as they bent down to place their parched tongues to the licking stone.

High up in the keep of Carlisle Castle they imprisoned Macdonald of Keppoch, who was captured during the Scottish rising of 1745. His little window looked out to Scotland ; and the red sandstone is worn an inch deep to the shape of his fingers as he stood there month after month gazing hungrily towards the Cheviot Hills. Is there in all England a more pitiful relic of the struggle between England and Scotland ?

Macdonald covered the walls of his prison with the most remarkable carvings, executed, so they say, with a nail. There is nothing so elaborate in the state cells of the Tower of London. Notable among his carving is the figure of a naked woman with enormous hips. She recurs frequently in his painstaking designs. She could be sold at Sotheby's as a good example of primitive Egyptian art.

This castle is the abiding memory of Carlisle.

* * *

There is, too, the famous Tullie House Museum, known to all who are interested in Roman Britain. Here is gathered everything that is left of those distant days, and among the relics is a fine collection of that red Samian pottery made in Gaul and used by the troops stationed along the Wall of Hadrian.

§ 4

One of the most unlucky things that can happen to a
man travelling from Carlisle to Lancaster through the Lake
country is a wet day. There is no happy medium about a
wet day in the Lakes. The rain falls with a deliberate
enthusiasm. If it stops it is through sheer weariness. Then
it is succeeded by a white mist that wipes out the lovely hills
and the great stretches of water that lie between them. I
I had not already seen, and described, the Lakes I would
have been forced to take them on trust.

But, even so, it was difficult to believe that beyond the
immediate blanket of fine drizzle the hills were rising in green
grandeur towards the sky.

I pulled up at the lakeside at Windermere and lunched in a
hotel full of storm-bound people. They sat gloomily eating
with their eyes on the lake and on the water falling on the
lake, pricking its dark surface with millions of pin-point
splashes ; and they seemed to have lost all initiative.

As a matter of fact a wet day in the Lakes can be the most
stimulating experience if you walk and climb and enjoy the
rain on your face and the rain on your clothes. If I were a
doctor I would prescribe wet weather in the Lakes for a variety
of complaints, from over-eating, which is one of the most
common diseases of this age, to melancholia, which is another.
But while I love to walk in rain I detest motoring through it.
I utterly loathe the greasy drops that trickle down the wind-
screen, the slithery splash of the wheels on a wet road, the
nasty glide round a corner.

Lakeland rain has, however, a romantic quality. It finds
its way into the soul. There is, also, a type of girl who looks
better in a rainstorm than in a ballroom. I do not think
any other country produces them. (Strangely enough they
are generally blonde !) Heaven help the bachelor who finds
himself with such a girl in a rainstorm in Cumberland. . . .

Just before Lancaster the rain ceased.

§ 5

Every one who has explored Carlisle Castle should go to
Lancaster and see the castle, still called the Gaol. It is very
similar. It overlooks the Lune as Carlisle Castle overlooks

he Eden. Although no longer used as the county gaol, the
ssizes are still held there in the most remarkable modern
Gothic court in England, hung with heraldic shields and
ooking more like a room reserved for the Knights of the
Round Table than a law court.

I was shown over the castle by a man who remembered it
when it was a gaol. He was a satisfactory guide. He knew
he history of Lancaster from A to Z. We went down into
he depths of this place, and stood in a round Roman watch-
ower, one of the most remarkable Roman relics in England,
nd one which should be better known. The place where the
Roman legionaries tramped with their spears, the same arrow
lits through which they looked across the river valley are in
xistence, magnificently preserved, in the heart of Lancaster
Castle. We climbed many flights of winding stairs, and from
he ramparts we looked down to the splendid gateway built
y John of Gaunt.

We entered the dock in the criminal assize court. At the
ack is an old iron 'holdfast', one of the last in position, I
nderstand, in England. When a criminal was sentenced to
e branded on the fleshy part of the thumb his left hand was
cked in this iron vice.

'Then,' said my guide, holding up a branding iron, 'the
entence was fulfilled in open court. The warder entered with
his iron, red hot. He came here into the dock, pressed the
on against the criminal's thumb until he had made an
mpression, then he would look up to the bench and cry to the
udge: "A fair mark, my lord!" and when the old man
odded from the bench the criminal was untied!'

*   *   *

The famous trial of the Lancashire witches took place there
a 1612, and a few paces away is the room in which men about
o be executed in public walked into eternity to the sound of
tumultuous crowd gathered on the walls and in the graveyard
f the parish church.

'There are still people living round here,' said the guide,
who can remember seeing people hanged. I was talking to
a old lady only yesterday who lives in the cottages at the
ack there. She said her brother brought her to see a man
nd a woman hanged together! The criminal spent his last
w hours in that cell there and he could hear the crowds

gathering, the noise of eating and drinking, the taunts, the songs made up about him. It must have been terrible for him ! Then in the morning they strapped him up ; and out he walked through this very door. . . .'

It is rather strange to realize that the last public execution in England took place as recently as 26 May 1868. One of the prison chaplains of Lancaster is said to have attended no fewer than one hundred and seventy criminals who were hanged.

' But it isn't the criminal who needs sympathy,' said the guide. ' That's over too quick ! It's the warder who does the last four hours with him ! In the old days I remember how the warders used to take four-hour shifts with the condemned men, and how they used to work it out days before the execution to see who would have to do the last four hours. . . .'

*   *   *

I have spent a thoroughly morbid day ! I looked back at the massive towers of Lancaster, and, remembering Carlisle and its two pitiful stones, I thought that you would go far to find in England two places so near together and so drenched in sad and terrible memories.

FROM THE RAMPARTS OF LANCASTER CASTLE

CHAPTER NINE

§ I

I CAME into Manchester over a road as hard as the heart
of a rich relation.

This road, which might have been made by a Roman
legion, began at a fried-fish shop miles away from Manchester,
and it ran on in undeviating flintiness, its surface formed of
small, granite-like Derbyshire stones in shape and colour
resembling little loaves of petrified brown bread.

A terrifying road! Any Dick Whittington going over it
in search of fortune in the great city could be forgiven for
turning back after one glance. It seemed to say: 'The way
of ambition is indeed hard!' and it led, more or less logically,
into Manchester.

It was that time between dusk and the full blaze of electric
light when the streets of Manchester fill with a curious uniform
blueness which I have seen in no other city in the world.
The streets are high jet-black banks. Between them flows this
blue river, the colour of those large expensive Colmar grapes
which one buys for people in convalescent homes. It seems
as though the smoke has in some way become damp and is
hanging in the air.

I have been told that it always rains in Manchester. This
is a lie; it had just stopped.

Over the shining, greasy road-stones clattered the dray
horses pulling wagons piled with white cloth. The rumble of
wheels and the sharp clatter of hooves on stone is the characteristic sound of Manchester. It begins early and ends late.
There was a clang of tram-car bells. Down the Colmar-blue
avenues rang electric cars painted red and white, the only
organized colour in the streets of this sable monster.

Manchester was going home after the day's work, not violent as London does, but leisurely, with calm. I came to a central blaze of light where Queen Victoria, sunk—I might even say collapsed—in a hopeless depression, sat regarding Manchester with the utmost disapproval. This place, I was told, is called Piccadilly.

And against the lit windows of Piccadilly was an exciting movement of crowds, the flash and twinkle of yellow silk stockings. I saw a girl wearing Russian boots and a Lancashire shawl.

Certain streets in Manchester die at six every night, while others remain alive until eleven. The dead ones smell of horse and cardboard, the live ones of Jockey Club. The dead ones are dark; the live ones are brilliant with the gold windows of the closed shops. Manchester is as London would look if you can imagine lower Oxford Street and the Strand marching up into the City and settling down haphazardly in the neighbourhood of Lombard Street and Tower Hill. Manchester is an elusive city; one is always searching for its centre and never finding it.

I came to a place where Oliver Cromwell, standing on a rocky plinth, seemed to have been flung out of the opposite hotel without his hat. Near at hand was a jet-black decorated church beside an undecorated jet-black river. Still night-prowling, I came to a huge Gothic stronghold, black as the very devil, with a little moon of a clock high up in a tower. Opposite I saw, with some emotion, that the Albert Memorial has had a little son almost as incredible as itself. Albert the Good stands, the luckiest statue in Manchester, protected by a roof.

*   *   *

There is in Manchester a little area sacred to tripe, oysters, and beer. I call it Greedy Street, but Manchester calls it Market Square. It is, I imagine, the last vestige of old Manchester. You come suddenly upon it from a modern street and you find yourself in the atmosphere of an ancient market town. The buildings lean confidentially together in the friendliest way. One of them is half timbered and calls itself an ' inn '.

The whole area is a sanctuary of food and drink. The lights of bar windows shine in the narrow alleys. I slipped into one of them. The place was packed, blue with smoke, loud with talk. They seemed to have come there for the evening. A man thumped a piano and a vocalist had a great battle with the conversation. He had, it appeared, passed by some one's window when the morning was red. There were, he told us, larks overhead and no one was near ; and he went on passing by. . . .

' Less noise there ! Not so much noise ! ' shouted a young man in a white apron, walking through the congregation threateningly ; and the song still went on.

The hero finished and passed away into the smoke, and a large white woman with yellow hair stood herself another stout. It was extraordinarily hearty : a kind of Lancashire cabaret.

*   *   *

It was raining. The rain came down with enthusiasm. I saw at once the reason for those hard whinstones. If Manchester was paved with rubber or wood blocks there would be gondolas in Deansgate and punts in Piccadilly within a week. The stones of Manchester act as a filter. The water drains off between them.

In the hotel lounge I met a Spaniard who had come all the way from a sunny land to see a man in Manchester about some oranges. Many others in the lounge had come from Jerusalem. A dance band played ' Lady Be Good ' ; and in a gold room at the back Manchester and its visitors gyrated slowly to appropriate music from the land of cotton and the coons.

A faint air of exile filled the lounge. We were all strangers who had come to Manchester to see somebody about something. Two men at the next table were talking German. On the left an honest Manchester man was having a terrible time with a client from the Levant.

' I know Manchester,' said a Spaniard. ' This rain ! ' He made a wide circle with his cigar which included the whole of Lancashire, and shrugged his shoulders. ' If you in England had a hot climate you would not be the great commercial nation you are. You concentrate against your climate. It gives you energy. It strengthens you. Look how big and hearty are the men of Manchester and how full of jokes. They have to be ! Now in the south where I come from . . .'

The rain was still falling when I looked out of my window ; and, down below, the last tumbril bumped and rumbled over the stones.

§ 2

If you would observe the Manchester business man you must drink gallons of *café au lait*, because the wheels of northern commerce are lubricated with coffee, as in the Orient. The city is a labyrinth of underground meeting places, technically cafés, but in reality business clubs or exchanges. Each café is used by members of a certain branch of the cotton and allied industries. The brokers meet at one, the bleachers at another, the dyers at a third, the insurance men at a fourth, the shippers at a fifth, and so on.

No woman is ever seen in these cafés until tea-time. They are sacred to Manchester's business. They are packed full. The air is blue with smoke. Your first impression is that of hundreds of large heads bent together over hundreds of little white cups. . . .

There can be no city on earth in which so many funny (and almost funny) stories are told every day of the year. A Manchester man thinks nothing of keeping you out in the rain for half an hour while he tells you the story which you told him yesterday. Whenever you see two or three sitting together you can be certain that one of them is spinning the yarn. The loud laughter of Manchester men is in fine contrast to the weeping skies under which they live.

Story-telling and business go hand-in-hand in Manchester.

It is rather difficult at first to know whether a man is telling his companion the story about the tackler who ordered soles in a restaurant or whether he is selling him cotton-waste ; but in time one recognizes the slightly different expression ! Why should Manchester be so anecdotal ? It proceeds not from a naturally dramatic temperament, as in Ireland, but from a feeling of good-fellowship. The Manchester man prizes above all things the fact that he is doing business with another Manchester man who is a ' good fellow '.

In London Manchester men frequently shut their mouths tight and say nothing. At home, among their own, they are the world's schoolboys ; they are either ' good fellows ' or in Coventry.

And a Manchester story, like the phoenix, lives for a long time, and then rises reinvigorated from its ashes. Some of them may seem to die, but this is not so. They retire to Southport and are brought back to 'Change by elderly men who wear orchids in their buttonholes and travel in first-class smokers.

* * *

A man comes down the steps of the café in search of a business friend. He spots him in his usual seat (Manchester is full of 'usual' seats), and he advances, in the cheerful Manchester manner, as follows :

' Hallo, Ted ! '

' Hallo, Bill ! I say, old man, have you heard this one ? (Another white coffee, miss !) A Welshman came down from his native hills into Wrexham. Have you heard this one, Bill ? '

' No.'

' Well, Bill, he came into Wrexham for Preston Guild ' (a ceremony held once every twenty-one years) ' and the first chap he met was another Welshman he hadn't seen since his last visit.'

' " Well, Parry," said his friend, " I am indeet glat to see you, deed to goodness ! I don't think I've seen you in Wrexham since the Great War ! "

' " What war ? " says Parry.

' His friend describes the war, and at the end Parry says : " Oh, Queen Victoria will be annoyed ! "

' " She's dead," says his friend.

' " Dead ? " says Parry, " then who's King now ? The Prince of Wales ? "

' " No," says his friend, " King George."

' " What ? " says Parry, surprised, " that little devil from Criccieth ? " '

The other Manchester man takes a drink of coffee quickly and jumps in before his friend can spring another one :

' What about this, Ted ? Near Great Harwood they got up a goose club in one of the pubs. There were ten members. The money was paid in regularly every Saturday night, and then the treasurer and the secretary adjourned to the bar with it and got drunk. As Christmas approached the secretary got the wind up. " Don't you worry, Bill," said the treasurer, " I'll see to it."

' So one dark night they set out towards a lonely farm where an old widow woman kept twelve geese, ten fat and two thin ones. They picked out the ten fat ones, one for each of their members, and they were just getting over the fence when the cackling of the geese awakened the old widow. She popped her head out of the window, and cried :

" ' Aw doan't know who you are, but you mun answer for it on Judgment Day ! " The treasurer, who was the last to get over the fence, said :

' " If we're goin' to wait all that time A'm goin' back for t'other two ! "

' And he did, Ted ! '

' Did he ? ' says Ted. ' By the way, a chap got married and took one of these new council houses and he was very proud of it. He'd just knocked a nail in, and had hung up the family portrait and was standing back to admire it, when a knock came to the door. A lad said : " Please, father wants to know if he can use the other end of the nail to hang his coat on ? "

' " Oh," said the man, " you live next door ? "

' " No," replied the lad, " next door but one ! " '

*   *   *

' Tried this tobacco, Ted ? '

' No, Bill ! '

' Got anything for me, Ted ? '

' Let's see, now. . . . '

*   *   *

Note-books come out. Pencils are produced. Figures are written : and in ten minutes four thousand new shirts have been assured to civilization.

That is how Manchester deals with Manchester.

§ 3

Every city should have some one place in which unhappy people and people in love—which sometimes is the same thing —may hide themselves from facts.

The London City churches, for instance, offer to the lovers of London a sanctuary outside time—a quiet patch of peace where a man can feel like his own ghost, which is very good for his sense of proportion. But Manchester, at first sight, offers no escape from itself. A stranger tramps the black streets for miles, looking vainly for a green park in the centre of the city.

The time came when I wanted to be alone, away from the sound of the cotton carts rumbling over the whinstones, and went to the cathedral, which is five hundred years old, black as pitch outside, and the colour of dusty chocolate inside.

Vibrations of an organ practice hung above the nave, and the sun, which was shining brilliantly, flung a saintly patch-work of colour through oak screens and at the base of pillars. Behind the altar I met Sir Humphrey Chetham.

He looks as one would like to think Shakespeare looked. He is the handsomest man in Manchester, and, in fact, the best-looking Elizabethan I have ever seen.   He is carved in white marble, and at his feet sits a Chetham schoolboy, reading a book.   Sir Humphrey Chetham belongs to that fine company of godly English gentlemen who, by founding a school for poor boys, a home for poor people, or a hospital for the sick have spread their influence over centuries.

Such men must be among the happiest in Heaven.   In Chetham's School I found the loveliest thing in Manchester. I have been there four times.   I go there every day, and I could never tire of going there.   It is the one thing in Manchester stronger than time.

A black gate in a black wall opposite the cathedral leads to a wide recreation ground, on which small boys in dark-blue clothes, their Tudor bonnets like little blue pancakes, kick a football about ; and beyond them is an L-shaped building, which has been standing there for the best part of seven centuries.

You ring a bell under a Tudor arch that might be in Oxford or Winchester and they lead you up a wide oak stairway, through the first free library in all England, into a splendid room like the admiral's cabin in a galleon.

As you admire the shining oak tables, the panelling, the coats-of-arms above the great fire, a little Manchester boy, holding his Tudor pancake in his hand, enters, bows, smiles, and, clearing his throat, says in a loud and confident voice: ' Chetham's Hospital was founded in 1656 by Sir Humphrey Chetham for the maintenance and education of a hundred poor boys,' etc., etc.

He tells you, if you ask him, how he was admitted to the school.   He comes, let us say, from Moss Side, and in accord-ance with the ancient regulations he had to stand up before the Governors, recite the Creed, the Lord's Prayer, and the Ten Commandments, and read a passage from the Bible. A boy who cannot do this is not admitted.

The belief that Chetham boys are orphans is not founded on fact. They are the sons of poor but honest parents.

' What are you going to do when you leave the school ? ' you ask.

' I go into a shipping office at Easter.'

' And you have been happy here ? '

He smiles and looks at you in a way that tells you what an ass he thinks you are.

Every day a cook prepares a hundred dinners in a Norman kitchen in the Chetham Hospital. You could drive a motor-car into the vast grate, and the walls are, in parts, eight feet thick. This kitchen was once the hall of the old castle (afterwards Manor House) of the Greslets and the De La Warrs—Manchester's first ground landlords.

It is surely a lucky chance that, in a city which has so completely obliterated evidence of a past, the ancient manor which was the germ of its social development should still exist beside the old church. I cannot think of another great city in which the manor-house and the church still stand shoulder to shoulder, unaffected by change.

The dining hall in which the Chatham boys sit down to meals at scrubbed white oak tables, has a high, beamed roof and Gothic windows. They call the fireplace the most comfortable spot in Manchester, and I am sure it is. They show you a chair in which Sir Walter Raleigh is said to have sat when he came to see the remarkable Dr. Dee, the greatest fortune-teller of Elizabethan times.

One of the most dramatic pictures in the history of old Manchester is surely that of Raleigh watching, on the eve of his great voyage, the doctor gazing into his famous crystal. Did Dr. Dee see there, I wonder, that melancholy rampart in the Tower of London and the executioner's block ?

They have a sideboard made from the head-posts of a bed in which Bonnie Prince Charlie slept when the bagpipes came south in the reign of the second George ; and in the private rooms of Mr. W. S. Fielden, the house governor, is a table at which, it is said, Guy Fawkes whispered gunpowder treason and plot.

Manchester is singularly unfortunate in its monuments, so that it is good to meet here, in a cloister of the Chetham

Hospital (I wonder how many know it ?), the best small war memorial of its kind in England—and I have seen and regretted hundreds.

If you are interested, the librarian will show you the most valuable book in the Chetham Library. It is the famous manuscript history by Matthew Paris, which was missed from Westminster Abbey shortly after the Dissolution. It was given to the Chetham Library by a Lancashire man several centuries ago.

I was amused and interested to know that the first thing a new Dean of Westminster does is to write a sentimental letter to Manchester asking for Matthew Paris. (I have a feeling, Mr. Dean, that this is a waste of your time.)

When night comes the hundred blue boys of the Chetham Hospital go up to bed in three long dormitories, where a hundred little cots stand side by side under a timbered roof. It is silent and rather dim, like going to sleep in a church.

Modern Manchester is spread around them mile on mile, warehouse after warehouse, great street after great street, but here, in this sanctuary, in the very heart of this great city, is nothing to tell that the Irk and the Irwell do not run still between green banks, and that the bells of ' t'ould church ' are not going over the water meadows.

Men leave their names engraved by various acts and thoughts, but I think that Sir Humphrey Chetham has in those hundred little beds standing side by side century after century a sweeter immortality than many a more famous man.

§ 4

Before you can judge a city you must seek out its moods and know its contrasts. . . .

Manchester plunges into its day like a man who sings in his bath. He (for Manchester is even more masculine than London) attacks each morning with loud gusto ; he seems to believe that life is real and earnest, and the workhouse is not its goal. The pavements teem with their crowds ; the counting-houses, the banks, the warehouses swarm with their varied workers, the stations set down in Manchester thousands of men from other cities, come to buy or sell, and the black giant of the north assimilates them, satisfying them or denying them, from the rising to the setting of the sun.

This is a side of Manchester which all the world knows. It

is so familiar that thousands believe there is nothing else to know. But . . .

In Deansgate is a Gothic building set at a slight angle to the road, so that it seems as if about to retire to a monastery. It looks, among the shops and offices by which it is surrounded, like a shy saint in a crowd. It is the John Rylands Library. This is Manchester's greatest contrast. This is a little peaceful acre in the miles of buying and selling given over to the other things.

The most remarkable fact about it is that Manchester owes this library to a woman. It is the only great library in the world founded by a woman : it is the only great library which owes its existence to the love of a woman for the memory of her husband.

' It is,' said Dr. Fairburn, of Oxford, when the Rylands Library was opened in 1899, ' entitled to take its place among the deathless creations of love.'

*   *   *

John Rylands made money in Manchester. He died, leaving Mrs. Rylands with the responsibility of great wealth and the desire to erect a monument to his memory. How this woman planned her scheme, sought the best advice, the best architect, bought the famous Spencer collection for a quarter of a million—as a beginning—how she watched every detail of the enterprise, is vastly more interesting to me than the history of the Rylands fortune.

I imagine, after studying the shrewd Puritan face of John Rylands, that nothing in Manchester would probably surprise him more, could he come back, than the John Rylands Library !

In universities all over the world Manchester means not cotton but this library, and it is interesting to remember how often in history commercial capitals have produced great centres of learning, beginning with Alexandria, by way of Florence to Venice, three great trade centres of the ancient and the medieval world. It is surely a fine instance of historical repetition that since the discovery of the Americas moved the commercial centre of the world from the lagoons of Venice to the wet hills of Lancashire, a library constructed on the grand scale should have found its way to Manchester.

You go up a fine Gothic staircase into a rich brown cathedral

of books. The Rylands Library is the colour of Chester
Cathedral. Its great nave adapted to books, beyond each
arch of it a little nest of shelves ; its cloistered corridors, its
stone fan vaulting, its windows, make you catch your breath,
for here is that rare thing, a perfect modern Gothic building,
exquisite in proportion, decoration, material, and perfectly
adapted to its ends.

It is very quiet. The only outside noise is the occasional
scream of a tram-car turning a bend in Deansgate. And
you might be in the Bodleian at Oxford, or in the Vatican at
Rome.

If you sit in an alcove you will see another side of Manchester. Here gather strange visitors to this city, professors
and men of learning from many countries. They are forced
to visit the Rylands Library because, among the 300,000
printed books and the 10,000 manuscripts, are thousands
which can be handled nowhere else in the world.

Above the reading alcoves is a gallery split up into a number
of little studios where an author can establish himself for a
long time. They will empty the shelves for him and allow
him to fill them with the books he needs. He can come in
every day and work surrounded by the knowledge he requires.

Many men famous in the world of learning have camped
out among the books in these alcoves, writing their works
day by day. These are visitors of whom Manchester knows
nothing. They are difficult to sum up. You can never tell
by the length of their beards or the height of their brows
whether they have come to Manchester to write a learned
book on the apple legends in Arthurian romance or whether
they are painfully translating a Demotic script in the hope of
throwing new light on the Gospels.

Down below in the other alcoves neat girl undergraduates,
cramming for examinations, hold their shingled heads in
their hands and read about life in the Rome of Nero and
St. Paul.

Were it not for them and their shingled heads, their sandy
stockings, and their occasionally lifted eyes it would be
possible to believe oneself back in some monastery of the
Middle Ages.

*   *   *

Outside is the traffic of Deansgate ; thousands of men and
women passing by unaware of the treasure house which

stands back a little from the road in unconscious symbolism.
Here is ancient peace, detachment from the common world,
a sanctuary of the mind ; and the woman who made it all,
who visualized it, who carried it out, stands in white marble
looking over the length of the great nave towards a statue of
her husband.

' To multitudes,' said Dr. Fairburn in 1899, ' it will simply
be the John Rylands Library, built by the munificence of his
widow. . . . but to the few, and those the few who know, it
will for ever remain the most marvellous thing in history, as
the tribute of a wife's admiration of her husband and her
devotion to his memory.'

§ 5

In the maze of side streets round Smithfield Market
thousands of men, women, and children, tightly packed
together, move slowly in the flare of naphtha jets. Whole
families are out shopping. The weekly feeling of a little
temporary wealth stimulates mind and body. There are
women in clogs and shawls, mill girls who dress like city girls,
young men arm-in-arm with their sweethearts, older men
with their responsibilities round them. It is a hearty carnival ;
a drab festival in monotone.

The thin tongues of light lick and flicker in the wind. The
streets smell of pear-drops, shell-fish, and paraffin. Great
vats of toffee boil and bubble, and above the shuffle of the
feet and the mutter of the crowd rise the voices of the stall-
holders, hectoring, bullying, ordering the white faces that
ring them round—white faces as expressionless as cows'—to
buy, buy, buy. . . .

What a queer, varied thing is a great city. A few streets
away are Piccadilly, Market Street, Deansgate : another
world.

The trades in this market are grouped together street by
street, as in the bazaars of Cairo or in the souks of Tunis.
In one are the patent medicine men, in another the sweet
sellers, in a third the china merchants, in a fourth men sell
that eternal gold watch. It is cold, it is raining, a cruel little
east wind creeps round the street corner, but here men and
women lean against walls in the darkness and eat ice-cream,
and cough. They lean against railings, moving their tongues
round frozen yellow cones.

You can buy anything in this market from cod steak (by way of a camisole) to Plato's *Republic*.

And in a dark, furtive by-way lurk the dog men. They prowl up and down. Little faces peep from their waistcoats. These men sidle up and whisper (dog men are always slightly husky) :

' D'ye want a reet good poop, mister ? '

In the shadows along this street shine that most pathetic thing : the eyes of a dog looking for a new master.

A peculiarity which singles out this market from, say Birmingham's Saturday Rag Fair, or Nottingham Market, is the Manchester desire to be weighed. Elaborate plush-cushioned, brass-railed weighing machines, which look as though they should either electrocute you or revolve to the sound of music, invite the passer-by. A Saturday night crowd in Manchester invariably weighs itself. Why ?

The street doctors do good business. One stands with his hand upon the head of a partially bald child, a pale, wispy little girl, who looks as though she had never laughed. What a picture ! The hair doctor, his manner faintly suggestive of a frayed surgery somewhere in the background of his life, the dull crowd listening, only half interested, and the pale child standing there like a patient little animal, her eyes downcast and her small hands on the edge of the stall.

There is the nerve-tonic man : a loud voice, a red face, flinging himself into an ecstasy, ordering the crowd to buy a white packet, as Peter the Hermit might have told them to recapture the Holy Land. And so different is the young medical student in horn-rimmed glasses, one hand in his tweed coat pocket, in the other a bright green influenza remedy.

' My governor was a doctor,' he says, ' and he died in debt ! I paid his debts, and here I am ! If I had the money I wouldn't be here ! But if you take the advice of a medical student, if you'll do as my old house surgeon told me to do ever I became a doctor—" Keep their lungs clean ! " he said, " whatever you do clean their lungs ! " Now, ladies and gentlemen . . .'

Over the way is a barrow piled with books. A lean young man picks them over eagerly. A working lad : a hungry-looking young man. He counts out six pennies, and buys a book. I am curious. I edge up and look. Milton's *Paradise Lost* ! And he so hungry ; and lucky, too, in the long run !

A thing you always remember happily is the way you starve yourself for books.

He pushes his frayed shoulders through the crowd, hungry looking in body and mind.

The public-houses are crowded in Manchester on Saturda night. Manchester will be the last city in England to g dry! (Norwich will, I think, stand by her to the end Pianos play! In all the main streets of Manchester there the sound of song. The men drink beer, and the wome drink stout, or port and hot water. A large woman in a je dress goes to the piano and sings 'Annie Laurie' with grea expression. There is applause. All the time the door opening and shutting, and the barman's tray is awash i beer.

Belle Vue! This is an amazing sight. It is ten o'clocl Three thousand boys and girls have paid sixpence each t dance in this enormous ballroom. There is hardly one persc present over twenty-five years of age. The girls come fror factory and mill. Some of them are very pretty, and hundred of them are very small; the neat undersized people whic cities produce in the third generation.

Some have carried fashion to extremes, and a few hav made themselves evening gowns of bright taffeta. Hundred of them dance in coat and skirts. The annexe to the bal room is an enormous bar. It is crowded with boys an girls. The noise kills the sound of the dance band in tl ballroom outside, and a group of boisterous young men sir together as they drink.

The three thousand dancers, all the same age, all from tl small homes of Manchester, provide a spectacle which I hav found in no other city.

In the popular dance halls of London there are always few middle-aged people, but Belle Vue is a carnival of youth modern youth, eager, energetic, dance crazy, pleasure seekin and, of course, uncontrolled. A great artist should paint picture of it at ten o'clock on Saturday night, and call 'Anno Domini 1927'.

He should stress the sparkling eyes, the laughter, tl white arms which end in hard-working, competent, litt spatulate fingers, the sudden, too-daring flash of colour, tl legs, the little girls in coats and skirts who neither powd nor paint, who dance together quietly like little brown mice and the laughing hobbledehoy youths who blunder round

ne another's arms like a couple of bears, wearing their over-
oats, smoking cigarettes, kicking out their feet, danger to
ny girl's one and only pair of real silk stockings.

He should also indicate the camaraderie of Anno Domini
927, the ease with which a boy raids the assembly for a
artner. If he began as his grandfather might with ' May I
ave the pleasure . . .' the girl would probably be suspicious
nd refuse to consider him, but ' Hello, kid ! ' and off they go
n one another's arms, engulfed in the epileptic chaos, stopping
o execute the Charleston, or perform some elaborate side-step.

The keynote of the picture is the almost startling capacity
or enjoyment. The palate is unspoiled. There is no fake
bout it. There is no simulated gaiety. They do not need
alse noses or filleted French dolls to make them forget
hemselves. There is hearty enjoyment about Manchester's
aturday night sixpenny dance hall before which a man who
nows how many rich people in fashionable places are sighing
iiserably at their asparagus feels slightly abashed.

In the tram-car on the way back a young boy of about
ighteen strap-hangs, swaying with closed eyes, and a girl
as gone to sleep on the shoulder of her partner.

It is Saturday night.

§ 6

The old mill stands beside the same stream that gave it
ower in the days of Arkwright's water frame. It saw the
oming of Hargreave's ' jenny ', Crompton's ' mule ' and
Vatt's steam engine ; it saw the end of spinning and weaving
s a cottage industry ; it saw the black smoke pall grow over
ancashire ; it witnessed that sinful slave trade in children
vhich entangled England's conscience in the spinning-jenny
ver a hundred years ago. The stream is now black with the
efuse of the works upon its dreary banks, and the old mill,
built many times, has grown great and prosperous.

The manager came into his office, changed his coat and put
n a cap.

' Keep your hat on ! ' he said. ' You'll find it better.'

He was a fine type, characteristic of Lancashire : young,
nergetic, quick-minded, all his energies gathered and directed
1 one direction, and behind him a technical education and
ears of night schools. His ambition is to save capital and
ecome his own master. Lancashire is full of young men

like him, and there is no other county in England where
ambition and ability have played such social football with
families. That is the romance of Lancashire. There can be
no other part of England in which so many men lie back
in saloon cars while their brothers go clack-clack in clogs
over the cobbles through the mill gates in the early morn
ing.

All is well, I have been told, until the rich brother sends
his sons to Oxford, and then, in many instances, that old
Lancashire saying justifies itself—'three generations from
clogs to clogs '.

That, perhaps, is why Lancashire is so suspicious of the
social graces, or, as they say, with a fine contempt, ' swank '

We went into a great store-room where cotton from Texas
lay in compressed bales, bound with wire—dirty, yellowish
and full of dust. All the way from Texas ! What a marvel
lous command man has taken over the conditions of life
(That also is the romance of Lancashire !) I remembered
the story, as I looked at this Texas cotton, of the Tartar
bandits who plundered the silk caravans from China to Rome
in the sixth century. Gibbon, in *The Decline and Fall of the
Roman Empire*, tells how the Emperor Justinian tried in
vain to protect the silk trade for the benefit of the Roman
aristocrats, but the problem was solved by two monks who
brought the eggs of Chinese silkworms to Constantinople in a
hollow cane, and so the silk industry came to Europe.

And now the ships come to the Mersey and the Ship Canal
with cotton from America ; and no one thinks it marvellous
How the safety and the simplicity and the cheapness of it
would have astonished the Emperor Justinian !

We followed the Texas cotton through a series of refining
machines into a great workshop that smelt of burnt oil. The
air was full of disembodied cotton-wool. It got into the
throat, into the nostrils, and stuck like thistledown to the
clothes. Men moved among the machines looking as though
their moustaches had been left out all night in a heavy
snow-storm.

The raw cotton was pumped into this shop in long, fat, soft
white snakes. The machines did everything it is possible to
do to cotton except set fire to it. They teased it, compressed
it, drew it out over wire prongs like a thin grey mist, all the
time refining it and leading it gently but firmly toward
its spinning machines. At the other end of the room hundred

of bobbins revolved violently clothing themselves at each revolution with tough thread.

On our way from the spinning mill into the weaving sheds we passed through a room in which a number of mill girls were hanging up their coats and hats. They did not immediately notice us, and they were singing ' Madame Butterfly ' ! I have been through hundreds of factories in the midlands and in the south, but I have never heard opera in them.

' We produced the " Bohemian Girl " last winter,' said the manager.

*   *   *

He opened a door, and we were in an organized pandemonium. Hundreds of looms stood side by side swinging their arms violently and clacking like a lot of lunatic hens. The noise of the looms is so great that weavers have perfected a lip language. I saw a girl move her lips when we entered. The news spread silently round the shed, so that when we arrived at the far side we were expected !

They were weaving artificial silk and cotton. Above certain looms danced a series of perforated bath mats. They told me that these were Jacquard looms. Every time the bath mats did their little Charleston steps a bit more ' art ' silk pattern arrived on some one's pyjamas ! It was at this fascinating moment that I saw my first tackler.

Now London has probably never heard of a tackler, but here he is famous. The tackler is a man who ' tackles ' a tired loom, and he is the official clown of Lancashire. When you begin a story : ' There was once a tackler who . . .' a Lancashire man smiles and gets ready to howl with laughter. The comic character of the tackler seems to date back to a time when conditions of work were harder and the mill tacklers used their authority against the mill hands, with the result that the Lancashire sense of humour ' got back ' on them unto the fourth and fifth generation !

I will give you a few typical tacklers' tales. The point of them lies in the complete asininity of the tackler. (By the way, the slang for a sheep's head is ' tackler '.)

A young tackler who was engaged to be married went to buy a ring.

' Eighteen carat ? ' said the jeweller.

' No,' replied the tackler, ' A'm chewin' 'bacco, but what the 'ell's it got to do wi' thee ? '

9

Two tacklers on a camping holiday forgot their pillows, so they found two drain pipes. In the morning one said he had a stiff neck. The other said, ' I've been all reet, Bill. I stuffed mine wi' straw.'

Two tacklers were bathing at Blackpool. One said : ' Tha didn't half want a weysh, Bill.'

' I'm three years older ner thee ! ' said Bill.

A tackler was observed one holiday time walking about all day with an empty wheelbarrow. When asked about this he said :

' Missus has gone to Blackpool, t'bull pup's sick, and a chap feels lonely walkin' about wi' himself.'

A tackler on his way to the mill turned round to face a high wind in order to light his pipe. Half an hour later a friend stopped him : ' Where arta goin', Ted ? '

' To mi wark ! ' Then a surprised look crossed his face. ' By gum,' he said, ' Aw forgot to turn reaund again ! '

The classic tackler story which is quoted all over Lancashire is this :

A tackler bought a piano. A friend met him one day wheeling the piano on a hand-cart.

' Hasta sowd it, Dan ? '

' No,' said Dan, ' I'm goin' to have my fost lesson.'

You may imagine, then, that I approached my first real tackler with interest and diplomacy. He seemed quite normal ; in fact, rather intelligent. He had a roving eye and a suit of blue dungarees. We got talking, and I eventually tackled him about tacklers. To my surprise he said :

' Hasta heard this one ? '

And this was the ' one ' he told me :

Once upon a time a tackler bought a big hen-coop, and he persuaded two friends, also tacklers, to help him carry the thing two miles to his home. They had a rough time with it. When half a mile from home they missed their friend, the purchaser.

' Where's Ted ? ' asked one.

' A' reet, lads, a' reet ! ' came a voice from inside the hen-coop, ' A'm carrying t' perches ! '

§ 7

If you are looking for the heart of Lancashire you will find it every Tuesday and Friday in the biggest building in

Manchester, the Royal Exchange. It is the largest exchange in the world ; you could put the Royal Exchange, London, in a corner of it, and they would say : ' Hasta seen t' new cloak-room, lad ? '

The cotton towns which are the daughters of Manchester, also Liverpool, which is Manchester's wife (a superior, beautiful lady, as I will show you some day), send their bosses and their managers into Manchester to the cotton market twice a week to tell funny stories, and, if possible, to take orders. They have luncheon in a gigantic grill-room—trying hard not to spin their best yarn until they go on 'Change—and then they walk up a flight of steps into the noisy temple of cotton. By two forty-five p.m. there are often over seven thousand members on the floor.

The view from the strangers' gallery is one of the sights of England. There is nothing like it in any city in the country : a slow, moving, seething—I tried hard not to use that word, but the temptation is too much for me—black mass of masculinity. I feel sure that there is no other commercial gathering this size on earth without a woman in it. I have heard that there was, or is, one woman member who has never been seen, but the story may be apocryphal. Women are not nervous, as men are, and they love to be conspicuous, but the Royal Exchange, Manchester, the last stronghold of the male, would, I am sure, daunt the bravest of her sex.

There are so many men, however, that one immediately thinks of the women represented by such a gathering. What a marvellous sight 'Change would be if the wives and daughters of the gallant seven thousand gathered instead ! How brilliant in colour and, I am sure, in beauty ; how sweet in tone ; how altogether different from that dull, black monster with its thousands of little black hats, its thousands of black jackets. . . .

They cover the acre and three-quarters of floor like a dark rash. Your first impression, as you open the gallery door and walk forward to look down on them, is that of sound beating against the ears in a constant, arrested wave that never breaks. It goes on and on in the same key ; the sound of the Cotton Industry ; the sound of seven thousand men talking about cotton, cotton waste, piece goods, grey cloth, printed cotton goods, artificial silk, bleaching, dyeing, shipping, money, and what the cook said to the policeman.

And it is not a human sound at all ; it is a forest sound,

or a sea sound, if you like ; a curious, resonant agitation of the air.

As I look down with a faint Olympic feeling, from the Strangers' Gallery, I try to follow one little man through his adventures on the floor. I see him moving through the monster, a part of it, yet, to me, the most important part of it, because I am thinking of him as an individual, and I watch him stop at various groups, edge his way in, say his little bit and move on, watching, searching, trying to make money, and the whole thing so casual—so removed from roll-top desks and all the paraphernalia of business.

He stops to make a joke. Some one tells him a story that makes him laugh just a little bit too much. He is anxious to please. Now he looks grave and rubs his little chin with his little hand and shakes his little head. Did some one try to sell him a pup ? Sometimes a man comes to him, or rather seems swept against him in the chaos, and they bring out note-books and look solemn. They have booked an order ! That was good !

Old men wander importantly through the crowd wearing buttonholes. They have a retired look about them. I have a feeling that the retired cotton magnates who live richly at St. Annes or Buxton, cursing the gardener and getting gouty, are kept alive by the Royal Exchange. This is also the place to see the young Lancashire man, the man with his way to make ; energetic, pushful, blunt, spatless. I wonder if the story is true of the man from the south whose business in the north was hampered by white spats. I believe it.

But I am losing sight of my little man. He is, I am sure, having a good day. He is a cheerful little man. I watch him tell the same story time after time to different groups. Often I see him standing politely, waiting until a conversation ends before he introduces himself. 'Change is the only place in Manchester where a man will not butt into a conversation, no matter how much he wants to. It is not done. And the little man, just as I am beginning to like him, just as I begin to hope that he is kind to his wife and always takes her home presents when he has been busy on 'Change, goes and loses himself in the rather grim impersonality of the monster. And the Voice of Cotton goes on and on and on. . . .

It is nearly three p.m.

This is a critical time. The other side of this moment is in America. It is nearly ten a.m. in New York. The New

York cotton men, the juice of the grape-fruit still fresh upon their shaven lips, are gathering at the Cotton Exchange, and in a moment the prices will go up. (How amazing to explain all this to Christopher Columbus, who hoped, poor ghost, that the wealth of the New World would be devoted to another crusade !)

Sharp at two minutes past three p.m. a figure arrives on a big board. The black crowd turns pink with upturned faces, and the Voice of Cotton changes a tone just for one second. Two minutes to cross the Atlantic ; two minutes from New York to Manchester ! That is the climax ! Slowly the floor grows bald in spots. And this is interesting. As you look from the Strangers' Gallery the left-hand side of the gigantic hall empties first. That is the new side. The Exchange was enlarged between 1915–1922, and the old Exchange stays longer on duty than the new. The reason is, I suppose, that all the old Manchester firms are stationed in the old hall, and the bulk of the new hall is occupied by men who have to go home to Blackburn, Bolton, Rochdale, and even to more distant towns.

And on duty in the Strangers' Gallery is William Satchwell. A letter addressed ' Satchwell, Manchester ', would, I understand, find him. He has been on duty in the Parliament of Cotton for fifty-three years. He knows more members of the Royal Exchange than any man, and he remembers a time when the black monster wore thousands of silk hats. He is an old man with a silver-white beard, a peaked cap, a long blue coat, and a great sense of humour.

He once told a story (it was about a rather disreputable parrot) to a member of 'Change, and some days after the member came to him and said :

' Satchwell, I want to thank you. That story got me a two-hundred pound order ! '

But William Satchwell has many other stories, gathered during half a century ; and there is something about him as he sits quietly with the sound of Manchester beating in the air about him which suggests that he could have retired long ago had he liked.

I think he prefers to sit quietly at the heart of Lancashire listening to the strange, insistent Voice of Cotton.

§ 8

In the early morning, just as it has become light, you turn uneasily in your sleep with the instinct that something has invaded your dreams. It marches on and on ; a thin, distant rhythm that is not yet a tramp, a steady, insistent something that drums against your drugged senses for a few seconds until, with a start, you awaken to the unforgettable sound of Lancashire clogs going by in the morning.

How can I describe the cold, hard clatter ? There is nothing else quite like it in England. I have heard it, but not so well done, in parts of Holland. . . .

Clack-clack go the clogs over the early pavements ; clack-clack over the cobbles. Down in the street the first mill girls pass by shawled, bent against a drizzle, the rain polishing the slate roofs, shining on the greasy road-stones, gleaming on the smooth iron-like tops of the clogs . . . clack-clack-clack they go, toneless, hard, the very expression of a wet Lancashire dawn. The mill workers chatter together in vigorous voices, talking, I suppose, about work and other realities, filling the until-now dead street with harsh echoes.

What shall I remember as most typical of Lancashire ? The sea-drone of the Manchester Cotton Exchange ; the swinging arms and the cackle of looms at work, black puddings hanging ready for sale, windows full of tripe like white astrakhan—tripe that is good to eat cold, with vinegar, so that it tastes like an iced bath-sponge—hot-pot, potato cakes, brown and warm, and then this strange clatter in the early morning.

These belong only to Lancashire. . . .

Suddenly the clogs quicken.

The beat of the marching men and women sounds like the march of a cavalry brigade ; hundreds of sharp hooves on the stones. The voices rise up also, now and then some cheery soul sends a great laugh into the air. (A tackler has perhaps taken the wrong turning !) Sometimes a girl's voice is raised coyly or in anger, and, in the minutes that follow, the clatter of the clogs turns from a walk to a trot, from a trot to a canter, from a canter to a gallop, and from a gallop to a charge ; so that you expect to look out and find them all on horseback ! And, at the height of the stampede, the air is cut by the high, undeniable siren of the mill.

Then the awakened sleeper lies listening to the dying down

of the clogs. In a few minutes the pace slackens, the echoes fade, the crowd has passed through the gates, and the only sound is the quick clack-clack-clack of a late comer hurrying along in the rain, then two, then three, then an interval of silence, then one, the last, going by loudly under the window.

This is a sound that is dying. The clog and the shawl are dying in many parts of Lancashire. They are being killed by the Cuban heel and the little felt hat, but in Oldham and Burnley, I imagine, the clogger will be an important man for years to come.

The clog came over with the Flemish weavers centuries ago. It was a wooden sabot called the *klomp*. It has a lining of lambswool to protect the upper part of the foot. Its descendant is not so soft. A hundred years ago there were, at every Lancashire assizes, many charges of murder against men for ' up and down fighting ' which permitted kicking.

How Lancashire has changed! How the standard of living has risen in all the mill towns! How the houses have improved! You can gauge something of the prosperity of these towns by looking at the windows of the houses. A bright line of gilding is a sign that a man has bought his own house. In Bolton, Blackburn, Oldham, Clitheroe, Nelson, Rochdale, you will see many a gilded window to-day. How eloquent are the windows of the drapers' shops in these towns! The mill girl of to-day likes *crêpe de Chine* and silk stockings.

I imagine that a Lancashire man—could he return from a hundred-year-old grave with memories of the industrial north as it was before England found a social conscience—would not believe himself in the same world or recognize his own town.

*   *   *

Thus it is that no man should mind very much when the clogs go clack-clack down the street, awakening him in the morning. He is listening to an historic sound : a sound his grandchildren may never hear, at least so vigorously : a sound which reminds Lancashire men all over the world that there is a place called home.

§ 9

Two miles outside Bolton—a town of great character—the road twists up and round to Hall i' th' Wood. The wood has gone long ago, but the hall that once gleamed through the trees remains ; a black and white Tudor country house, whose windows gaze out over Eagley Brook towards the tall mill chimneys of Bolton.

Every cotton spinner who has made money in Lancashire should put peas in his boots, wear a hair shirt, and go fasting to Hall i' th' Wood, for here in this lovely little house Samuel Crompton played his home-made violin and invented his famous spinning ' mule '—poor Samuel Crompton, the clever, irritable, unworldly man who died poor while his brains piled up fortunes for other men. The hall is now, thanks to the imagination and money of the late Lord Leverhulme, the property of Bolton Corporation, and has been fitted up, as only a millionaire can fit up an old house, as an intelligent museum. It is not advertised. I suppose thousands pass through Bolton every day who have no idea that this place exists. And what an astonishment it is to the man who comes across it by chance ! How surprising to find here in a little black-and-white house overlooking the chimneys of Bolton two fine portraits by Peter Lely and two Van Dycks !

When the Hall in the Wood ceased to be a country house towards the middle of the eighteenth century, it was let off as tenements to farmers and weavers. Among these tenants was the father of Samuel Crompton. From his earliest years Crompton was made to spin yarn on Hargreaves' spinning-jenny, and he hated it. It annoyed him. He thought it was the worst bit of machinery he had ever set eyes on. He was enraged by the ever-breaking ends of the thread, and one day he became so sick of Hargreaves that he decided to think out a better spinning machine.

He was forty-six years of age before his ' mule ' was completed. It was called a mule because it was a cross between the water-frame and the spinning-jenny. It had both rollers and spindles, and its importance lay in the manufacture of a finer and stronger thread, which enabled the Lancashire weavers to rival the fine Indian muslins. This poor man in the tenement house thought out, alone and in the still hours of the night (for he worked by night to obtain greater secrecy) an invention which was one of the chief means of transferring an ancient industry from the eastern to the western world.

Like all poor men who have done great things, Samuel Crompton starved himself for an idea. He made himself a fiddle and he played it in a Bolton theatre so that he might earn extra money to construct his machine.

The financial world smelt out a good thing in the ' Hall in the Wood Wheel ', which was the first name given to the ' mule ', and Crompton was pried on. He hated that as much as he hated the breaking threads. He became more irritable than ever, and (how one would like to have given him legal advice !) he made one of the most absurd gestures in the history of invention and gave his ' mule ' to the public !

What a cynical mood fortune was in ! Within thirty years from the invention of the mule five million spindles were being worked on Crompton's principle ; and the inventor was still a poor man. Parliament was to be asked to vote him £20,000 (surely this should have come from the pockets of the men whom he had made rich and not from the nation), but even here Crompton's bad luck became again evident. Spencer Perceval, the Prime Minister, was assassinated in the Lobby of the House of Commons with the Crompton memorandum in his hand !

The inventor was eventually given £5,000, which he invested badly and was again penniless. He died, aged seventy-three, in receipt of a miserable £63 a year, and they buried him in the parish churchyard.

One more ironic thrust, and then Fate seemed to forget the family. In 1862 Bolton erected a statue to the man who helped to make it. The most notable figure on the platform was a poor old man of seventy-three, Crompton's surviving son.

*   *   *

When I entered Hall i' th' Wood it was difficult to believe that so much bad luck and unhappiness had been harboured there. A lovely house : the kind of house that turns a rich American's eyes bright green.

The caretaker took me through panelled rooms. We admired ceilings and Tudor fireplaces. I looked at the Van Dycks and the Lelys, most unexpected treasures to discover in such a spot. I saw objects which illustrate the spinning industry, and, most pathetic surely of all Lancashire relics, Crompton's home-made violin. What a subject for a Lancashire poet ! Poor Crompton's old fiddle, on which he used to wring out music to serve the dream that came true only to hurt him, as dreams, of course, can.

'These wooden spoons,' said the caretaker, 'used to be carved in the old days by young men in love and were given as a sort of token to the girls. That is the origin of the word spooning. And that is Shakespeare's comb.'

That Bolton should claim to possess Shakespeare's comb struck me as interesting, but irrelevant.

Go to see Hall i' th' Wood if ever you are in Bolton. Stand in the little formal garden where the trees are blackened by smoke and you will, I think, feel that you are between two worlds. Hall i' th' Wood is sweet as an Elizabethan madrigal, and its background in the dip, where the Eagley Brook still runs, is a dark smoke-cloud, and, could you hear it, something very like the sound of Crompton's mule.

You still inevitably think of the poor old man who beat his brains out on this hard world, and is now, however, an historic character, and his town's most famous and respected son.

That is the last joke of all.

§ 10

I looked at the sky and knew that I wanted to climb a hill in wind or rain. I took the road to Pendle Hill beyond the town of Clitheroe, the best hill, I am informed, in all Lancashire. In fact, they say, and have said for centuries, 'Ingleborough, Pendle Hill, and Penyghent are the highest hills between Scotland and Trent', although I believe that the Ordnance survey has proved this to be inaccurate. . . .

Clitheroe is all that London imagines a Lancashire mill town is not. It has retained its ancient shape. The main street is still feudal-looking ; it climbs up to a Norman castle and curves, as all good English lanes do, seeming to have been designed long ago in beautiful aimlessness by a herd of lost cattle. In Clitheroe you can see cotton mills and crocuses. To the south drifts the smoke of Preston and Blackburn, to the west and to the north stretch the wild Lancashire fells, rolling hill against rolling hill as far as eye can see.

In the autumn I think hares come from the north to sit up in the long grass and listen to the looms of Clitheroe making artificial silk pyjamas. Clitheroe is half in Lancashire and half in fairyland ; that is to say, half in new England and half in old.

Pendle Hill lifts his head beyond Clitheroe to a height of

1,831 feet. He is a real hill. He looks like ' a living creature stretched in sleep ', a great whale of a hill jutting out sharply over the valley which he guards. This hill is to Lancashire almost as the Wrekin is to Shropshire ; it is the one great physical feature of Lancashire steeped in local sentiment.

We went through the village of Downham, and there, in a lane which reminded me of Somerset, I left my car and struck off over a watery meadow in which there were lambs.

Lancashire lambs remain white for a month or so until the chimneys of Blackburn and Preston from the south, and Rochdale, Burnley, Nelson, and Colne from the east, tone them to the shade of their sires. These lambs were enjoying their distinctive infancy as lambs do, running timidly beside their dams on disproportionate legs and with a dangle of long tails, lifting their pretty blunt faces to make toy-shop noises, stumbling over the grass so unsure of themselves and, in fact, of anything. I never see a lamb without deciding to become a vegetarian.

Now the wind comes over Pendle like a storm at sea. Pendle seems to have its own private supply of wind. When the rest of the landscape lies at peace the south wind tears over Pendle Hill in a splendid fury, and the colour of this hill is deep brown.

As you begin to climb in the steep track of a watercourse your feet strike chips of grey limestone, and Pendle smells good, on a sunny morning with the wind racing over it, of clean grass, heather, and wet vegetation.

Half-way up, unless you are in good training, you collapse gratefully on a hummock and feel proud of yourself as you look back down the lonely hillside at the chequer-board of green pasture lands, so neat, so smoothly green, that merge gracefully into the blueness of the Yorkshire moors. Or you swear to give up cigarettes as the wind of Pendle takes you by the throat, as the height of Pendle hits you above the knee, as the wild beauty of Pendle adds another beat to your heart. . . .

Near the summit the wind ceases suddenly. There are parts of Pendle over which it skips with a shrill whistle ; you can hear it, but you cannot feel it until you climb up to the summit, where a post vibrates ; and here the wind comes for you suddenly with an angry whistle anxious to hurl you back far down into the green valley from which you came.

* * *

I sat down on the top of Pendle and surveyed the most interesting view in Lancashire. Is there, I wonder, a more varied view in England? To the right of me, far away, lying against a slope of the Pennine Chain, were the manufacturing towns of Rochdale, Colne, and Nelson, lifting their tall chimney-stacks into a smoke-cloud. All round this cloud the sun was shining brilliantly, and into this blue mist it shot faint shafts of light in a vain attempt to reach the earth.

In the valley of smoke I could see little gasworks, little streets of houses, mills, high stacks, now and then a puff of smoke from the railway, sudden and white as a bursting shell, and reservoirs shining like silver spoons in the haze. A grim panorama of effort, made more effective by the shadowy, high outline of the Pennines (the hills which bring down the Atlantic rain-clouds and make Lancashire safe for cotton spinners to live in!). Over these hills was another, fainter blanket of smoke which suggested the distant, invisible chimneys of Leeds, Halifax, Huddersfield, and Sheffield.

And the other side of this picture? To the left of me was old Lancashire—old England! The lovely green valley of the Ribble, bounded by the wild fells of Lancashire and the blue moors of Yorkshire, lay comfortably, little field against little field, bridges, white threads that were roads, little white farms, church spires among trees. To the right, industrial England; to the left, rural England. Is there a greater contrast anywhere than these views from two sides of one hill?

I am told that you can see York from the top of Pendle Hill, but I searched the sky in vain for it.

I fought against the wind to the Malkin Tower, where the 'Lancashire Witches' are said to have held their grand council. A fine spot for them! Here it was that, in 1612, on the top of Pendle, in the mists and at night, with the wind screaming down into the valley, the Pendle witches, ten of whom were executed at Lancaster, were believed to celebrate dark deeds. There was old Mother Demdike, whose real name was Mrs. Elizabeth Southerne, a sort of local agent for the devil. She confessed that she had sold her soul to Satan. I suppose it was on the crest of Pendle that the little imp called Tib used to wander with one half of his coat brown and the other half black. . . .

I stumbled down Pendle, down to the fields and the black-faced lambs, coming at length to a small inn in which a burly farm labourer in a blue shirt and clogs talked about the lambing.   (It may be news to some that shepherds guard their flocks within thirty miles of Manchester !)   And this old countryman, who has lived in the shadow of Pendle all his life, told me that before the war people came from all the milling towns to see the sun rise over Pendle on the first Sunday in spring !   They were called the ' Springers '.

That surely is the Roman Floralia ?   Did they light fires on Pendle, I asked.   He thought that they did.   Then it may be an even older superstition.   They started to climb the hill at midnight, said the shepherd, and you could hear their feet through the village, their voices singing, and in the first light of day, if you looked up at Pendle Hill, you would see them standing in a bunch, all facing the east, waiting for the rising of—the sun god !   (But they thought it was only a picnic !)

So Pendle, with its pagan rites, its witches, its stubborn ruggedness, seems to be like the grandfather of Lancashire. I raise my hat to him with respect ; but wearily !

§ 11

Four miles of boarding-houses—waiting.   Hotels, big and small—waiting.   Furnished apartments, whose windows are like wide, eager eyes—waiting.   Three piers, from whose extremities small boys catch dabs—waiting.   Miles of yellow sand—waiting.   The largest and whitest open-air swimming bath in the world—waiting.   The Tower—waiting.   The Wheel, with its wide circle of empty cars—waiting.   Hundreds of shops full of broadly comic postcards, full of ' Presents from Blackpool ', full of Blackpool rock, cafés, restaurants, dance-halls, cinemas, theatres—all waiting for the Lancashire ' wakes ', and for the deluge of free men and women who will soon descend on Blackpool like a riot migrating to the sea-coast.

Blackpool is just on the edge of its season.   It is about to make sufficient money in three months to keep it for a year, and—to maintain the rates at 7s. 6d. in the £ !   The land-ladies of Blackpool have ' welcome ' written not only on the mat but also on their faces ; there is a sound of hammering from the Tower, where carpenters are making a midget city of little houses, little garages, little shops to be inhabited by a troupe of English-speaking midgets ; and men with paint pots wander about the town putting the final touches to England's greatest experiment in organized pleasure.

Blackpool is the logical result of Lancashire. It is the silver lining to all the smoke-clouds. It is as eloquent of Lancashire as the smoke-stacks of Bolton and Oldham : it is Lancashire's idea of the earthly paradise.

There are millions of people all over the north of England who have been saving up for the past twelve months for a glorious week's ' fling ' at Blackpool.

The ' wakes ' are something we do not understand in the south. They are a contradiction of the northerner's traditional thrift. He is thrifty, but he can be open-handed. He arrives in Blackpool with his holiday money, and he spends every penny, and goes home ' broke ' to start all over again. But he carries back with him the memory of a week's careless affluence. He has known a week free from the nagging humiliation of slender means. He has scattered his pounds, shillings, and pence nobly like a millionaire ; but with much greater satisfaction !

And Blackpool has been designed for him and by him. Its red plush, its gilded cornices, its wine bars, its oyster saloons, its side-shows, its roundabouts, its fortune tellers, its postcards, its winking lights, and its music minister to a soul free, for a little while, from the dull monotony of granite ' setts ', and the sound of the siren in the morning. Blackpool is a perfect reflection of Lancashire's repressions.

Two things interest me about Blackpool : its inevitability and its uniformity. There is something in the salty air which makes it the inevitable playground of Lancashire ; the wide sands were designed by Nature to recreate the mill hands of the north, there is something in the wind which suggests that Blackpool could not help being the natural corollary of Manchester !

Its uniformity ! Popular seaside places are frequently self-conscious. There is a democratic quarter and a superior quarter. Blackpool has no self-consciousness. There is no invisible boundary between its cheapness and its expensiveness : it is all Blackpool. This is also characteristic of Lancashire. The mill hand and the ' boss ' both go to Blackpool. It belongs equally to them. Its democratic four-mile-long promenade rightly makes no distinction between them.

It is natural that the millions of pounds which have poured into Blackpool for the past thirty years should have had an effect on its appearance. The gaudy little vulgarities of a popular seaside place have vanished.   Even the side-shows are housed in the grand manner.

It is the professional seaside place developed as nowhere else in England.

'It looks quiet now,' said a Blackpool resident, ' but come back in a few weeks' time !   You will see the sands black with people, you will see the promenade tightly packed with them, you will see them coming in with their money, having a good time and going off again to save up for next year ! '

It is right and natural that Blackpool should have two sunsets !   You see one from the ground level, and if you rush to the top of Blackpool Tower you can see it over again. . . .

CHAPTER TEN

LIVERPOOL AND THE GREAT DOCK ROAD, A GLANCE INSIDE
THE ' KING'S PIPE ', AND THE PLACE WHERE MEN GAMBLE
IN COTTON WHICH IS NOT YET GROWN

§ 1

A GALE from America was delivering itself in the Mersey. Beautiful women were being blown up Lord Street in a most enchanting way, fighting and winning each corner.

Liverpudlians—this is the last time I shall use this grotesque word—clutched their hats, tucked in their public-school ties and butted on against the wind to see men about things happening, or about to happen, in Brisbane, Lagos, or Texas. The two Liver birds on the skyscraper at the Pier Head held to their green domes like grim death as the gale swept past and the sun was shining, the air was crystal clear.

Above the rattle of the tram-cars and the steady tramp and jingle of the dock road sounded the high, thrilling hoot of a tug in the river calling to its mates !

I, who have lived in the solid self-assurance of Manchester for many days, felt, as the gale hit me, that I had escaped from a directors' to a lovers' meeting. Manchester—a man among the cities of the earth—inspires admiration, respect, loyalty even, but—how easy to fall in love with Liverpool, this elusive, moody city, so full of variety, beauty ; so full of warm vitality.

The queer thought came to me as I walked the streets that the City of London was taking a holiday by the sea. There is about Liverpool something strangely London-like and poised : I find it in her men, her women, and her streets. There is an elegance here which I think exists in few places outside the capital. Liverpool has rubbed off her rough corners against the map of the world.

' Oh,' said the secretaries of three important business men, ' Mr. So-and-so's in London to-day ! '

Half the lifetime of Liverpool is spent in the Euston express !

Manchester seems to have happened ; Liverpool has been designed. Like London, she has a logical pattern. She groups herself round the stupendous St. George's Hall, the Town Hall, and the Pier Head : three definite centres as distinct as the Bank, Charing Cross, and Piccadilly.

Liverpool has a beautiful figure.

The Pier Head . . .

This is a magnet. All roads lead you there ; it is the end of all tramway journeys. Red funnels slide smoothly over the galvanized roofs of landing-stages, there is a gleam and movement of grey water, a thrilling nearness of great ships, a sound of their sirens shouting 'Safety first' up and down the Mersey.

I went down an inclined bridge to the floating landing-stage with a crowd of men and women. They were going home to the growing town of Birkenhead or to the many towns across the estuary which are the bedrooms of Liverpool.

Every morning and every night as the people of Liverpool leave or return home by the ferry they see the liners gliding from their berths, going out to the ends of the earth, or they see them returning, weather-beaten, low in the water, with the produce of many countries safe home at last from the hazards of the seven seas. What a difference this must make to the imagination of a city !

And how lucky surely are the wives in Egremont, New Brighton, West Kirby, and Hoylake ! A train journey nurses a man's temper, especially in London during the rush home. I am sure many a domestic tragedy has been born in a crowded train. But crossing water is an adventure : it is a definite breaking away from solid land : a symbolic act, a leaving behind. Can a temper or a hard thought survive that windy minute over water which separates the desk of a Liverpool man from his home ? I hope not.

I think my worst rage, my deepest mood of self-pity, my most painful sense of injustice would fly downwind at sight of those ships' funnels and the Liverpool chimneys rising side by side against the sky, those little tugs with red smoke-stacks beating up against the tide with the Mersey water, which is like melted ice-water spread with clotted cream, breaking over their blunt bows.

Not for me the Mersey tunnel !

Something is always happening on the landing-stage.

10

It may be a liner leaving for a foreign land, the crowd cheering, laughing—or trying to laugh—as the inch between the ship and the land widens to a yard.

Or it may be the *Daffodil* or the *Royal Iris* chugging over from the other side with a cargo of pretty girls—the *Daffodil* and the *Royal Iris* which took such a different cargo one dark night under the bloody Mole at Zeebrugge.

I saw a cattle boat come over from the largest landing-place for live-stock in the world at Birkenhead. The arrival of the cattle on the Liverpool side is a characteristic sight : the red-brown steers, bunched together in the ferry, their wide, frightened eyes, their slipping, blundering steps on the landing-stage, heads down, long trickles of saliva swinging from their dewlaps, a breakaway and a clumsy, galloping steer scattering the crowds. . . .

The varied assembly looks on : business men waiting for the New Brighton ferry, neat typists, women who have been shopping, dockers, a Japanese, a negro, a sailor. . . .

I stood beneath one of the Liver birds which crown the towers of the Liver building, and watched the sun set over Liverpool. Three miles off the mouth of the Mersey was cut across by a bright silver bar, which was the sea. I looked down over eight miles of docks : eight miles of great warehouses : eight miles of cranes : eight miles of ships at anchor.

Behind, mile after mile, the roofs, towers, chimneys of Liverpool lifted gently to the heights of Everton. The wind dropped, the smoke settled down over the city in a blue mist. The mighty red sandstone cathedral, the greatest building of its kind since the Middle Ages, begun twenty-two years ago yet only half finished, rose up on its hill grandly like a great stronghold above the mist.

The sun went in a stormy smother of cloud ; little cargo boats, jet black against the bright silver of the Mersey passed left and right ; the last wagons going by below were just a faint vibration in the air, and from the Canada Dock a liner with yellow funnels came slowly into midstream and took the way to America.

§ 2

Liverpool Cathedral is unquestionably the greatest thing in the city. It has been building for twenty years. Some say that it will not be finished for another fifty years. Although much has been written about it, the most interesting things will not be written until A.D. 3000, when men will sit down and decide how and why it happened in Industrial England of the twentieth century.

It is the greatest piece of church-building since the early Middle Ages, and it is conceived on an immense scale. When completed it will be larger than Westminster Abbey and York Minster. It will be the largest church in the world with the exception of St. Peter's in Rome.

It is the third cathedral to be built in England since the Reformation. The other two are St. Paul's and Truro. Truro was built in sixteen years ; St. Paul's, after the Fire of London, was rebuilt in thirty-five years. The only other cathedral which can be called the work of one generation is Salisbury, which was originally founded on the now desolate hill of Old Sarum and rebuilt on the plain during the thirteenth century. Even Salisbury was a quick work compared with Liverpool Cathedral : it was built in about forty years !

Another of Liverpool's many records is the fact that her two greatest buildings were designed by men in the twenties. The great St. George's Hall was designed by Harvey Lonsdale Elmes when twenty-four ; the winning design for the cathedral was made by a young man of twenty-one, now Sir Giles Gilbert Scott, aged forty-seven. He may be an old man of ninety-seven before the work which he began at twenty-one is finished.

The windows in the Lady Chapel perpetuate the lives and deeds of great women. There are windows to Eve and Queen Victoria, and to such different women as Grace Darling and Christina Rossetti ! There can be no question about the saints of the Prayer Book Calendar, but when we come to women of historic times the choice becomes provoking. Who are the twenty-one greatest women in English history ? I am sure that Liverpool has chosen many.

Her windows are dedicated as follows :

Juliana of Norwich, and all who have sought the inner light.
Susanna Wesley, and all devoted mothers.
Elizabeth Fry, and all pitiful women.
Josephine Butler, and all brave champions of purity.
Charlotte Stanley, Countess of Derby, and all steadfast women.
Queen Victoria, and all noble queens.
Angela Burdett-Coutts, and all Almoners of the King of Heaven
Catherine Gladstone, and all loyal-hearted wives.
Christina Rossetti, and all sweet singers.

Elizabeth Barrett Browning, and all who have seen the infinite in things.

Lady Margaret Beaufort, and all patronesses of sacred learning.

Anne Clough, and all true teachers.

Margaret Godolphin, and all who have kept themselves unspotted in a corrupt world.

Mother Cecile, and all women loving and large-hearted in counsel.

Louisa Stewart, and all the noble army of martyrs.

Dr. Alice Marval, and all who have laid down their lives for their sisters.

Anna Hinderer, and all missionary pioneers.

Grace Darling, and all courageous maidens.

Kitty Wilkinson, and all poor helpers of the poor.

Agnes Jones, and all devoted nurses.

Mary Rogers, stewardess of the *Stella*, and all faithful servants.

I do not know how many people could pass an examination on the lives and deeds of these women. Margaret Godolphin would have ploughed me. I find that her fame rests on the fact that she lived a pure life at the Court of Charles II ! John Evelyn immortalizes her in his *Diary*.

I looked vainly and long for :

Edith Cavell, and all dauntless women.

Florence Nightingale, and all women who have carried a light into dark places.

Catherine of Aragon, and all unhappy wives.

Lady Jane Grey, and all wronged women.

I also searched for ' Queen Elizabeth and all business women ! '

The gigantic red sandstone temple is Liverpool's contribution to the monuments of England. One would like to be able to show it to the men who built York Minster and Westminster Abbey. The Gothic style has been adapted with magnificent ease by a genius born in an age of machines, of skyscrapers, of man's control over matter. It is not a slavish copy ; it is a creation.

It is perfect in detail as in mass : it is, like all our cathedrals, the gift of Catholicism to Protestantism. There is no surprise in the knowledge that the architect was educated at Beaumont College !

You stand in the half-built nave, which ends in a blank wall, conscious that you are in one of the great churches of the world ; and the thousands who every day visit Liverpool and do not see this building are missing one of the notable sights of England.

From the top of the Royal Liver Building its towering mass of red stone is seen to dominate the city of Liverpool, rising high above the shipping as St. Sophia rides above Constantinople. Its site can be compared with that of Durham and Lincoln. It is, I imagine, the first landmark that catches a sailor's eye as his ship comes up the Mersey from the sea ; the last sign that dips below the horizon as, outward bound, a ship goes into the west.

If, in the uncertainties of a thousand years, the docks of Liverpool are silent, if the cranes rot and rust on their iron perches—an unlikely fate, but one which has overtaken many an English port as famous in its time as Liverpool in hers—men from every part of the world will still visit Liverpool to see the only cathedral of the twentieth century.

§ 3

I met him in the overhead electric. He was in the twenties, had red hair, a college tie against a silk shirt, and a great sense of what he called ' the realities '. He told me that he had come over to see the honest-to-goodness England. He was dead set on our ' realities '.

' None of your dead-town bunk for me ! ' he said. ' I guess my sister can have your cathedrals. I wanta see the people at work, I wanta see them living, I wanta see the places where you *do* things—the cotton mills of Lanca-shire ; and all that. I guess we folk get right off the track in England, mooning around like a lot of poor stiffs listening to all that Edward the Confessor bunk. It's all dead, but, see here, this is alive, it's happening, it means something, its important. . . . Geewhillikins ! look at that ! '

The train banged over the girders, shot past a high wall, and gave us a left-hand view of ships discharging their cargoes and a right-hand view of a road that runs for nearly eight miles at the back of the docks. I pointed out this road to the realist as one of the most remarkable in England.

' That looks mighty good to me ! ' he said. ' That makes the British Mu-seum look like a hen-house to me, sir ! That's alive. . . . Oh, say, look at those cotton bales ! From the States, I guess ! '

His enthusiasm nearly carried me away. There is some-thing about the drama of the Great Dock Road that stirs the imagination. Eight miles of straight, hard road filled with the exports and imports of Liverpool.

The sound of the Great Dock Road is the voice of Liverpool. It is the sound of hooves, of iron-bound wheels bumping heavily from stone to stone, of carters clicking their tongues, geeing and whoaing, of whips cracking.

It is more than a road : it is a barometer of commerce.

When the rumble of the Great Dock Road falls a tone a Liverpool man knows at once that trade is bad. When the Great Dock Road rumbles, bumps, jingles, gees, and whoas from early morn until late at night he knows that men all over England are buying and selling, that ships are loading and unloading, that the Port of Liverpool, and cities and towns far beyond Liverpool, are thriving and content.

' Listen to the sound of it ! ' said the realist. ' Isn't it good ? '

We looked out of the window, and, as far as we could see, the carts and the wagons went by left and right like the baggage trains of a great army.

This road is the spine of the north country. It is a magnificent epic of commerce. The heavy draught horses strain against their loads, lifting their hairy feet slowly, ploddingly, methodically, going past with a jingle of chains.

All the produce of the world goes by upon the Great Dock Road. There is cotton for Lancashire, tobacco for Nottingham, metals for Birmingham, wool for the north country, raw material which will find its way into the far-spread, intricate machinery of British manufacture. More than a third of British exports pass along the Great Dock Road.

The longer you study it the more fascinating it becomes. The peoples of the earth have laboured to fill its wagons. You identify the origin of boxes and crates as the lorries go past : a name here, a sign there : oranges from Jaffa, lemons from Naples, onions from Egypt, from Valencia, grape-fruit from Cuba, wool from the West, frozen meat from the Argentine . . . just a few haphazard boxes in the convoy.

Over the high walls of the docks rise the warehouses, accepting and discharging their stores. Through the prison-like gates is many a glimpse of a ship home from sea, a long line of empty wagons approaching for her cargo, or a ship loading, men swarming up her gangways, the cranes screaming, dipping their thin steel arms to the dockside and lifting boxes in an arc through the air to drop them into the omnivorous mystery of the hold.

All day long from every gate a slow line of carts and wagons joins the main stream upon the Great Dock Road.

At the back of the road is Liverpool, her fine buildings, her frequent touches of real grandeur, her many signs of elegant opulence, her busy men and women, split up and divided between a thousand endeavours, but most, in some way, vitally concerned with the long procession that winds all day along this road.

There are so many angles to remember of this varied city, but Liverpool to me means first a ship coming up the Mersey from the open sea, and then a mighty shire horse, his immense flanks shining, his muscles moving like steel under velvet, plodding steadily along the Great Dock Road pulling the ends of the earth together into Liverpool.

*   *   *

There is another side to the story of the Great Dock Road.

It is grey and cold over the docks. A sharp wind blows down the road, empty now of its wagons, its lorries, its motor-vans, and so strange in this still hour. The ships are awakening beyond the high dock walls. Ships awaken with fine breezy hammering sounds and to a smell of fried bacon and strong coffee. Their riding lights have grown pale ; the last star has faded in the sunrise, and a new day begins.

Before the massive gates of a dock in which a ship waits to be unloaded stands a crowd of perhaps five hundred men. Look at their faces, and read there the humiliating tragedy of casual labour. It is not peculiar to Liverpool ; I have seen the same good, bad, and indifferent faces waiting in the early morning outside the Port of London. The uncertainty of it, the vague, shifty eyes, the hopefulness of it (and the hopelessness) shake the heart. Even a beast is rarely unwanted, but to be a man and to be unwanted day after day, rejected day after day. . . .

Many of them are rough, debased, down-trodden, many poor and tragic, many of them are thinking of their labour only in terms of liquid, many of them are thinking of it in terms of bread, with a woman somewhere in a slum, and children. All of them have been drawn out of bed in the dawn, unwashed, most of them unfed, to stand in the pale, growing light and offer their arms and their backs as they did in Tyre and Sidon. (It was, I think, better for them in those days, because they belonged to some one; a slave must at least be fed, but a free man has the right to starve.)

They do not speak much. A cold, breakfastless morning does not encourage conversation. There is something more —they are all, at this moment, enemies. There are five hundred of them, and the ship will need only sixty-two.

The dock gates open. An air of intense eagerness vitalizes the waiting men as if they have been charged with electricity. Some rub their rough hands as if already they are hauling at the boxes and the bales; some stand sullenly waiting; a few look threateningly with pursed lips; and more than one or two—pale, poor creatures, hardly strong enough, it seems, to lift a kitten—square their shoulders and try to look strong enough for the job.

Two men, one with a note-book, walk from the dock gates. They have come to choose the 'casuals' who will reinforce their regular gang. The grey faces edge near. A ring is formed. The man with the note-book looks round.

'You!' he says in a sharp, firm voice, as he points round the ring, 'and you, and you with the green cap, and you— no, not you there, get back! The man behind you—and you with the pipe. . . .'

So it goes on in the grey morning, like something happening long ago in a slave market.

The man behind the foreman watches carefully in order to prevent the rejected from insinuating themselves into the commerce of the Port of Liverpool; and this they try to do cunningly.

When the moving finger, having written, moves on, see how they slink out and creep round after it, thrusting their faces forward in the crush, attempting to catch the foreman's eye; and generally in vain.

'How do you choose them?' I asked a foreman.

'I know my casuals,' he replied.

The affair ends suddenly. Sixty-odd men have slunk away from the group; four hundred-odd are left standing a moment dully, while the realization that they have been passed over once again sinks into their brains. But perhaps it does not. Possibly the sharpness of rejection has blunted itself against them. Do they just think: 'Perhaps there'll be something to-morrow. . . .'

They melt away in slow groups, talking now, swearing, drifting off up side streets to become lost in the mystery of their casual lives.

I suppose it ends for most of them before a woman's eyes. No need for a woman to ask questions as the rejected body hunches home, head down, hands in pockets. . . .

Over the dock walls the cranes scream and dip towards the cargo, the carts come up, the gangs bend to their burdens.

More riches have come to Liverpool.

§ 4

A man who buys cotton for Lancashire to spin and weave led me to the Liverpool Cotton Exchange. He took me as a man takes a stranger to the temple of his fathers ; and we stood outside and paid graceful compliments to this building . . . dignity, proportion, Doric, Ionic, Renaissance, and so forth.

In view of what followed I must say that my first impression was one of calm sanity. In this fine building, I thought, they can buy as much cotton as they can afford—and even a bit more now and then—in perfect harmony. They must indeed be glad to make their fortunes in these spacious surroundings. We went inside, up a stairway, through a door, and out to a colonnade of pillars of dark, polished granite. Here, as I looked down to the floor of the Exchange, my first impression was shattered. I seemed to be in a luxurious asylum.

A hundred men, some bareheaded, some wearing hats, stood outside a wide circular rail set up in the centre of the great hall. They were shouting at each other and making urgent gestures. It seemed to my puzzled and ignorant eye that they were ordering drinks from an invisible barman. The centre of the ring, at that moment vacant, seemed to lack a man in a white shell jacket with a cocktail shaker.

They crowded shoulder to shoulder, shouting, flinging up their arms, making signs with their fingers, the resultant noise a deep masculine babel from which it was not possible to tell whether they wanted dry martinis or whisky and soda.

The same gestures, the same time-driven anxiety, the same quick glances at the clock are seen in certain north country bars at closing time every Saturday night.

I took my friend firmly by the shoulders and shouted into his ear :

' Is it a revolution or do they only want the manager ?

' No,' he managed to tell me, ' they are buying cotton !

' How do they know ? I asked him, but this he could not, or would not, answer.

The ring was the ' Cotton Futures Ring. The cotton— or much of it—which was causing so much excitement was, I gathered, not yet grown ! They were buying cotton as far as twelve months ahead. New York was egging them on, sending them encouraging or discouraging messages every few seconds, while the only calm person present, a little tow-haired boy, put up the prices on a great black screen which resembled in its mathematical obfuscation a senior wrangler's idea of a pleasant Sunday afternoon.

There was a smaller ring near at hand, but the storm did not touch it. It looked like a bit of the Hyde Park rails at lunch-time ; two men were leaning on it casually and chatting.

' Egyptian cotton ! ' shouted my friend. ' Not much doing.'

There was an even smaller ring, uninhabited.

' Empire cotton ! ' shouted my friend. It had evidently all been sold.

The whole drama was concentrated round the American ring. Cable Company boys, wearing peaked red caps, came in chewing toffee, unconscious of their importance as slaves of that god of commerce, the Atlantic cable, and men sat in little areas of detachment manipulating telewriters or quietly adding to the mathematical obscurity of that important blackboard which held the secret of cotton prices for twelve months ahead.

As I looked down on the Cotton Ring, trying to find out how it worked, I became aware that its violence was fitful. It was a moody riot. It blew hot and cold. Now it would be cold and suddenly silent—but watchful—then it would in a second blaze up so that every man seemed to be shouting down the other fellow. I noticed that it responded to men lurking on the outskirts, who received cables and telegrams from time to time ; messages which they read quickly and furtively ; messages telling them to sell or buy. They would then enter the ring and get busy, and the ring would react at once.

When a sharp spurt was dying down I heard voices crying :
' I'll sell five June ! '
' I'll buy five at seventy-one ! '
My friend shouted to me :
' It's really like an auction among friends ! '
I patted his arm sympathetically and tried to appear
convinced.

I went back to an importer's office. I sat down impressed
by the Cotton Ring, hoping that the wives of ' ring merchants '
are always kind to them, for these men, so long as they do
not shout in their sleep, deserve peace and kindness.

A senior partner opened the door an inch and said
rapidly :
' It's dropped since five ! '
The whole cotton trade seems to be conducted in these
short, cryptic sentences.

The senior partner came in again, quickly, excitedly.
reeled off some more figures, and went back to his listening
post, and I realized that the shouting men at the Futures
Ring were not a badly conducted riot : they formed an
astonishing nerve centre, a queer, intricate, delicate bunch
of nerves created by years of trading, nerves linking New
York with hundreds of Liverpool offices.

' Up two points since three ! ' said the face of the senior
partner between the opening and the slamming of the door.

And in hundreds of offices where they buy ungrown cotton
the same nervous tension was, I suppose, felt as men followed
the moods of the market minute by minute. . . .

I walked out, still puzzled, but vaguely glad to know that
the price of a cotton vest was fixed for April next year !

§ 5

' No smoking ! ' said the man at the gate as I stepped into
the largest tobacco warehouse on earth.

Round us were millions of bales of tobacco, tobacco of
every kind in thousands of tons, pipe tobacco, cigarette
tobacco, and the complete cigar in boxes, yet he made me
throw away half a cigarette ! I went into the office, where
they took away my matches !

' Now this,' said my guide, ' is the largest warehouse in
the world.'

' Yes,' I replied, having heard all about it. Liverpool has

collected the greatest number of ' record ' achievements in
the country :

The largest spot cotton market.
The largest electrically-driven clock.
A cathedral which is to be twice as big as Westminster
Abbey.
The largest organ in the world.
The first overhead electric railway.
The first under-river tunnel.
The first enclosed dock.

This does not exhaust the ' records.' I believe that the
wind straight from America puts these inspiring ideas into
Liverpool's charming head.

' It certainly looks like the largest in the world,' I said,
leaning back against a wall and gazing up at a red brick
mountain.

' And it *is*,' said my guide finally.

Had I been an American and ready to argue about it I
believe he would have knocked me down.

Leaf tobacco comes over from America in gigantic wooden
casks which hold a tun. It smells like malt. Indian tobacco
comes in square sacks.

The Customs officers roam about a tobacco warehouse
like pirate kings. Nothing escapes them. If you absent-
mindedly chewed a bit of leaf I think they would charge
you duty on it. And the duty on American tobacco is 8s. 2d.
a pound. There are 1,120 lbs. in a tun, so that each one of
the thousands of hogsheads in the largest warehouse on earth
helps Mr. Winston Churchill to the extent of over £457.
I looked reverently at the hundreds of thousands of hogsheads, wishing earnestly that every one of them could come
out of bond at once and bring down the income tax. The
only manner in which I can convey the majesty of the sight
is to say that in the crypt alone I consider that there must
have been at least a possible 6d. off the income tax. If you
take 6d. for each one of the nine floors it is clear that Liverpool's largest warehouse holds the secret of our happiness.

We went up to floor after floor, each a gloomy, dark, evenly
temperatured, malt-smelling prairie stacked with hogsheads.
Some of the tobacco had been in bond for years. Hundreds
of tons of it will not be smoked for years to come.

This warehouse contains tobacco which our infant sons

will smoke ; cigars with which our unborn grand-children will comfort their declining years.

When my guide was not looking I stole half a Virginia leaf, which is a serious crime, but I did it in the interests of knowledge. This was the kind of tobacco that Sir Walter Raleigh smoked, right from the plantation. The first tobacco that came to England probably looked like this. This brittle brown paper was the tobacco which the mariners of Bristol and Plymouth crammed into their pipes on the quays in the reign of Gloriana.

We came at length to that which I was to learn is the tragedy of the largest warehouse on earth.

Half a floor was stacked with wooden boxes bearing those magic, but almost forgotten letters : ' N.A.C.B., B.E.F.'— The Navy and Army Canteen Board, British Expeditionary Force. These boxes contain 10,000,000 Canadian cigarettes in packets. They arrived too late to help to win the war. Poor gaspers ! A matter of a few months and they might have gone up in blue smoke along the roads of Flanders.

' To whom do they belong now ? '

' To no one.'

He explained to me that no one can afford to take them out of bond. The duty is too high. It would be possible to buy much better English-made cigarettes for less than the duty necessary to release the ' gaspers.' When the N.A.C.B. faded away to become a happy memory in the lives of ex-quartermaster-sergeants, the 10,000,000 cigarettes were sold by auction to firms, who quickly came to their senses and disowned them. The cigarettes then got into debt for storage, and the Mersey Docks and Harbour Board entered into ownership.

' But we don't know what to do with them. No one can afford them. We cannot do anything unless the duty is paid on them. We did, however, offer them to the Navy and the Army.'

' And ? '

' They both said " No, thanks ! " The only way out is for us to destroy them. We shall have to put them in the King's Pipe.'

*　　　*　　　*

The King's Pipe is the only dramatic feature of the world's largest warehouse. They used to call it the Queen's Pipe in Victorian times.

It is a vast furnace with a high chimney-stack rather like a giant's briar. Into this furnace in the course of a year go hundreds of pounds' worth of tobacco, cigarettes and cigars ; dutiable articles on which no one will, for one reason or another, pay duty. The Customs officers come in state, unpadlock the King's Pipe, and kindle the valuable bonfire.

I went inside the royal pipe. Lying on the floor were two sacks of perique which had gone bad, the sweepings of nine gigantic warehouse floors, a miscellaneous assortment of pipe and leaf tobacco, cardboard and a few boxes : a fine medium mixture.

Whenever a dense aromatic smoke issues from the chimney-stack the dockers outside, the loungers round the ' Green Man ' and the proppers-up of walls sniff the air sadly and say :

' King's havin' a smoke to-day.'

They sniff and sigh. What a waste of good stuff ! Plug, probably ! Twist, perhaps ! What a waste.

*   *   *

It only remains for me to say that if Sir Walter Raleigh brought home from Virginia the kind of leaf tobacco which I stole and smoked in my pipe with some historical emotion, he must have made hundreds of enemies.

CHAPTER ELEVEN

TELLS HOW I FOUND THE HAND-LOOM WEAVERS OF MACCLES-
FIELD, AND HOW I SLIPPED OVER THE DERBYSHIRE PEAK
THROUGH A SNOW-STORM INTO BUXTON—THE TOWN OF
BLUE WATER. HOW I ENCOUNTERED AN AMAZON IN
BREECHES, HOW I VISITED A VILLAGE THAT STILL TALKS
ABOUT THE PLAGUE OF LONDON AND HOW I CAME INTO
THE VARIED SMOKE OF SHEFFIELD

§ 1

I FLED from Liverpool as men occasionally fly from
affection. The city is too full of things worth writing
about for any man who is supposed to be making a
motor-car tour. I took the Cheshire road to the Derbyshire
Peak, and on the way I was driven by hunger into a town
called Macclesfield, where the dogs have no fear of death.

Macclesfield stands on the edge of Cheshire, lying against
a great ridge of hills. These are the Pennines, the spinal
cord of England, which illuminate spiritually, while they
separate physically, Lancashire and Yorkshire. At first sight
Macclesfield had nothing to recommend it to a casual visitor
except the medievalism of its street names and a white,
crumbly kind of Cheshire cheese which does not bite the
tongue as it does when it goes to London.

I noticed all over this town vacant-looking top stories to
the houses with little leaded panes, curtainless, dusty.

'Those,' said the old man who was leaning against the
local fountain, 'are called garrets. Before the factories came
the silk weavers used to keep their looms there.'

The older streets of Norwich are distinguished by this relic
of the pre-factory era, but the looms of the Flemish weavers
in that city were housed in Dutch eaves like inverted V's.

'And Macclesfield is still the centre of the silk weaving
industry, or is it Spitalfields ? '

The old man looked annoyed.

'It's Macclesfield,' he said ; and spat.

In a side street, against the window of a mill, I saw what i now surely a most remarkable appeal in the north of England

WANTED

Six thred figured hand-
loom weavers.

I went in to see about it. Macclesfield is the last strongholof the old hand-loom. The power loom may have conquerethe rest of the north, but there are things done in Macclesfielsilk which can only be done by hand. There are workinin this town about two hundred and fifty hand-loom weaverThey have a trade union of their own.

'Our mill,' said my informant, 'employs sixty hand-looweavers. The highest grade of silk weaving will always bdone by hand-looms. We could employ more than sixty we could find them, and the prospects are so good that ware starting an apprenticeship system. . . .'

'I suppose you weave expensive things for women?'

'On the contrary, we make silk ties for men of fashion.'

'You mean those expensive silk ties which they almossell you in small streets off the Burlington Arcade ? '

'But they are worth it ! ' he said indignantly. 'Theare distinctive ! There are very few alike. A man of refinement likes to have a tie made up for him from a small pieof hand-woven silk. Many rich men who dress well wounever dream of buying a ready-made tie.'

I felt properly rebuked.

In a long shed I heard the slow, steady clatter of hanlooms : a sound which Lancashire has now forgotten : thsound to which she rose to her greatness.

Contrasted with the uncanny, quick, intelligent, chatterinsheds worked by power, this long shed, with its sixty deliberathand-loom weavers, was a surprising glimpse into the pasAll the weavers were men. This was so in the old days. Thwomen were spinsters and the men were weavers. Many the men were over seventy. One of them allowed me to trthe pedal of his loom ; he was treading a hundredweight lead every time he pedalled.

'No,' he said, 'I don't notice it ! I've been used to it amy life. My father taught me, his grandfather taught himWe've been hand-loom weavers right away back. . . .'

He liked it. It satisfied him, he told me, to weave silk patterns. He had created something. It was not just minding a machine. The power-looms were marvellous, but—they couldn't weave like he could !

'It is a curious thing,' said my guide, 'but if the same pattern was woven by a power- and a hand-loom I believe I could tell which was which almost in the dark. There is a touch about hand-woven silk—a personality—that only a hand-loom can give.'

The hand-loom is surely the most clumsy instrument in the world. To the untechnical eye it seems more than marvellous that such delicate things as those cobweb threads of coloured silk can be passed through this Heath Robinson-like wilderness of twine, leaden fringe, foot pedals, weighted boulders, shaking arms, and other queer gadgets which beggar description into a tie which a ' man of fashion ' buys before he meets ' a lady of quality '.

Long may the hand-looms shake the sheds of Macclesfield !

*   *   *

I took the high road over the bare hills into Derbyshire.

§ 2

If a Londoner can imagine Dartmoor moved into Essex he will have some idea of the meaning of the Peak District to the crowded industrial cities of the north. At the very doors of Manchester, and, on the east, Sheffield, are miles of the wildest country in England. Men and women from these cities can be lost in untamed hills in less time than it takes a Londoner to ride in an omnibus from the Bank to Hammersmith.

The ease with which the workers of Manchester and Sheffield can reach open country would be astonishing to any southerner who does not know this part of England. A Cockney in search of a similar escape into the same refreshing wilderness would have to go to Devonshire ! Every week-end thousands of men and women leave the northern cities to fill their lungs with the sharp moorland air, for Peakland invigorates the body and the mind of the industrial north.

As I took the Cat and Fiddle Road over the hills—one of the highest roads in England—I met in a sudden and unexpected manner this wild thing that is at the very heart of the north country.

It was raining : a fine, persistent drizzle. The road twisted gracefully round and up to a desolate land of peaty moors, cut across by low limestone walls, brown and shining in the wet. Curlews were flying over the brownish grass, sheep grazed mournfully above the walls, and the clouds, flying low, steamed gently across the crests of the hills, so that I was continually running in and out of mists.

A keeper with a retriever at heel passed me on the road. Derbyshire grouse are fiercely guarded.

So I climbed slowly on, the road hugging the edge of the hill. The map told me that I was twelve hundred feet above sea-level. I stopped my car and looked back across the distant panorama of long hills folded one upon another against the weeping sky ; a grim, forbidding landscape. It was as bleak and untamed as Dartmoor. There was not one sign of human life. One hour from Manchester. . . .

Round a bend in the road I came on a man in trouble with a motor-car :

' It's nothing,' he said. ' Only this ! '

He picked a large frozen snowball from between the running board and the chassis.

' It's snowing like the devil up on top,' he said, ' and the wind's blowing a gale.' He looked at my car. ' You'll have a job to hold her to the road.'

It seemed impossible. Snow on a typical April day !

I asked him how far off this quick-change weather might be :

' You'll strike it,' he said, ' in about a mile ! '

The Cat and Fiddle road at this part rises two and even three hundred feet every mile.

Suddenly the rain became chilled. Far off to the left a moor sloped away dusted with white. It looked as though it had been sprinkled with lime. Still there was no sign of the storm. I looked to the right and there I saw it ! Snow was blowing before the wind in wild eddies and spirals. It was blowing down to the distant moors which showed dark and green through the moving whiteness. At a point far below the white flakes vanished and fell as rain.

I climbed on. Snow began to fall, timidly at first, very slowly. It melted into the icy slush of the road ; it was licked up by the stone walls. The flakes became more

IN DERBYSHIRE

frequent as I advanced. It was bitterly cold. Very still. I had left an April world and had come, in a few short miles, to the depth of winter.

The highest (but one) inn in England stood in the very teeth of the gale on the highway. The snow cut across its chimneys, drifted against door and window frames. It was a typical December sight.

The Cat and Fiddle Inn stands sixteen hundred and ninety feet above sea-level. The Tan Hill Inn, Yorkshire, is said to stand seventeen hundred and twenty-seven, which is not a great victory. One or two snow-bound travellers thawed their hands and feet at the fire and felt their red-hot ears.

We watched the snow falling outside. We were cut off from the world in this unexpected blizzard. I think we rather enjoyed it. A physical struggle with the elements gives you a fine spiritual glow. I felt sure as I watched my companions that they would boast about their fight in the blizzard when they dropped down into the milder world of Manchester. I would be doing the same thing in Buxton! I would seek out some fat, over-fed man and tell him how fine it is to battle with the head wind; how glorious it is to plough through the snow. . . . I could see his eyes goggle:

' Snow? Where? '

I liked Peakland in this wild humour.

*　　　*　　　*

How the wind sprang up as I splashed along the exposed road towards Buxton! It tore at the wind-screen, it held back my car, which shook itself and rocked in the sideways gusts that threatened to lift us and fling us to the rocks beneath.

The road dropped. So did the wind. The snow was melting. The grass was green. I had left Derbyshire's little Switzerland behind me. I passed a house with a garden full of daffodils. April again.

In Buxton the streets had dried after an April shower. The snow-storm seemed like a dream. I looked back at the hills. It was true after all! Right at the top was a little patch of white the size of a saucer!

The water of Buxton is the most beautiful water in England. It reminds me of Capri. It is a palc shadc of blue. In official circles here they call it aquamarine, but the colour is the lovely tint of a bowl of water in which you have washed a not too dirty fountain-pen nib. Bubbles of nitrogen float slowly up through it to burst on the surface, sometimes with a slight explosion.

I defy any man or woman to look at a big bath full of this pale-blue water without wanting to undress at once and get into it. It bubbles generously from the earth through nine springs at a convenient temperature of eighty-two degrees, so that Buxton is I think the only spa in this country in which your bath water is heated entirely by the lower regions. (The waters of Bath gush out at too high a temperature ; they have to be diluted with cold water.)

Half a million gallons of blue water are delivered in Buxton out of the earth every day ; the quantity and the temperature never vary.

The waters of Bath look like pea-soup, and tasted to Charles Dickens like warm flat-irons. I have described the taste of Harrogate water. But Buxton water, no matter whether it cures you or not, is a pleasure to contemplate. All water should look like that. There is probably a huge fortune awaiting the man who can popularize coloured bath water. Surely in a world that bristles with societies there is room for a Brighter Baths Association.

It is very quiet in Buxton. There is practically no sound but the soft bursting of nitrogen bubbles on blue water. It is a soothing town, and as clean as Hereford on a May morning.

It is the highest town of its size in England. It appears as you approach it over the hills from Goyt's Moss just when you expect it least ; it springs out suddenly nestling in a cosy, affectionate manner between the bare, rounded hills ; a delightful little elegance on the wild roof of England. Fashion in scenery changes almost as notably as in humour. The eighteenth century considered Buxton's situation ugly ; to-day it is much appreciated.

I like to be here watching the nitrogen after the more strenuous sights of Liverpool and Manchester. It is almost as excellent a way of doing nothing as leaning over a bridge.

The full force of the country's sciatica has not apparently invaded Buxton yet. I went into the Pump Room to taste the blue water. A neat maiden stood beside a big oblong marble pool into which the holy well of St. Anne was passing at the rate of fifty gallons a minute. The maiden placed a glass in a socket at the end of a long metal rod, she swished the glass several times round the bubbling bath and handed me the radio-active tumbler.

Buxton water tastes triumphantly of—nothing.

It is not good for people like myself to be left alone in a spa. There comes that inevitable moment when you pick up in a smoke-room one of those booklets which the local authorities produce in copious quantities, and you begin to read about the diseases cured by the waters—or if not actually cured, alleviated. You then notice a suspicious ache. You wonder whether it is the first twinge of rheumatoid arthritis or possibly a warning of fibrositis.

You turn over hurriedly to ecstatic pages which glorify the natural beauties of the spa : ' The moorlands,' you learn, ' are the home of grouse, snipe, curlew, blackcock, merlin, sparrow-hawk, kestrel, and a number of small birds. To the lover of nature . . .' ' How difficult it must be,' you think, ' to love nature and at the same time have gout. Arthritis ! Hardening of the arteries. Active people get it ! You just slow down and end. . . .'

You turn over :

' On almost every hill,' you read, ' a low mound marks the burial place of a chieftain, and the place-name " low " (Anglo-Saxon hloew, a grave, mound) occurs frequently. Those interested in archaeology . . .'

You stop to watch one of those dear old ladies who inhabit all spas—old ladies who wear châtelaines and a thin black velvet band round their necks—hobble across on two sticks. Some one says that she is getting better. She smiles bravely, and goes on. Or one of those old men, paying the debts of the Eighteenth Century in a wheel-chair, goes past ; and you realize that the hour for treatment has arrived.

You begin to feel quite ill. Perhaps if you are not actually suffering at the moment, you think, neuritis, sciatica, arthritis, are only staying their hands so that they may leap upon and seize you suddenly. A bath in time may save years of Harley Street. . . .

So you follow the painful crowd.

*   *   *

I came to the marble baths of Buxton.

I told a man in a white coat where I thought my pains were, and he thought that a plunge bath would do me no harm. This is a most attractive treatment. It is the hypochondriac's heaven.

Five or six marble steps lead down to a marble tank, in the corner of which is a seat. The attendant turns a wheel, and the marvellous blue Buxton water swirls and gushes and gurgles into the tank until it is level with the top step. You then walk out unashamed and descend into the water. It is blue. It is warm. The nitrogen bubbles burst and tickle you. It is like bathing with invisible goldfish. The attendant tells you to sit down on the seat, but this is not easy, because in such a depth of blue water you do not trust your sense of direction.

If you find the seat your face will then be floating like a lily above the blue water, looking, it occurs to you, rather ridiculous. Still, in the interests of health . . .

The attendant then arms himself with a powerful hose and, standing like a fireman on the dry ground above, aims a fierce stream of hotter blue water at those portions of you which require massage. He will then make your spine purr. He will run his stream of hot water up and down your back. This gives you the illusion of being full of radium.

There will come a time when he will suggest that you get out. You will refuse. He will say that you are taking in too much sodium, potassium or magnesium, but you tell him you don't care. You tell him that you would like a bath of this kind at home, and you argue with him about the backwardness of British plumbing.

He is not interested. You tell him that the time will come when all true bath lovers will combine and demand better and bigger bathrooms. . . .

Then probably a real pain will shoot through your left arm, and you will leap out in great alarm, with the feeling that you have asked for, and received, neuritis.

*   *   *

Buxton, with its hills, its curlews, its mounds, its caves, its harriers, its sciaticas, and, above all, its fascinating springs, is a town to which I shall return some day when it is definitely established that I need calcium, barium, magnesium, aluminium, manganese, sodium, potassium, ammonium, etc.—or, in other words, nice blue water.

§ 4

She was eating eggs.

Her long legs were in khaki breeches, her long arms in the sleeves of an old tweed jacket, her feet in stout walking boots. The wind had pulled her yellow hair all over her head, and the rain had given it a temporary wave. She was enjoying herself. She liked eggs.

The inn parlour contained also a fat dog asleep on a mat, a number of archaic drink advertisements showing men in silk hats driving gigs containing women with wasp waists and leg-of-mutton sleeves. There were also a few desolate-looking benches. Beyond the window the moors of the Peak district rose and fell, vast and smooth as the curved backs of sleeping cattle. It was raining. The thin shower pin-pricked the window, and the rain-drops raced one another down the glass in a way that rejoices the heart of Lancashire because it is possible to bet on them !

I watched her eat eggs. She was a Peak Walker, or ' rambler ', if you like. There are thousands of them, men and women. Some, like Kipling's cat, walk by themselves, others conquer Derbyshire in mass formation, or clubs, every Sunday. There are two kinds of Peak Walker—the ordinary rambler and the storm fiend.

The ordinary rambler rambles (weather permitting), but the storm fiend loves hardship. He, or she, likes nothing better than to drop down from the moors into Manchester or Sheffield, as the shades of night are falling on the already thick gloom of Sunday, looking as though he, or she, had been blown up, flung into a stream, dragged through wire netting, ending up with a triumphant victory over sixteen game-keepers and a dog. These splendid storm fiends with their ruddy cheeks and the moorland wind in their eyes, are a weekly rebuke to the softness of poor city dwellers.

You can't help liking them.

During the week the Walkers of the Peak are ordinary

people who serve Commerce in banks, shops, counting-houses, and factories. When Sunday arrives they become conquerors. They are the despair of their landladies. They rise with the lark, cut sandwiches, fill thermos-flasks, bang about the house in dubbined boots, seek out ash sticks which have been planted on a hundred hills, and depart heartily to seek new hardships. Their clothes are a revolt; their trousers a declaration of independence.

I think that much of the revolt felt by healthy youth for the artificiality of any great city is walked off every week-end in the Peak. Derbyshire is the safety-valve of Manchester and Sheffield. Here, on the roof of the north, Lancashire and Yorkshire meet every Sunday : here they drink beer together while the girls drink tea ; here they eat eggs and tinned pine-apple ; here they sing songs together.

*   *   *

She finished the eggs.

Mrs. Innkeeper entered. She said that Miss Jones had passed that way earlier in the day on her way round the Scout. Mr. Brown and ' his young lady ' had taken the high road to Edale, the Misses Robinson had got to be back early because they were taking part in a sacred concert, and Mr. Jackson had not yet been seen.

(The Peak knows its Walkers almost as well as they know the Peak. . . .)

The rain came in gusts against the window.

' Wet on the Scout to-day,' said the Amazon vaguely.

' Jolly to walk in rain,' I ventured.

' I like it best,' she said.

Where was I going ' this Sunday ' ? To Edale. I had to pick up a car there. She looked at me in disdain. (Storm fiends hate cars, and they despise bicycles !) Which way was I going ? Rotten. She knew a much better way across country if I'd like to go. I did like.

' Let me carry that for you ! '

Another glance of disdain as she swung her rucksack on to her shoulders, wriggled them like an old soldier, felt the pack settle down, tapped the stones with her ash stick, and was off over the moor. . . .

' Come on ! You've got the wrong kind of shoes on. You'll slip ! '

The pale Amazon walked like a man. She had that slow, steady mountain step which they teach you in Swiss climbing centres. I gazed in admiration at her wet profile. She might have been her younger brother.

She was, she volunteered, a secretary. How impossible, I thought, to dictate a letter about cotton-waste to this striding Diana of the moors ! (On Monday, however, the Walkers of the Peak, are, as I have said, different people !) We tramped the wet moors, over footpaths, across streams— brown streams with smooth, round stones in them—talking all the time like a couple of men.

On a wet stone wall we collected two other Walkers of the Peak, a man and a woman, who had come by train from New Mills and were going back with a walker's ticket from Edale. They talked of their victories, of the Peak in its winter and its summer mood, of the time when a man was lost on Kinder Scout, and all the walkers linked hands round the Peak and covered every inch of ground until they found his dead body.

So we came at length, with wet knees and red faces, to the inn at the end of the road. It was blue with smoke. It was full of men and women in all stages of weariness. You will see no healthier sight in all England.

The rucksacks lay about the floor, the ash sticks near them. The tables were covered with the remains of a mighty feast of boiled eggs and tinned fruit. The men drank beer, the women drank pints of tea from china tankards thicker than the refreshment-room cups at Crewe. Some had come from Manchester, some from Sheffield, some had walked alone, many had come together. There were unattached maidens, young men, men and their wives, and men and their sweet-hearts. A young fellow rose up and called for a song :

' The more we are together, together, together. . . . '

Lancashire and Yorkshire sang it with fine heartiness ; thirty miles of hard going does not affect the voices of the Peak Walkers. . . .

Some one looked at the clock. Time to go for the train ! They rose up, among them the pale Amazon ; they slipped their arms through their rucksacks, grasped their sticks, and clumped heavily out, still singing, into the rain.

§ 5

In the quiet Derbyshire village of Eyam, men still talk about the Plague of London as though it had happened last week. Eyam is the last place in England with a vivid memory of the terrible pestilence of 1665.

Eyam is a mile-long street of fortress-like stone houses set in a cosy cleft of the wild Peakland moors. There is a church, a manor-house behind a wall, and the remains of the village stocks. I went into the church, where the elderly caretaker began to talk, as they all do in Eyam, of the Plague :

' We used to leave our money in the well, where the water washed it clean,' she said. ' And people from other villages would bring food for us and take the money out of the well. We used to put vinegar in the water to disinfect it. It was terrible. Every one was frightened of catching the Plague. . . .'

(She might have been talking about that year's influenza !)

The great Plague of London, which came before the Fire of London, lives for us now only in the diary of Pepys, in the fine journalism of Defoe's *Plague Year*, and in the sweet herbs with which the Guildhall is ceremonially disinfected when the new Lord Mayor of London is elected on Michaelmas Day. So many things have happened to London since the reign of Charles II that the Plague is not even a memory ! But it was the last thing that happened to Eyam !

This is the story.

In the autumn of 1665 a box of clothes was sent from London to a tailor in this village. They were damp. The servant who dried them at a fire became ill and died of the Plague. So also did others in the house. The horrible thing had taken root among the clean, windy moors of Derbyshire.

No one knew where the next plague death would occur. No one knew when he or she might develop the swelling symptoms which were literally a death warrant. There was a stampede from the village. People wanted to get away, to reach the windy moors, to put miles behind them and the village which had suddenly become a place of horror.

Then an extraordinary thing happened which must give Eyam a foremost place among the courageous villages of England.

The rector, William Mompesson, saw that the stampede

from Eyam might spread the Plague through the north of England. He assembled the villagers and persuaded them to remain and defy the pestilence. He promised that he would stand by them to the end. He drew a line round the village a mile from its centre, and beyond this boundary no man, woman, or child from Eyam was to move. At various points along the line were established food dumps. People from other villages would come up at given times with supplies, which they left on the boundary. So Eyam was fed.

When Mompesson appealed to the courage of his parishioners three hundred and fifty people remained in Eyam with him. The Plague continued for over twelve months, and when it ended, as it did suddenly, two hundred and sixty-seven had died.

Only eighty-three remained to tell the story of a year's horror.

Surely there are few villages in England which can point to a braver story. . . .

*   *   *

It is difficult to visualize that year of death. The old cottages are so small and snug. Children laugh and play about the street. Untroubled faces look through the very windows which saw, two and a half centuries ago, the passing of the Plague carts ; a wife going to bury her husband or a husband his wife.

It is strange, too, to see cottages which in any other village would be inevitably ' Rose Cottage ' called ' Plague Cottage '. I entered one, a small sweet-shop, in which a young girl discussed the Plague, like the caretaker, as though it had just occurred. The story of the Plague is the first story which prints itself on the imagination of Eyam's children.

That distant year of death has left a scar on the memory of this village : the story will never die. I am told that the last generation was even more fearful. A lingering horror of human bones existed in Eyam until recent times, and any bones dug up in a field were hastily reburied because the fear of infection lasted for centuries.

Among those who died was the rector's wife, Catherine Mompesson. Her memory is still revered in Eyam. She sent her children to safety, but refused to leave her husband. There is in existence a touching human document in which

Mompesson tells his children about their mother's death, and recounts her virtues to his 'dear hearts' so that 'the knowledge thereof may teach you to imitate her excellent qualities'.

I think the most touching Plague relic in Eyam is a little cluster of graves in a field some distance from the village. They are protected from wandering cattle by a low stone wall. They are very lonely, with the wind blowing over them, the green moss eating into them, and about them still an air of haste and disaster. Among them are the graves of the Hancock family, seven of whom were buried in eight days.

As you stand among these tombs in the middle of a field you realize a little more clearly what it must have meant to live for a year locked up with death. The full story of the agonies, the heroism, the faith of this little village community defies description.

How often during that year must the temptation to desert have come to men and women, to get clear away over the green moors, in the wind, to forget the very name of the place where death sat waiting on every man's doorstep.

If an English village had to be given a V.C. I would vote for the cool, deliberate bravery of little Eyam.

§ 6

Tall chimneys were smoking. There was grey smoke, brown smoke, black smoke, quick jets of snow-white steam. The sun was quenched, the sky was darkened, the outer rim of hills was a hard shadow beyond the haze. A Sheffield man stood with me and said :

'Things are getting better. We are recovering from our bad times. . . .'

Smoke is to Sheffield as the traffic of the Great Dock Road is to Liverpool. It is the barometer of trade. The darker the sky the brighter is Sheffield ; the thicker the smoke the thinner the crowds of idle men at street corners. As one by one the black chimneys of Sheffield come to life, as one by one the orange flames of the blast furnaces return to the night, the spirit of this grim city rises, and her men are encouraged.

The hard ugliness is queerly grand. You cannot make gun shields in a rose garden. It is right that shells and the great guns that fire them into human flesh should have been made in Sheffield : she has never pretended to be beautiful : she is the hard, cold mistress of steel. She is a city of machines that bend steel, that bore holes in steel, that shave steel in long, curling lengths as easily and smoothly as a knife cuts bread.

In the evening she looks queerly inhuman. The chimneys lengthen, the furnaces glow red, quick, snake-like flickers of orange light dart and play against the sky, and she seems like a city built not by men but by gnomes. She is perhaps the most spectacular expression in England of man's control over the rough materials of his existence.

She is the antithesis of the cathedral city : the opposite of York and Canterbury.

Steel to her is a thing to be conquered and beaten to a hundred uses. Theorists have often spoken of man's subjection to his machines. One might expect the people of Sheffield to be as cold and hard as the intelligent machines they control. But human nature has a knack of confounding the theorist. The people of Sheffield are jolly. They are surprisingly varied. They come from all the neighbouring counties and from Scotland. They smile through the smoke. The more smoke there is the broader is their smile.

And Sheffield glorifies its women. Against the blue-blackness of the smoke bath a pretty girl wearing a scarlet hat is more marvellous than in any city on earth. . . .

The big crucibles swing from the furnaces to the mould, smoking with the white heat of the metal in them. Slowly they tilt, slowly the liquid metal runs in a livid stream into the mould, sets, hardens, and—Sheffield has added more armour plate to the sum of the world's woes ! Or it may be a gun. . . .

Just now, however, one of the largest things made in factories which helped to win the war are steel tyres for railway carriage wheels. The smallest object is, I believe, a gramophone needle.

Every gramophone needle takes a month to make. Its working life is at the most five minutes. Experts have worked it all out. They say that a gramophone needle travels a track along the record seven hundred and twenty feet long, and that it carries a load of three and a half ounces. As the area of the point is three-thousandths of an inch, this means that pressure on the point of a gramophone needle is twelve tons to the square inch. They are made of specially tested and hardened steel.

I entered a factory where girls were making gramophone needles. They take bundles of thin steel about a foot long, and run them through machines which sharpen both ends. The next machine cuts off the sharpened ends, and the now blunt steel is sharpened, cut, resharpened, and cut until the last two needles are taken from it.

Trays containing millions of needles travel through a long furnace. As they advance they change colour; they become millions of bright orange needles, sparks flicker over them, and when they have been adequately baked the trays tip up and millions of needles fall with a splash into an oil bath.

They are then polished in revolving machines. A month from the time they are sharpened and cut they are ready to play ' Zampa.'

       *   *   *

One is liable to become too fascinated by the smoke of Sheffield and to forget that one of the most remarkable things about this city is the ease with which it is possible to escape from it. A Sheffield man took me in half an hour from the centre of the smoke into the wildness of open country. There is no other great industrial city with so many swift and surprising escapes from itself.

Sheffield also possesses the finest suburbs of any city with, perhaps, the exception of Bristol.

But smoke is the sign of Sheffield. To thousands of people the very name calls up a picture of chimneys sending their brown, grey, black and white smoke down the wind. In this smoke you can see gunboats and cruisers and guns, safety razor blades, knives and forks, gramophone needles, electro-plate : all the things, great and small, which the ingenuity of man can fashion out of the hard heart of steel.

CHAPTER TWELVE

BIRMINGHAM, AND HOW THIS CITY SAVES ITS MONEY, THE BULL
RING ON SATURDAY NIGHT, A MEMORY OF CHARLES
DICKENS, WITH SOMETHING ABOUT GOLF BALLS, MACHINES,
AND JEWELLERY.

BIRMINGHAM. . . .

The train spins on over the points. Men in the dining-car fidget with luggage, as the promise of Edgbaston, home and beauty illuminates their honest features. A talkative commercial traveller considers that with luck he will have time to absorb his fifth whisky and soda. And the train spins on.

It is evening. The sun has retired resentfully into a sullen mist of smoke. Imperceptibly the lovely green fields of Warwickshire have merged into black acres; grim streets lie to the skyline; factories with yellow windows flash past; and the eye takes in a dreary ant-hill of endeavour in which men and women are just ending the day's work.

The commercial traveller puts down an empty glass on the green baize table and says :

'Birmingham is unlike any other town. They make every blessed thing but ships . . . from pins to railway carriages. That is why Birmingham can never feel unemployment like a city with one big staple industry : there is always so much happening.'

He rises and takes down a suit-case.

'It's a tough spot, too,' he says. 'If you can sell things in Brum you can sell them anywhere on earth.'

He takes down another suit-case.

'Hard-headed lot !' he says.

He pulls down a third, and, casting a cautious glance round the dining-car, whispers confidentially :

'Rotten hole—I hate it ! Goes to bed at ten !'

The train dives through a tunnel and out into a grimy conservatory called New-street Station, prompt to the minute —two hours from Euston !

I step out on the platform with the feeling that some kind of a thrill is due : the faint thrill, perhaps, of meeting a self-made man who by hard work, self-denial, acuteness, and the ordinary human virtues has pulled himself into fame. Birmingham !

This is the city that walked quite recently into English history with a brass bedstead ; the city which clasps metal rings on the arms of African chiefs and turns out tropical gods by the gross ; the city whose buttons hold up the trousers of the world ; whose pins assist civilization in a million ways; whose nails go into cradle and coffin.

' Keep to the left there ! '

Behind an indignant moustache is a station policeman. With the sure instinct of the Londoner for the wrong side of a street I have broken the written law of ' Keep to the left ' on the long footbridge of New-street ! It is a crime they dislike. Birmingham is an orderly, disciplined city.

The first thing the traveller notices is a lily-white policeman dressed evidently for the Russian ballet. His helmet is pipeclayed, his gloves are white, and a long white macintosh falls to his heels.

These ghostly point-duty men are symbolic of Birmingham ; they tell the world the secret of Birmingham, that there is nothing Birmingham adores more than a mild flirtation with a new municipal idea ! A girl with a new dress is not to be compared to a Birmingham committee with a new kind of sign-post, a new police whistle, a new note-book for the gas man—anything that will enable the business men who manage this obviously well-run city to clasp hands in a council house sacred to the memory of the first king of Birmingham, Joseph Chamberlain, as they cry with one voice, ' Forward ! '

For me the great thrill in Birmingham is the Town Hall. It stands there as if attempting to make up its massive mind to walk down Hill Street and catch the last tram back to Rome. Its solemn, classic grandeur kills every building in the locality stone dead. The shadows play between its tall columns, and the darkness is kind to its rather solid proportions. If you fed the Madeleine in Paris on underdone rump steak for a month it might look like Birmingham Town Hall. . . .

Down the steep hill of the Bull Ring, where a market begun in Saxon times, is a church. It is, perhaps, generous to believe that more than two per cent of one million people have been inside more than twice.

In the chancel four stone men sleep, three in full armour, one in full canonicals, the de Berminghams, the old lords of the manor. They lie, inexpressibly remote in the silence, deserted, forgotten, the men who pegged out the claim, who had no idea that they had founded anything larger than a green village.

§ 1

It takes you ten minutes to realize that as a city Birmingham does not exist. It is a myth. No city with a million population has greater municipal enterprises and fewer evidences of civic grandeur. But it takes you several days to realize that if Birmingham is not a city in the sense that squares are wide and streets majestic, it is, as a series of industrial encampments held together by the tramways department, the greatest workshop the world has ever known. . . .

Soon after dawn there is a whine in the air. The early tram-cars are running. Each day they irrigate with human life forty-three thousand, six hundred acres of dull streets. They drive on with their packed loads, their cloth-capped crowds, pausing at little street corners, where platoon after platoon from the great battalion of workers descends and makes off to the day's task.

I look at their hands : capable, grimy hands born to control machinery, made to fashion objects, to beat new life into white-hot metal : to do a million tasks for which the world has need. This is Birmingham ; this is the real Birmingham.

There are girls : small, sturdy girls with nimble fingers practised in quick work in a packing room, in dabbing a speck of paint on a thousand objects which, one by one, go past them on a moving band all day long. Sprightly, smart girls, loud of voice, independent, laughing, giggling, full of life that must be repressed throughout the long day's task.

Near the centre of the city the streets are here and there composed of old dwelling-houses that fifty years ago were turned into workshops. They wear that sad, insulted look common to factories which once knew how to behave at a dinner party. As you go on and on through a drab uniformity—district after district each with its own shops—it is possible to trace how wave after wave of manufacturing prosperity added acreage to Birmingham ; a city with a Georgian core and a Victorian red-brick casing.

So you travel to the outer crust of ugliness, where on the

very outskirts of Birmingham stand those great camps of industry, little towns in themselves, where small houses cluster round a huge mass of stone and brick from which tall chimney stacks spire to the sky.   Here men live side by side with the machine.   Beyond lie the green fields and the hills wilting a little, it seems, in the gusts of smoke ; wondering how long it will be before the great, black footsteps of Birmingham stride up and go on down the valley. . . .

A hush falls over the streets of Birmingham.

It is as if a monster has been fed.   From workshop and factory there comes a whirr of bands, a scream of machinery. The great jig-saw puzzle of the midlands is at work : they are making jew's-harps and corsets, rivets and buttons, steel pens and cartridges, saddles and wedding-rings, motor-cars and cutlasses, rifles and cradles.

There seems to be nothing they are not making.

The small employer arrives on the tram-car. In nine cases out of ten he looks and talks like a foreman ; in nine cases out of ten he could show his foreman how to do a job.   Twenty years ago he worked at the bench. The large employer arrives in a discreet limousine.   He is the same type : grown up out of Birmingham : grown rich out of Birmingham, a voice and a mind made in Birmingham, a man who knows his own business inside out, as he should do ; for that is his life.

It is one of the virtues of Birmingham that the grandfathers of so many prosperous natives arrived in the city over a century ago with nothing on them but a shirt.   The only aristocracy is the aristocracy of successful commerce.   Grandfather went to work, and soon some one was working for him. His sons became rich and carried on ; and now their sons, having been to Oxford, possess all those advantages necessary for the wrecking of the apple cart—or a greater success ; a wider field. . . .

*   *   *

Now, perhaps, you understand, why Birmingham is a city of three short, select streets.   Not only has it been too busy to look grand and important : it is also lacking in local millionaires anxious to speculate in putting up big shop property.   It is a city of moderate wealth, of moderate men. Money is perhaps more evenly spread here than in any other big industrial city.

Birmingham is not a show place—it is a work place, a useful city, a city that cares little for appearance but much for results, a city that looks at life in terms of material achievement. A great sense of beauty or wide learning will always be unhappy in Birmingham ; for Birmingham is a great machine that knows only production.

There is nothing for the stranger to admire in Birmingham but the vigour and drive of its hard-working people and the proud achievements of their rulers, their omnibuses with pneumatic tyres and covered tops, their smart police, their smooth Welsh water that comes from seventy-three miles away (without affecting the pronunication) ; but sometimes— sometimes—you catch a face in the crowd that shines out from the uniform, dull, expression. . . . a face that belongs, not to Birmingham, but to all humanity ; and you realize with almost a shock that beneath the ceaseless effort is the play of the human comedy, desire, failure and success, but well in hand, well controlled, most marvellously disciplined.

Here work is life.

*   *   *

In every city is a place where crowds mass on Saturday night, their work done, their pay—or portions of it—in their pockets.

For hundreds of thousands this is the only social occasion in the week. It is interesting to note that such meeting-places are invariably the oldest portion of the town, generally the site of an ancient market to which generation after generation of workers have remained faithful long after the fashionable shopping centre has marched off elsewhere. In Birmingham this spot is the Bull Ring. . . .

It is 8 p.m.

The Bull Ring lies at the foot of a steep incline. It is a cup filled to the brim with life. Thousands move in the large square, gazing at the booths which stand in the centre and line the pavements. You are immediately conscious of that queer something remarkable about a Birmingham crowd : they are almost silent ! They are moving about, jostling, laughing, buying roots of celery, kippers and potatoes, going in to drink at the frequent bars, returning to swell the throng, and yet, so quietly, with such unusual orderly calm !

Beneath a statue of Nelson—who seems to have been washed up in good form with part of a wreck—are grouped orators and religious meetings.   Here you can listen to whatever faint Bolshevism is blowing round, but generally speaking, politics are seriously damaged by those self-contained groups who do so much good in all great cities, even though they praise the Lord in a flat key. . . .

' Come along there, Ma, take a couple o' kippers back to the old man ! Lovely, they are ! Feel 'em ; smell 'em ! Go on—don't be bashful ! '

That is how a London hawker does business on Saturday, striving to create an atmosphere of intimate cheer around him ; but the Birmingham hawker is a sad, morose individual, who limits himself to short, sharp, technical descriptions, such as : ' Bananas ! Penny each—all C'naries. . . .'

No street salesman attempts to sweep a woman off her feet with glowing words as they do in London ; the romantic method of selling cod-steak is unknown.   The reason may be that in Birmingham a careful shopper feels a banana to see that it is well and truly inhabited before buying it.

Yet there is a kind of suppressed heartiness about the Bull Ring, but it is the heartiness not of a crowd but of stray individuals in the crowd. . . .

The gas and paraffin jets stream out in the wind, and the light flickers over white faces, caps pulled down over eyes, neat neckcloths tied at throat or Saturday collars and ties : wives carry baskets that bulge cabbage ; young girls, arm-in-arm, giggle discreetly and glance over their shoulders at a group of rather backward cavaliers.   Even in Birmingham youth does this.

You look over hundreds of cloth caps, moving slowly, changing pattern : you look into hundreds of faces all wearing the same expression, and it occurs to you that this is a nightmare inhabited by Robots.   It occurs to you that machinery is a vampire that sucks the blood of humanity and turns its back on life heartlessly as it turns out nails and pins, of a size and pattern, And there is something infinitely sad in the quiet contentment of the uniform grey people moving slowly about in search of something to eat on Sunday.

Who has not seen the Rag Fair has never seen Birmingham. No crowd such as this, filling the great covered market, can be seen in London.   The avenues between the stalls are packed with stationary people unable to move backward or forward. The place smells of peppermint, recent beer, and old clothes, with stray but important gusts of onion and fried potatoes.

Near the alleged entrance are the men who sell china. Nothing is too intimate for sale. One glance assures you that all the mantelpiece horrors of theatrical lodging-houses hail from Birmingham : those two silly eighteenth-century lovers who bow and curtsey to one another ; those incredible pseudo-bronze horses who apparently have torn every shred of clothing from the men trying to control them ; pots and vases of every calibre, colour, and uselessness ; and . . .

' How's this for a vase ? ' cries an auctioneer, leaning above the crowd with a terrible urn encrusted with gold. ' Ain't it a fair treat ? Who says five bob ? '

Nobody does.

' Look at it ! It's lovely ! It's a possession, that's what it is ! Half a crown, then ? '

And somebody buys it ! In a dull little home that awful ' possession ' will stand perkily on the mantelpiece inviting a boot, reverenced, cared for, even loved. In hard times it may even be one of the last things pawned.

By marking time on the feet of the man in front it is possible by degrees to enter the Rag Fair : to appreciate piles of spectacular toffee, stalls full of iron odds and ends and literary stalls hung with promising paper novelettes with such titles as *Poppy's Last Chance* (with a jacket showing Poppy on the verge of this event), *Love Locked Out*, and *Her Lover's Word*.

The crowd presses and heaves and makes little progress. Men sell lace curtains with astonishing speed, others sell clothes, old and new, moth-bitten furs, silk stockings, old shoes. You are struck by the absence of the Jewish trader. . .

Prompt on closing time one of Birmingham's remarkably smart policemen enters the Rag Market. The orderly, disciplined mob melts, the vast barn gradually empties, the china merchants suck a throat pastille and count piles of silver. It is over ! A Saturday night which cannot be called exactly gay and hardly sad, but just dull, is over.

The Bull Ring also empties.

Here and there a man, wrestling with some rebellious spirit within him, takes off his hat and waltzes slowly all alone. A policeman regards him with professional interest mingled perhaps with sorrow. The man puts on his hat and walks rather too steadily away, leaving behind him the impression that he has had a good time in some way not clear to the observer. . . .

Up in New Street, a few paces off, the shuttered shops
stand in deserted streets.   The Bull Ring has a popularity
all its own—the weekly haunt of whatever heartiness is left
over when the machines are stilled.

§ 2

If you go watchfully about Birmingham you will see—not
in the main streets, but in busy side streets, in factory and
shopping districts—a large illuminated key hanging over a
building.   There are over thirty such buildings in Birmingham.
On the prongs of the key are the three words : ' Security with
Interest '.

This key is the symbol of the most remarkable organization
in Birmingham : the only bank in the world run by a city for
the people of that city !   The Bank of Birmingham—or the
Birmingham Municipal Bank, as they call it, dates from the
end of the war.   It has attracted one hundred and eighty
thousand working class depositors, who have to their credit a
balance of £6,000,000 saved out of wages.   How this was done,
how one hundred and eighty thousand men and women living
in a hand-to-mouth atmosphere, in a condition of society which
has no thought of banking, have been encouraged to entrust
their hard-earned money to this city bank is a marvellous
triumph in applied psychology.

When the war ended, Birmingham sought power to transfer
£325,000 accumulated in her War Savings Department as a
kind of nest egg into her projected Municipal Bank.   You will
notice that the unpleasant word ' savings ', which calls up a
horrible vision of an empty tankard and a cold pipe, was
eliminated, and crusaders set out into the factories to tell
men and women not to save that they might in the misty
future become rich, but to save in order that in the immediate
future they might spend well and wisely.

They understood that.   It sounded like sense !   Their
money was not going off into dark regions of compound
interest ; they were told how it would accumulate week by
week and take them to Wales next July !

The bank caught on !

Sums from one penny upwards came pouring in every
Saturday night.   Children caught the habit, and home safes
were manufactured.   Soon over ten thousand were in cir-
culation.   They are small, heavy boxes, from which a dissolute

parent cannot extract treasure with a bread knife, a hammer
or even an axe !

'When the history of the early days of the bank comes
to be written,' said the chairman, 'it will read like a romance.
We opened branches in all kinds of queer, makeshift places.
We begged an ancient watchman's hut from the public works
department and dragged it to Saltley—one of our most
crowded districts. Here we opened for business. In five
years in this old hut we had collected £170,000, and
had on our books five thousand depositors. We built an
annexe to the hut, and recently we opened a proper branch
office. . . .'

'But how did you make the worker hand over his cash ? '

'We talked to him. We explained things to him. We
told him how much money runs to waste every day. We also
realized that if the bank was to be a success it would have to
be different in many ways from a joint stock bank. Our
£6,000,000 has come from people who would never be clients
of a joint stock bank. We realized that we should have to
work at night to take the money at the week-end, and we saw
that our managers and clerks would not have to observe joint
stock manners. That would freeze out our customers ! We
have opened a friendly bank. We smile at the pennies as
they come in ; we take a pride in the depositor whose account
is doing well, and we are sufficiently human not to show
annoyance when he draws it all out and " blues " it, for he
will come again and build up again ! '

Anyone with £20 to his credit in the Bank of Birmingham
can buy his own house ; the city will lend him the necessary
money to purchase a house under the municipal housing
scheme. In five years over four thousand workers became
owner-occupiers through the bank, and new houses are rising
up all over the district.

'The bank is increasing its business year by year,' said the
chairman of the committee, 'and has become part of the
municipal organization of this city. It will grow. It will
extend its usefulness. Customers can buy their homes
through it, they can pay their rates through their accounts,
they can arrange to have their wages paid straight into the
bank. The service side of the bank will develop.'

So the Sign of the Golden Key shines over the Bank of
Birmingham, and behind that £6,000,000, which, believe me,
split up into shillings and even sixpences saved with grim

courage from a weekly wage, is the story of men and women denying themselves the little they have for the sake of—it may be a new hat, it may be a first sight of the sea . . . it may be a painfully courageous approach to a municipal house of neat red brick, with confetti lingering over the mat. I do not know ! (But the branch managers do !)

* * *

It was about seven o'clock in the evening when I entered a busy branch office in a district famous for its chips and fried fish. The bank was busy. Men and women crowded to the counter in a kind of desperate endeavour to hand over spare shillings to the municipality before they became squandered. Among the crowd were workers, in neckcloths, who had not troubled to wash since leaving work ; factory girls who had come straight from the pay desk to the bank ; young clerks fingering a slender weekly ' packet ' ; typists with their gains ; and numbers of old men and women who were putting away half-crowns.

' Notice,' whispered the manager, ' how many people are saving up to be married.'

I looked round and spotted them : young men and girls each placing a few shillings a week into separate accounts, their heads bent over balances. Some faces registered no emotion. Possibly the credit side of the account did not justify any optimism. Now and then a couple smiled as they handed back their cards before going out arm in arm with a triumphant hopefulness over them that made you see a front door key and as much of Paradise as anyone sees in Hockley, Duddleston, Saltley, or Aston !

When they are married they return and say :

' We want to open another account, please.'

' A joint account ? ' asks the manager.

This puzzles them. He explains. A quick look of mutual distrust flashes between them :

' Er-yes,' they say. ' To be taken out on either signature ! ' Another quick look of distrust ! They go out a bit silent, pondering it, and return on Monday to say that on full consideration they think that both signatures should be required for a withdrawal.

Safety first !

An untidy old man who had been lingering on the fringe

of the depositors edged a way to the counter and in a rather
threatening voice asked :

' 'Ave you got it still ? '

' Got what ? ' asked the clerk.

' My blinkin' money ! ' he whispered.

The clerk was young and scrupulous. He called the
manager.   This lit a horrid doubt in the mind of the depositor.
He leant on the counter and glared round the bank as if he
expected to be told that his money had been lent to a foreign
Power for the making of a new war.

' Of course we've got it ! ' cried the manager.   ' You're
Mr. X. Of course we have ! Twelve pounds fifteen and
ninepence ! '

The man appeared soothed.   Then a dogged look came
into his eyes, and, leaning over the counter, he whispered :

' Then let's 'ave a look at it ! '

I wonder what would have happened in a joint stock bank !
The manager, however, appeared in no way surprised.   He
lifted the counter flap, led his depositor into a back room,
opened a safe, and showed him bags of silver and a few piles
of Treasury notes.

' Do you often have people like that ? ' I asked.

' Oh, yes,' he replied.   ' Quite a number of my clients
come in, draw out every penny, count it, and put it back
again. I help them all I can. If I didn't they wouldn't
come to us !   You see they are just learning to trust a bank ! '

Every bank manager in the Bank of Birmingham can tell
queer stories of hoarded wealth.   Hundreds of old women
are walking banks.   They often carry as much as £100 sewn
into their clothing—the savings of a lifetime.   When they
become converted to the banking habit it is necessary to
show them a dressing room.

' One day,' said the manager, ' an old woman came in
and, after telling me the story of her life, placed a petrol tin
on the counter.   " Can you do anything with this ? " she asked
apologetically.   Inside was over five pounds' worth of half-
crowns.   I explained to her how safe it would be, and that it
would breed interest, and that any day she might take it out.
She was delighted, and placed another tin on the counter
containing another five pounds in half-crowns.   Finding that
I was pleased she asked me to come round and take an old
leather suit-case, which also was full of half-crowns !   Altogether I suppose she had about £40 in silver.   As she was

going she invited me to tea, and told me that she had a lot more money at home !

' I went to a tiny house at the back of an entry. The bedroom floor, under the boards, was lined with silver ! Some of the half-crowns were black with age ! We nearly pulled that house down ! We took over £500 from it, which now stands to this old woman's account ! She often comes in to see it. It appears that her husband, who lived to a great age, was always hiding half-crowns, and before he died he said, ' Pull up the bedroom floor and you'll be all right ! '

' Just imagine what this bank means to people who keep money so dangerously ! . . .'

Near closing time a burly, middle-aged man came in, added something to his account, and chuckled :

' My old gal won't half be surprised when she knows . . .' Then he went off.

' That's funny,' said the manager. " His old gal " has an account and he doesn't know it ! She comes in and says much the same thing. " My old man won't half be surprised when he knows," she says. How they are going to surprise each other is not yet clear. I suppose I shall know some day ! '

Almost the last depositor before the bank closed its doors was a wispy little girl of about seventeen, who shyly put down sixpence.

' How much have I got ? ' she whispered.

' Eleven shillings and sixpence.'

' Oh,' she said, and seemed to be calculating.

' I wonder what she is saving up for ? ' I said, as she went off. The manager cast a shrewd eye after her.

' A new hat,' he said definitely.

Under the Sign of the Golden Key the day's takings reposed in neat piles, and then there came the encouraging sound of a safe door closing on the sacrifice.

§ 3

I suppose not more than one Birmingham man in every thousand knows of the secret cider drinkers of Snowhill. Near the station goods yard, tucked away in a row of old and rather mean buildings, is a fruit shop which at first sight seems nothing more than an ordinary small fruit store in a not too smart district. Behind the crates of red apples rise tall black

casks bound with metal : they are full of draught cider.
Behind the shop, but entered from an ill-lit alley at the side,
is a kitchen known to the elected few as ' The Old Cider Shop '.
Its licence is, I have been told, the only existing one of its
kind in Great Britain : it is for the sale of cider and nothing
else.

Night after night men who would not insult their throats
with beer or whisky meet in the kitchen to drink the apple
juice. The two rooms are small, but they are always full.
The stranger who blunders in by chance feels that he has
trespassed ; for the cider drinkers meet like members of a
club banded together under an invisible apple-tree, ranking
themselves against the heathen ale drinker and the greater
barbarian of whisky.

It was dark. My companion pulled me up at the entrance
to the alley.

' Here we are,' he whispered. ' Follow me, and when they
ask you if you'll drink " sweet " or " rough ", say " rough ",
or they will know that you are not a cider man ! '

He opened a door, and we found ourselves in a remarkable
room. It might have been plucked up, china mugs and all,
from some little Herefordshire or Somersetshire village. A
big fire was blazing in an old-fashioned grate. An ancient
sporting gun hung in the smoke over the broad mantel. A
brass sign bore the words ' Home Sweet Home '. A stag's
head protruded from a wall bracket, and lying across the
antlers was a big wooden bludgeon.

' That's a paying-out stick,' whispered my companion.
' A client brought it back from India or Ceylon. It settles
any argument about back pay !'

Round the room, sitting on wooden benches at wooden
tables, were the cider drinkers : a marvellously varied
gathering. City men, workmen, a man wearing a railway
uniform. Each man grasped the handle of a big china mug.
Over the sawdust of the floor passed and repassed a girl in an
apron with her hands full of empty mugs.

' All these men are regulars,' said my friend. ' They come
here night after night. That big man with the grey hair is
a farmer from Hereford. That man talking to the railway-
man is an ex-city councillor. They are all cider men. They
all know each other, rich man and poor man. . . .'

A curious, attractive atmosphere. How different from a
four-ale bar ! Your cider drinker is a cool, calm, thoughtful

person who likes to drink sitting in an ingle nook with his feet
to the fire. I looked round the room, half expecting the
door to be pushed open by the squire in a pink coat with the
mud of a day's hunting on his white breeches !

The serving-maid opened the glass door which separates
the kitchen from the second, even smaller, room. Inside
this room four women and four men were drinking bottled
cider. One of the women gave a brilliant champagne laugh :

' They are drinking the best ! ' said my guide. ' That's
1915 vintage cider ! It's three shillings a bottle, and you can
hardly tell it from bubbly. The effect anyhow is exactly the
same ! During the war certain dealers shipped a lot of it
to America with champagne labels on the bottles. I wouldn't
mind betting you that nine women out of ten would think it
champagne if they didn't see the label ! '

One or two new arrivals entered, were greeted by a series
of nods, settled down in their favourite seats, and, automatic-
ally, large china mugs appeared in their hands.

In the dark alley we met Mr. David Smith, an elderly man
in a white apron, who owns the cider kitchen. Mrs. Smith,
who is over seventy, was born in the cider shop and even then
it was an ancient institution. Mr. Smith refused all informa-
tion. He said he didn't want his place overrun by strangers.
He was kind but firm.

' You see,' he said, ' there's not much room, and if you go
and write a book about it we shall be overcrowded, and we're
quite content as we are ; we like to hide our light under a
bushel, as the saying is. Now an old customer came to-day
to cure his rheumatism ! I don't want my old customers
crowded out by a lot of curious beer drinkers, thank you all
the same. . . .'

We turned and looked back at the cider shop. A man
could pass it every day for years and never know that it
existed. Such places are the secrets of great cities. All
cities possess them ; little insulated patches of life which
never alter. The city grows up round them, changes,
matures, but they pursue an extraordinary existence of their
own, self-satisfied, careless of change, content to be as they
have always been.

So in the very heart of a modern city you sometimes find
a village kitchen.

§ 4

Modern critics say that Charles Dickens exaggerated. He did not. He happened to live in a world that had not heard of standardization in men or material. What we now call eccentricity was in his day the normal expression of a man's personality; it was an unself-conscious world; a world in which a man was not afraid of being himself. To-day, even in remote villages, outside influences react on a man and tend to whittle down personality to a common denominator. Here and there, however, tucked away in unlikely places, you may find the last outposts of the Dickens world. . . .

The house in Moor Street, Birmingham, was built in 1744. It has not altered. The fine old Georgian staircase is polished like brown glass by the hands of the men who came in coaches and groped their way up to bed full of port in the reign of the second George! It has been a commercial hotel for well over the last half-century. Commercial travellers talk about it all over England and regard it as the most interesting, the most peculiar, and the last of its kind.

If you went there as a stranger seeking accommodation you would be led reverently to a room on the left in which you would find an old man with a close-growing white beard and a grey bowler hat to match. He would look you up and down through gold-rimmed spectacles and say in that gruff manner which often hides a kind heart:

'Where the devil do you come from, hey? Are you a fresh-catched one?' (Fresh-catched, or fresh-caught means a commercial traveller new to the road!)

Then, if he did not like the look of you, he would either tell you to go to hell, or he would raise his voice and shout:

'Sarah! Hi, Sarah! Full up, aren't we?'

Whereon the invisible Sarah would be heard in the affirmative and you would be turned out. At this precise moment the final touch to your rejection would be given by a fat Sealyham dog called 'Pat', who would bark twice and look extraordinarily like the guv'nor!

'Old John,' as he is known all over England, is the essence of independence! Ordinary hotels take in anyone: the honest man sleeps next to the criminal in the vast impersonality of the hive: 'Old John' shelters only those he knows or likes.

Birmingham men who have grown up with blunt ' John ', meet there every day, and bring their sons, to eat the kind of meal which seems to have come all the way from eighteenth-century England.

The company was assembled in the panelled bar. I was introduced formally. ' John ' looked in at his guests at the moment Frank, the boots, poked his head round the door and began to beat a tattoo on a tray. ' John ' gazed at the young man, and then, as if suddenly struck by a revelation, said :

' You get more like Sir Oliver Lodge every day, my lad ! ' and a smile tried to hide itself in his white beard.

We trooped upstairs, where a long table was set faultlessly for luncheon. A guest was appointed president and took one end of the table. ' John ' was Mr. Vice, and took the other.

We settled. For five minutes we called one another ' sir '. Two gigantic tureens of soup were carried in.

' Hare or tomato ? ' said ' John ' to me.

' Tomato,' I replied.

' I bet you six to four you don't know what you are talking about,' snapped ' John '. ' Hare's the best : you won't get any like it in Birmingham ! '

So I had hare ; and he was right !

There followed one of the few perfectly grilled soles in the world. The maid then appeared with, in swift succession, three gigantic silver domes, which she removed, revealing to the party a shoulder of mutton, a chicken swimming in a sea of parsley sauce, and a round of boiled beef escorted by carrots and doughnuts.

' John's ' eyes glittered wickedly behind his gold rims as the guests made their choice. Chaff and banter flashed round the table, beginning and ending with ' John '. He was like a swordsman dancing round an adversary, aiming a neat thrust here and parrying a lunge there, turning off a jest aimed at himself with an adroit retort. . . .

Men laughed and chaffed like this in old England ; the good, leisurely old England that is dying fast.

' Doris,' cried ' John ' suddenly, ' we want sherry with this pudding ! '

Doris poured out a glass.

' That's not sherry,' boomed ' John '. ' Let's smell it.'

He took the glass and drained it without a word. Doris,

with no change of expression, filled another and handed it round the table.

'Gentlemen, we drink to you!' said the opposite side of the table.

'And we to you,' said our side.

'And I to myself,' said 'John'.

'This is a bit of real old Brum,' said my neighbour.

'It's a bit of real old England,' I whispered back.

In the cosy bar, where a large open fire blazed, Sarah, in a white apron, was busy with bottles of port. The wine went round. The air was blue with smoke. 'John' sat with his grey bowler straight on his head, pretending to read a newspaper, but waiting to pounce on the conversation.

'The people who stay here are mostly the old-time commercial men,' said a man to me. 'Many of them have known "John" for forty years. We who lunch here are a kind of family. If we couldn't come the week would be all wrong. . .'

Personality! That is the secret of 'John's Club'. Here men are encouraged to be themselves, to speak the blunt truth like schoolboys. In this same atmosphere of fellowship and leisure, good talk, good food, good wine, good tobacco, grew up the great business of the nineteenth century before the modern god Hustle (which is often another word for muddle) crossed the Atlantic with dyspepsia and a quick-lunch sandwich!

I shook hands with 'John' and went through the smoke and the laughter into twentieth-century Moor Street.

§ 5

In the tumult of a thousand factories where dynamos throb, where saws scream as they bite into cold steel, where the thick scum of molten metal writhes and bubbles, you will find the Man who is 'Brum'.

He is wonderful in his unself-consciousness. He is, with all his shortcomings, symbolic of the industrial age, which began in Birmingham with the steam-engine of that dyspeptic genius, James Watt. He is physically slight, his face is grey with a factory pallor, and his eyes are bright and alive; for he has no time to dream—a poet on his job would soon be in a cemetery! His lungs are well developed by loyalty to Aston Villa, but his power lives in his hands: strong, virile hands on thin, stringy arms, pale as a girl's. A century of industrialism seems to have brought such hands into the world in endless numbers, as different from the hands of an agriculturist as a townsman's face differs from that of a yokel.

The Man who is ' Brum ' stands all day long with those famous hands—grimy, competent, ugly—on the lever of a great machine. The machine is powerful, possesses beauty of line, a blind efficiency, and it glistens with care. The only touch of pathos about the Man who is ' Brum ' is that he looks like the servant, and not the master, of this powerful monster.

A steel trackway runs from the machine down the factory. A gang of men are unloading heavy iron wheels which, one by one, they bowl along the track towards the Man who is ' Brum '. Each wheel is a complete circle save for a gap of about half an inch. The great machine welds the metal, closes the gap, and sends the scarred wheel on to be pressed into shape.

As a wheel comes lolloping down the track the Man who is ' Brum ' steps calmly out, catches it in those big hands and, with a dexterous movement of the wrist, twists it back into position on the machine. Then he steps back, catches his lever, and with a sharp, sure movement, draws it down as far as it will go. . . .'

Sparks fly . . . little violet pinpricks. They play over the gap in the wheel. They grow by millions every second. They splutter. They crackle. They snap. Then with startling suddenness they leap into the air, a fountain of red and yellow stars, big, spluttering stars that leap twenty feet into the air and fall alive to the stone floor.

Through the cascade of fire you look and catch sight of the grey face of the Man who is ' Brum ' standing there holding down the lever behind that wall of fire, expressionless, stolid. How much power he lets loose into the world each time he touches the lever of his machine it is difficult to say. It seems that his hand holds all the thunderbolts of Jove. Yet how unconscious of power he is !

The sparks die away. The last star falls. He releases the lever. He walks forward, catches the wheel quickly, gives it a push, and sends it on down the track, hobbling along on a great livid sore of red-hot metal where once was a gap ; a sore that glows and glows, turning from vivid pink to dull red and from red to violet.

Rattle-bang comes another heavy wheel down the track !
Those clever quick hands are ready for it !
Down goes the lever !
And I know what the Man who is ' Brum ' thinks about as
he stands there, the master of fire and stars. I know the
lonely dreams that light his vigil, for I heard him empty his
heart.
A whistle blew !
The gang stopped work.
The Man who is ' Brum ' straightened his back, wiped his
hands on a piece of waste, and a look of deep thought came
into his eyes. I could feel the delight with which he faced
a rest from the big machine. A group of men came towards
him down the factory. As they approached they smiled.
He smiled ! Then something between a war cry and the cry
of a soul released came from his lips :
' Up the Villa ! ' he shouted. . . .
If you don't know what this means you must go to
Birmingham and find out !

*   *   *

In high shops, warm with steam, men take raw rubber, boil it
and bake it until the air is rich with a smell that is almost
aromatic and not quite antiseptic : a curious, difficult smell
to describe. Then they hang up the rubber till it is in sheets
like warm wet blankets, and you might think that they would
let it rest. But no ! They mix in red powders (for inner
tubes) and black powders (for tyres) ; they pass the mixture
through rollers till the rubber creams and bubbles like hot
chocolate ; and, eventually, it is ready.
Each shop is itself a factory. In one the rubber goes in at
one end to emerge at the other as a pneumatic tyre, or an
inner tube ; in the next it emerges as a solid tyre ; in the next
as a golf ball ; in the next as a tennis ball. Each shop works
by numbers. The rubber moves in steady procession through
hundreds of hands, each hand does something different to
it ; and so it goes on down the line, becoming more like a tyre
or a tennis ball every yard.
Hundreds of girls sit in a shop making golf balls.
They take little hard balls of india-rubber and quickly wrap
rubber tape round them. These cores come along to them in
endless quantities, so that the mind reels at the thought of

the golfers they represent, the plus-four power involved, the language. . . . At every operation they are weighed on scales.

The balls run on to the next shop, where they are bandaged again, and they travel onwards to still more good looking, shingled maidens, who dress them in miles of thin rubber, like refined vermicelli. It is somewhere at this stage that a remarkable change comes over the young golf ball. It is put into an oven, and it emerges looking like a well-poached egg.

In the painting shop, girls, whose palms are covered with enamel, rub the finished golf balls, and send them on ; in the packing shop they lie in thousands, white and un-sullied by a tee, ready to start off on their horrible career, ready to provide untrue stories in club-rooms, to drive men to suicide, to separate husband from wife and wife from husband. . . .

There are also tennis balls.

The most interesting stage is that in which the ' uniform bounce ' is injected into it.

Girls sit administering the bounce, quietly, efficiently, with no thought that they may be creating an argument at Wimble-don ! The tennis balls arrive in two neat halves ; the ' uniform bounce ' looks like one aspirin and a pinch of salt. The girls weigh out the chemicals, quickly pop them into one half of the ball, while the next girl claps on the lid and seals it. Men then subject them to heat in vast ovens, where the aspirin and the pinch of salt are turned into chemical gas.

§ 6

No one will deny that a cold wind of fashion has blown along ' Gold Row '.

In the bricks you can read a drama. Among rows of fac-tories which minister to the vanity of man and woman you reach a blank, more factories and then another blank ; firms once famous for their jewellery which have gone out of business because women are not wearing gold chains, because men are not wearing the kind of ring for which such factories were noted, or because so many modern people would rather have a sparking plug than a sparkling finger.

And all these factories have made fortunes for two gener-ations, and nearly all began in the smallest way a business can begin—in a back or a front room of a man's house. So you can read in the bricks how they rose, how they prospered, and how they fell. . . .

Here stood a home. A century or so ago grandfather—and modern Birmingham stands on the shoulders of its grandfathers—began to make jewellery in his front bedroom. No doubt grandmother created a disturbance and objected in a sweet but stern manner to removing the furniture so that he might introduce a bench. Possibly she told him, prophesying ruin, that he was getting along ' quite well ! ' working for nice Mr. Brown round in Vyse Street, and that no good ever came of a man ' getting above himself '. Many great fortunes have had this send-off !

But grandfather was on a good thing. Whether he saw the chances or just plodded on is not known, but the fact remains that he stuck to his bench and melted down the sweepings each week to extract the last grain of gold.

Read the bricks.

In a few years he bought the house next door. He was getting on ! Grandmother, now convinced that she had been in favour of the enterprise from the start, occupied a large house in the suburbs and brought up a new generation of jewellers. All the time the two-house factory sent out a stream of wedding rings into the world, signet rings, good value-for-money goods, and also, capturing distant markets, something in the way of decoration that pleased the Chinese.

How the enterprise of those old men ate up a street in Gold Row ! Two houses, and then three, were engulfed by his factory. He was now successful ! He established a reputation for glittering solidity. German brides were married with his rings, and could he have stood looking into a jeweller's window in Moscow or Edinburgh he would have said, pointing to certain things : ' We made that . . . and that . . . and that.'

Friends who had worked at the bench with him were doing the same thing. Their factories hummed with activity, turning out chains for muffs, chains for anything and everything, brooches, rings, pendants, presents for men to give their sweethearts and for husbands to give their wives ; all the things that the world likes but can do without.

Read the bricks.

The new generation extended the business. The factory ran along the street. It was now a big place. It was difficult to realize exactly where grandfather began ; how exactly the ' gov'nor's ' room was once the dining-room of the house next door.

And the Colonies were making money. Women wanted nice solid gold rings to seal their marriages in Canada, in South Africa, in New Zealand, in Australia ; and grandfather's sons saw to it that they had them !

Then, I suppose, there came a little breath of cold wind from somewhere. Fashions were changing, perhaps. Some panicky people sold out while they were solvent rather than alter their equipment and tradition to suit the mode of the moment. But the die-hards stuck to it, giving the Georgian era those things which had made their fortune and reputation in the Victorian. When you have been making one thing for a hundred years with outstanding success it requires a lot of courage to make something quite different.

' This is just a passing phase ! ' you say.

But the chill of changing fashion had certain branches of ' the trade '—as they still call it in Birmingham—firmly in its grip when the war came and the gold went. The nimble fingers of craftsmen trained only in delicate, minute work were idle.

Over patches of Gold Row now broods a silence of defeat. Fashion has won the last trick.

The factory that began in the front bedroom is either vacant or in the hands of ' Messrs. Jones and Co., Machine Tool Manufacturers '. Slain by women all over the world is the business built up with grim perseverance over those two generations which, as experienced Lancashire says, separate clogs from clogs . . .

*   *   *

In the cold, November wind that blows along Gold Row at night you may, if you ever feel that way, imagine the ghost of grandfather looking for ' the business ' ; a little sad and worried and deeply puzzled ; and quite unable to realize that all the labour of his hand and heart was built upon the shifting sands of change.

§ 7

There is a quality about certain towns which prints itself on the imagination. Wolverhampton possesses it.

Such towns rouse curiosity. They are interesting and complex. They are not sudden industrial mushrooms like many of the big Lancashire manufacturing towns. They were living their busy lives long before there was coal ; long before James Watt put the world on wheels. They are market towns of Old England which, because fate planted them near coal and iron, have rolled up their sleeves, and entered the New England. Generations of human life, beginning with a shepherd who feared the baying of the wolves, and coming down to the daily tramp of the mechanic towards the chimney stacks, give to towns like Wolverhampton a strongly defined personality. Such places are alive.

The record of their strenuous history is like a great novel, or a pageant, packed with the adventures of countless men and women, a record of struggle, victory and defeat, but never of stagnation, a continuous narrative of human effort ending, so far as we to-day are concerned, with the shrill call of the siren in the morning and the departure of the goods train loaded with motor-cars, safes, locks, keys, and a hundred other things to every part of the world.

I stood beside the Prince Consort in the square—escaping death from a six-wheeled juggernaut known locally as an omnibus—and I watched a smouldering sunset glowing towards Tettenhall. A lovely glimpse is that view downhill on an afternoon in May.

Wolverhampton on its hill has not lost touch with its youth. Bits and corners of it are still in rural England. The ' lay-out ' of its lesser streets was patented in the Middle Ages. Even the vigorous modern mind of Wolverhampton, which would sweep away anything that stood in the path of progress and town planning, has not been able to banish entirely that curious knowing old look.

Its crowds proclaim Wolverhampton the capital of the Black Country which, by the way, is not so black as it is painted ; vigorous crowds of commercial men are reinforced by thousands of men and women whose skill with the machine is the latest epic of this ancient place.

' You must go to Tettenhall,' said a Wolverhampton man. ' We are proud of Tettenhall.'

Just as Bristol men are proud of Clifton, so Wolverhampton men praise Tettenhall, and I think that these two are the finest suburbs possessed by any large manufacturing town. (I would much rather live at Tettenhall than in Edgbaston !)

The character of the old English village has been preserved here. The fine houses bought and paid for in the town on the hill do not destroy the impression that the country has nestled down close to the town. On the cliff above the Church of St. Michael and All Angels, which has been standing there for nearly a thousand years, is the finest view I ever thought to see of the Black Country. To the east lies Cannock Chase, southward the chimneys of Wolverhampton rise up against the sky, in the evening light reminding one of a great dockyard full of ships, to the south-west lies Sedgley Beacon, Penn, and Wombourn ; and far on the western horizon is the line of the Clee Hills.

The greatest treasure of Wolverhampton is the magnificent Church of St. Peter, with its stately red sandstone tower. It is one of the most beautiful old churches of its type and size in England. It contains the most remarkable fifteenth-century stone pulpit I have seen. In this church is the tomb of Colonel Lane, who died in 1667. It was he who, with the help of his daughter Jane, contrived the escape of Charles II after his defeat at Worcester. . . .

In the churchyard of St. Peter stands an object which I regard as typical of the Black Country. It is a high stone pillar, smoke-blackened, and so corroded that the intricate mass of carving is almost obliterated. They call it the Dane's Pillar, but it is, I think, Norman.

I call it typical because it is one of those things which prove that Birmingham and Co. is as ancient as Winchester and Co. Most of these great towns in the Black Country, now overlaid with smoke and factories, are built on ancient sites. I do not know a more surprising experience than to enter little quiet churches hemmed in by shafts and stacks, round whose altars echo all day the beat of the steam-hammer and the roar of the furnaces and to realize here is enshrined some almost forgotten memory of the England of Alfred and the Danes. . .

Wulfere, a Saxon king, founded Wolverhampton one thousand three hundred years ago. The name means 'Wulfere's high town'. I do not know what he was like or who he was. I expect he chose the hill on which the Prince

Consort now stands because he liked to see his enemies coming. No doubt his great hands were equally firm on the sword hilt and the ale horn ! As I stood and saw the tall chimneys of Wulfere's town against the sky, I felt, as I have often done in such places, how astonished the world would be could one awaken such a man from the dead and interview him on the town he made.

Would he be pleased, I wonder ? Would he want to become a manufacturer of locks, safes, bolts, and keys, and live at Tettenhall, or would he take one look at it and ask for his tombstone again ?

§ 8

Behind the third hole of the Sandwell Park golf course, West Bromwich, lying low in a hollow at the edge of a thin wood stands the most authentic ghost I have ever seen. They call it Sandwell Hall.

It is the ancestral home of the Earls of Dartmouth, but it has not known an earl intimately for seventy-three years. ' Billy, my lord,' as the Earl of Dartmouth, who died in 1853, was affectionately called in the district, was the last of his line to live there. Before he died he saw the tall chimney-stacks marching nearer to his deer park ; the underground shafts which to-day scar the surface of the land had not appeared, but it was obvious even then that the industrial revolution had knocked out one of the stately homes of Old England. The famous family acquired an estate near Wolverhampton where they have lived ever since ; and so for seventy-three years the two hundred and fifty-odd windows of this immense house have seemed to be looking for some one. Now the end has come : Sandwell Hall is to be pulled down. Its melancholy vigil is over.

I approached it over the hummocky ground towards the end of a wet afternoon. To the left of the stables, in the middle distance, rose the high black tube of a factory stack ; drawn up in a field near the obliterated curve of the carriage drive was a chain of coal trucks. In front of the hall lay the eighteen holes of the ex-deer park. And the old abandoned house, with its dead stables, its dead rows of windows, its dead chimneys, its stable clock killed at half-past eleven, stood there in the thin rain like a poor old ghost at the edge of a wood. . . .

I wonder how many golfers, having driven a ball into the ring of evergreens that grows close up to the hall, have paused, aware of the old house watching them, looming above them in its portentous loneliness.

There was no one about as I pushed my way through the bushes, which have formed a kind of barricade, as if in protection, and I came out opposite the portico, upheld by ten classic columns, beneath which was the front door, leading to the main hall.

There was not a sound but the drip of the rain ; not a movement but the steady fall of the rain like mist drifting. Weeds had pushed apart the stone pavement in front of the hall, on which, I suppose, the hounds have met on many a cold winter's morning.

The personality of a large empty house is a tremendous thing, especially with dusk falling and a smoky mist creeping out of the woods. Through the stained windows of the door I saw the great hall empty. Beads of water dripped from the roof, forming a pool on the floor. I knocked with the hopeless thought that perhaps in some remoteness of the great shell lived a caretaker, but the eerie hollowness of my knocking drove me away, suggesting, as it did, the footman who would never come to the door.

Timidly, for the old house seemed not dead but asleep on a pile of memories, I peeped into room after room, each one empty, each one decayed, each one pathetic in its lost splendour, and as I went on it seemed to me that there was always the horrible chance that at some window I might see a face looking out over the park where the deer once grazed. . . .

I went through the stables, stall after empty stall, lofts and harness-rooms with shutters down, all this place which once was loud with the lovely bustle of men who care for horses, pungent with dubbin and sweet to the chink of burnishers, lying dead with the weeds sprouting.

Suddenly a dog barked !

In a portion of the old dairy, right at the back, a man and his wife live.

' You are not scared,' I said to her, ' to live alone in a corner of this great empty house with its hundreds of rooms ? '

She looked at me in amazement.

' We never think of it,' she replied.

I returned her amazement.

We went into the old hall. The great kitchen ovens, which have roasted many a haunch of venison and many a baron of beef, were rusted and cob-webbed. Rather pathetic was the butler's pantry, with the damp on the walls.

My lord's library still has the doors lined with imitation books so that when he closed them he was locked within a tomb of literature ; books round him and no way out but through books. Upstairs her ladyship's boudoir was dripping wet and scaly with the damp ; the floor of the private chapel was cracking and dangerous to walk on . . .

And people did say, went on the woman, that the Bishop of So-and-So was born in this room and Lord So-and-So in that . . .

Her voice was like the last whisper of the old house.

Through the tall cracked windows I looked over the once deer park. An electric tram-car went past to Birmingham ; at the back the high chimney-stack smoked steadily, like a gun pointed to the sky : the gun that shot this old hall stone dead.

Poor old Sandwell Hall, built for talk of foxes and corn-land, for the music of a quadrille, for the loud laughter of men in pink coats with their broad backs to the fire and their faces red with port . . . I could not have felt sorrier for it had it been my own home.

I turned from the height of a distant green and looked back into the hollow where it stood, ghostly, in a mist at the edge of a wood : a ghost of eighteenth-century England that can only be exorcised by a breakdown gang . . . but those suggestive windows, and those lonely corridors, and those high, elegant rooms from whose walls the marks of ancestral portraits have not quite faded ! . . .

' We never think about it ! ' said the woman.

Amazing !

For Sandwell Hall is an epitome of that new England, which is yet so young, the England that came out of steam as the genii in the fairy-tale sprang out of the bottle.

It has swept away many lovely things, it has planted its pit shafts in deer parks, it has driven its railway lines through the place where hounds once met on cold winter mornings ; and before it the Old England has retreated rather mournfully, understanding it as little as old Sandwell Hall understands the coal mine.

§ 9

I took to the road again one hot day in June, and the road led between high Warwickshire hedges to that place of blessed memory, the Forest of Arden. The spring which I had seen advance, leaf by leaf, flower by flower, was now merged in the rich splendour of summer. The trees cast a deep shade ; the corn was high in the fields.

And as I smoked my pipe in that good old inn on the high road at Henley-in-Arden I was seized, suddenly and surprisingly, with the desire for one of those sentimental journeys which occasionally afflict the souls of men in the middle thirties. This is a queer age. To be thirty-five is not to be young and not to be old. It is a good age because at thirty-five so many, many of the things which made you sad at twenty only make you laugh. Men of fifty regard you as a stripling, whereas they think of men of forty as contemporaries. At thirty-five a man has not quite climbed that hill whose reverse slope hides for ever those fair valleys of youth which stretch so alluringly to the distance.

I decided to go to Stratford-on-Avon because in this place is a flat grey tombstone, washed by the rains of a century, on which I used to sit when a boy on how many lazy summer afternoons and far into the dusk. It stands in the churchyard of Holy Trinity near the river wall. It is a beautiful place. You hear the Avon rushing through the mill race lower down ; you hear the wind shivering through the lime trees ; every hour you hear the bells of Holy Trinity chime above you out of the grey spire. I have remembered this in so many places and at so many times in my life. Lying in strange beds in strange countries I have closed my eyes and forced myself back to this melancholy seat above the dark river which moves so strongly between its meadows to the green tunnel of Wiers Brake.

As I covered the few miles between Henley and Stratford I looked forward to sitting there again with an eagerness difficult to analyse. I suppose that tombstone is sacred to the memory of my innocence !

Stratford-on-Avon was basking in the sun like an old dog. I lunched in a room full of Americans. They were talking of Shakespeare and John Harvard. A lean, sallow man and his exquisite daughters had been to Shottery, which they called Shattery. I stole off and walked past the Grammar School and round the corner to the left towards Holy Trinity. I always admired the wall flowers which sprout from the top of a high garden wall here.

Is there anything more satisfying than finding a beloved spot just the same? The rooks were cawing, the bells were chiming, the wind was going through the lime avenue ; and, as a background to these sounds and far off, there was a steady rush of water which I knew was the Avon tumbling past the mill. The sexton unlocked the gate of Holy Trinity, admitting me to the tinted coolness of the church, leading me gently, whispering to me as if I were a stranger, to Shakespeare's tomb in the chancel.

In the churchyard was a patchwork of brilliant light and gracious shade ; there were olive-dark yew trees, elms and beech ; and many eighteenth-century tombstones, green as the sea, stood propped against a wall. I went to the river side and found my seat. Cows were standing in the shade, their legs in cool water.

What a country ! My mind went back over the road to York, to Whitby, to the abbeys of the north, to the gold sands of Lindisfarne, to the wild Border Marches, to the sudden beauty of village and the energy of city. I tried to penetrate the minds of people who live in England yet spend their leisure out of England. I can conceive no greater happiness than that of going out into England and finding it almost too English to be true : the little cottages, which vary from county to county, the churches with their naves in Norman England, the great houses, the castles, the incredible cathedrals, the strange little places which will, let us hope, never quite emerge from an earlier and, I believe, happier world. England is one of the easiest countries to see because it does not matter whether you set off north, south, east, or west. Which ever way you go you will in the first mile meet something worth your attention and perhaps your respect. Nearly two centuries of settled life in a small island have crowded England with treasures. There is something almost too opulent in the way our ancient cities and their cathedrals nudge each other on the map. In what other country in the world could a man in one day's journey see anything to compare with Worcester, Hereford and Gloucester, or Cambridge, Ely, Peterborough and Lincoln, or York and Durham, or Jervaulx, Rievaulx and Fountains ?

And there will come a time in any tour of England when most men from a city will feel that no matter how life disappoints them there can be always one thing worth while at the end of the journey : the sight of the wind moving over their own wheat field ; the moon rising behind their own home ; the knowledge that they have fought their way back to the country and have planted their feet in the splendid sanity of English soil.

INDEX

PRINTED BY
JARROLD AND SONS LTD.
NORWICH

METHUEN'S
GENERAL LITERATURE

A SELECTION OF
MESSRS. METHUEN'S
PUBLICATIONS

This Catalogue contains only a selection of the more important books published by Messrs. Methuen. A complete catalogue of their publications may be obtained on application.

ARMSTRONG (Anthony) (' A. A.' of Punch)
WARRIORS AT EASE
WARRIORS STILL AT EASE
PERCIVAL AND I
PERCIVAL AT PLAY
ME AND FRANCES
HOW TO DO IT
Each 3s. 6d. net.
LIVESTOCK IN BARRACKS
Illustrated by E. H. SHEPARD.
6s. net.
TWO LEGS AND FOUR
Illustrated by RENÉ BULL.
5s. net.

BAIN (F. W.)
A DIGIT OF THE MOON
THE DESCENT OF THE SUN
A HEIFER OF THE DAWN
IN THE GREAT GOD'S HAIR
A DRAUGHT OF THE BLUE
AN ESSENCE OF THE DUSK
AN INCARNATION OF THE SNOW
A MINE OF FAULTS
THE ASHES OF A GOD
BUBBLES OF THE FOAM
A SYRUP OF THE BEES
THE LIVERY OF EVE
THE SUBSTANCE OF A DREAM
Each 3s. 6d. net.
AN ECHO OF THE SPHERES
10s. 6d. net.

BALFOUR (Sir Graham)
THE LIFE OF ROBERT LOUIS STEVENSON
Twentieth Edition. 7s. 6d. net.

BARKER (Ernest)
NATIONAL CHARACTER
10s. 6d. net.
GREEK POLITICAL THEORY
14s. net.
CHURCH, STATE AND STUDY
10s. 6d. net.

BELLOC (Hilaire)
PARIS 8s. 6d. net.
THE PYRENEES 8s. 6d. net.
MARIE ANTOINETTE 18s. net.
A HISTORY OF ENGLAND
In 5 Vols. Vols. I, II and III
Each 15s. net.
ON NOTHING
HILLS AND THE SEA
ON SOMETHING
THIS AND THAT AND THE OTHER
ON
FIRST AND LAST
ON EVERYTHING
ON ANYTHING
EMMANUEL BURDEN
A PICKED COMPANY
Each 3s. 6d. net.

BIRMINGHAM (George A.)
A WAYFARER IN HUNGARY
Illustrated. 8s. 6d. net.
SPILLIKINS : ESSAYS. 3s. 6d. net.
SHIPS AND SEALING-WAX : ESSAYS
3s. 6d. net.

BLEEK (Dorothea F.)
ROCK PAINTINGS IN SOUTH AFRICA
Illustrated. £2 2s. net.

BUDGE (Sir E. A. Wallis)
A HISTORY OF ETHIOPIA: NUBIA
AND ABYSSINIA
Illustrated. 2 vols. £3 13s. 6d. net.

CHESTERTON (G. K.)
COME TO THINK OF IT . . .
6s. net.
G.K.C. AS M.C. 7s. 6d. net.
THE BALLAD OF THE WHITE HORSE
3s. 6d. net.
Also Illustrated by ROBERT
AUSTIN. 12s. 6d. net.
CHARLES DICKENS
GENERALLY SPEAKING
ALL THINGS CONSIDERED
TREMENDOUS TRIFLES
FANCIES VERSUS FADS
ALARMS AND DISCURSIONS
A MISCELLANY OF MEN
THE USES OF DIVERSITY
THE OUTLINE OF SANITY
THE FLYING INN
Each 3s. 6d. net.
A GLEAMING COHORT 2s. 6d. net.
WINE, WATER AND SONG
1s. 6d. net.

CLUTTON-BROCK (A.)
WHAT IS THE KINGDOM OF HEAVEN ?
ESSAYS ON ART
SHAKESPEARE'S HAMLET
Each 5s. net.
ESSAYS ON BOOKS 3s. 6d. net.
MORE ESSAYS ON BOOKS
ESSAYS ON LIFE
ESSAYS ON RELIGION
ESSAYS ON LITERATURE AND LIFE
MORE ESSAYS ON RELIGION
Each 6s. net.
SHELLEY, THE MAN AND THE POET
7s. 6d. net.

CRAWLEY (Ernest)
THE MYSTIC ROSE
Revised and Enlarged by THEODORE
BESTERMAN. 2 vols. £1 10s. net.
STUDIES OF SAVAGES AND SEX
Edited by THEODORE BESTERMAN.
10s. 6d. net.

DAVIS (H. W. C.)
EUROPE FROM 800–1789
8s. 6d. net.

DERWENT (Lord)
GOYA. Illustrated. 10s. 6d. net.

DUGDALE (E. T. S.)
GERMAN DIPLOMATIC DOCUMENTS,
1871–1914
Selected from the Documents published by the German Foreign
Office. In 4 vols. Vol. I, 1871–
90. Vol. II, 1891–8. Vol. III,
1898–1910.
Each £1 1s. net.

EDWARDES (Tickner)
THE LORE OF THE HONEY-BEE
Illustrated. 7s. 6d. and 3s. 6d. net.
BEEKEEPING FOR ALL
Illustrated. 3s. 6d. net.
THE BEE-MASTER OF WARRILOW
Illustrated. 7s. 6d. net.
BEE-KEEPING DO'S AND DONT'S
2s. 6d. net.

EINSTEIN (Albert)
RELATIVITY : THE SPECIAL AND
GENERAL THEORY 5s. net.
SIDELIGHTS ON RELATIVITY
3s. 6d. net.
THE MEANING OF RELATIVITY
5s. net.
THE BROWNIAN MOVEMENT
5s. net.

EISLER (Robert)
THE MESSIAH JESUS AND JOHN THE
BAPTIST : according to Flavius
Josephus' hitherto neglected
' Capture of Jerusalem ' and
other Jewish and Christian
sources. Translated by A. HAG-
GERTY KRAPPE.
Illustrated. Demy 8vo. £2 2s. net

FIELD (G. C.)
MORAL THEORY 6s. net.
PLATO AND HIS CONTEMPORARIES
12s. 6d. net.

FYLEMAN (Rose)
FAIRIES AND CHIMNEYS
THE FAIRY GREEN
THE FAIRY FLUTE
THE RAINBOW CAT
EIGHT LITTLE PLAYS FOR CHILDREN
FORTY GOOD-NIGHT TALES
FAIRIES AND FRIENDS
THE ADVENTURE CLUB
FORTY GOOD-MORNING TALES
SEVEN LITTLE PLAYS FOR CHILDREN

FYLEMAN (Rose)—*continued*

TWENTY TEA-TIME TALES
Each 3s. 6d. *net.*

THE DOLLS' HOUSE
Illustrated by MARGARET TEMPEST.
5s. *net.*

GAY GO UP
Illustrated by DECIE MERWIN.
5s. *net.*

THE ROSE FYLEMAN FAIRY BOOK
Illustrated by HILDA MILLER.
10s. 6d. *net.*

A GARLAND OF ROSE'S : COLLECTED POEMS
Illustrated by RENÉ BULL.
8s 6d. *net.*

GIBBON (Edward)

THE DECLINE AND FALL OF THE ROMAN EMPIRE
With Notes, Appendixes and Maps, by J. B. BURY. Illustrated. 7 vols. *Demy* 8vo. 15s. *net each volume.*
Also, unillustrated. *Crown* 8vo.
7s. 6d. *net each volume.*

GLADSTONE (Mary) (Mrs. Drew)

HER DIARIES AND LETTERS
Illustrated. £1 1s. *net.*

GLOVER (T. R.)

VIRGIL
THE CONFLICT OF RELIGIONS IN THE EARLY ROMAN EMPIRE
POETS AND PURITANS
Each 10s. 6d. *net.*
FROM PERICLES TO PHILIP
12s. 6d. *net.*

GRAHAM (Harry)

THE WORLD WE LAUGH IN : More Deportmental Ditties
Illustrated by ' FISH '. *Seventh Edition.* 5s. *net.*
STRAINED RELATIONS
Illustrated by H. STUART MENZIES and HENDY 6s. *net.*
THE WORLD'S WORKERS
Illustrated by ' FOUGASSE '.
5s. *net.*
ADAM'S APPLES
Illustrated by JOHN REYNOLDS.
5s. *net.*

GRAHAME (Kenneth)

THE WIND IN THE WILLOWS
Nineteenth Edition. 7s. 6d. *net.*
Also illustrated by WYNDHAM PAYNE. 7s. 6d. *net.*
Also unillustrated. 3s. 6d. *net.*
See also **Milne (A. A.)**

HADFIELD (J. A.)

PSYCHOLOGY AND MORALS
Eighth Edition. Crown 8vo. 6s. *net.*

HALL (H. R.)

THE ANCIENT HISTORY OF THE NEAR EAST
Illustrated. £1 1s. *net.*
THE CIVILIZATION OF GREECE IN THE BRONZE AGE
Illustrated. £1 10s. *net.*
A SEASON'S WORK AT UR OF THE CHALDEES. Illustrated. £1 5s. *net.*

HERBERT (A. P.)

HONEYBUBBLE & CO. 6s. *net.*
MISLEADING CASES IN THE COMMON LAW. With an Introduction by LORD HEWART. 5s. *net.*
MORE MISLEADING CASES. 5s. *net*
LIGHT ARTICLES ONLY
Illustrated by GEORGE MORROW.
6s. *net.*
WISDOM FOR THE WISE
Illustrated by GEORGE MORROW.
5s. *net.*
THE WHEREFORE AND THE WHY
Illustrated by GEORGE MORROW.
3s. 6d. *net.*
THE BOMBER GIPSY 3s. 6d. *net.*
THE SECRET BATTLE 3s. 6d. *net.*

HOLDSWORTH (Sir W. S.)

A HISTORY OF ENGLISH LAW
Nine Volumes. £1 5s. *net each.*

HUDSON (W. H.)

A SHEPHERD'S LIFE
Illustrated. 10s. 6d. *net.*
Also unillustrated. 3s. 6d. *net.*

HUTTON (Edward)

CITIES OF SICILY
Illustrated. 10s. 6d. *net.*
MILAN AND LOMBARDY
THE CITIES OF ROMAGNA AND THE MARCHES
SIENA AND SOUTHERN TUSCANY
NAPLES AND SOUTHERN ITALY
Illustrated. *Each* 8s. 6d. *net.*
A WAYFARER IN UNKNOWN TUSCANY
THE CITIES OF SPAIN
THE CITIES OF UMBRIA
COUNTRY WALKS ABOUT FLORENCE
ROME
FLORENCE AND NORTHERN TUSCANY
VENICE AND VENETIA
Illustrated. Each 7s. 6d. *net.*

INGE (W. R.), D.D., Dean of St. Paul's

CHRISTIAN MYSTICISM
(The Bampton Lectures of 1899).
Sixth Edition. 7s. 6d. *net.*

KIPLING (Rudyard)
BARRACK-ROOM BALLADS
255th Thousand.
THE SEVEN SEAS
186th Thousand.
THE FIVE NATIONS
143rd Thousand.
DEPARTMENTAL DITTIES
116th Thousand.
THE YEARS BETWEEN
95th Thousand.
Four Editions of these famous
volumes of poems are now pub-
lished, viz. :—
Crown 8vo. Buckram, 7s. 6d. net.
Fcap. 8vo. Cloth, 6s. net.
Leather 7s. 6d. net.
Service Edition. Two volumes
each book. Square Fcap. 8vo.
3s. net each volume.
TWENTY POEMS FROM RUDYARD
KIPLING
482nd Thousand. 1s. net.
A CHOICE OF SONGS
Second Edition. 2s. net.

LAMB (Charles and Mary)
THE COMPLETE WORKS
Edited by E. V. LUCAS. Six
Volumes. With Frontispieces.
6s. net each.
SELECTED LETTERS
Edited by G. T. CLAPTON.
3s. 6d. net.
THE CHARLES LAMB DAY BOOK
Compiled by E. V. LUCAS.
6s. net.

LANKESTER (Sir Ray)
SCIENCE FROM AN EASY CHAIR
SCIENCE FROM AN EASY CHAIR :
Second Series
DIVERSIONS OF A NATURALIST
GREAT AND SMALL THINGS
Illustrated. Each 7s. 6d. net.
SECRETS OF EARTH AND SEA
Illustrated. 8s. 6d. net.

LINDRUM (Walter)
BILLIARDS. Illustrated. 6s. net.

LODGE (Sir Oliver)
MAN AND THE UNIVERSE
7s. 6d. net and 3s. 6d. net.
THE SURVIVAL OF MAN
7s. 6d. net.
RAYMOND 10s. 6d. net.
RAYMOND REVISED 6s. net.
MODERN PROBLEMS 3s. 6d. net.
REASON AND BELIEF 3s. 6d. net.
THE SUBSTANCE OF FAITH
2s. net.

RELATIVITY 1s. net.
CONVICTION OF SURVIVAL 2s. net.

LUCAS (E. V.)
THE LIFE OF CHARLES LAMB
2 Vols. £1 1s. net.
THE COLVINS AND THEIR FRIENDS
£1 1s. net.
VERMEER THE MAGICAL 5s. net.
A WANDERER IN ROME
A WANDERER IN HOLLAND
A WANDERER IN LONDON
LONDON REVISITED (Revised)
A WANDERER IN PARIS
A WANDERER IN FLORENCE
A WANDERER IN VENICE
Each 10s. 6d. net.
A WANDERER AMONG PICTURES
8s. 6d. net.
E. V. LUCAS'S LONDON £1 net.
INTRODUCING LONDON
INTRODUCING PARIS
Each 2s. 6d. net.
THE OPEN ROAD 6s. net.
Also, illustrated by CLAUDE A.
SHEPPERSON, A.R.W.S.
10s. 6d. net.
Also, India Paper.
Leather, 7s. 6d. net.
THE JOY OF LIFE
6s. net. Leather Edition, 7s. 6d. net.
Also, India Paper.
Leather, 7s. 6d. net.
THE GENTLEST ART 6s. 6d. net.
And THE SECOND POST 6s. net.
Also together in one volume.
7s. 6d. net.

FIRESIDE AND SUNSHINE
CHARACTER AND COMEDY
GOOD COMPANY
ONE DAY AND ANOTHER
OLD LAMPS FOR NEW
LOITERER'S HARVEST
LUCK OF THE YEAR
EVENTS AND EMBROIDERIES
A FRONDED ISLE
A ROVER I WOULD BE
GIVING AND RECEIVING
HER INFINITE VARIETY
ENCOUNTERS AND DIVERSIONS
Each 3s. 6d. net.
CLOUD AND SILVER
A BOSWELL OF BAGHDAD
'TWIXT EAGLE AND DOVE
THE PHANTOM JOURNAL
ZIGZAGS IN FRANCE
TURNING THINGS OVER
TRAVELLER'S LUCK
Each 6s. net.

LUCAS (E. V.)—_continued_
ROVING EAST AND ROVING WEST
5s. net.
Mr. Punch's COUNTY SONGS
Illustrated by E. H. SHEPARD.
10s. 6d. net.
' THE MORE I SEE OF MEN . . .'
OUT OF A CLEAR SKY
IF DOGS COULD WRITE
' . . . AND SUCH SMALL DEER '
Each 3s. 6d. net.
THE PEKINESE NATIONAL ANTHEM
Illustrated by PERSIS KIRMSE.
1s. net.
See also **Lamb (Charles).**

LYND (Robert)
IT'S A FINE WORLD   5s. net.
THE GREEN MAN
THE PLEASURES OF IGNORANCE
THE GOLDFISH
THE LITTLE ANGEL
THE BLUE LION
THE PEAL OF BELLS
THE MONEY-BOX
THE ORANGE TREE
Each 3s. 6d. net.

McDOUGALL (William)
AN INTRODUCTION TO SOCIAL
PSYCHOLOGY   10s. 6d. net.
NATIONAL WELFARE AND NATIONAL
DECAY   6s. net.
AN OUTLINE OF PSYCHOLOGY
10s. 6d. net.
AN OUTLINE OF ABNORMAL PSYCHO-
LOGY   15s. net.
BODY AND MIND   12s. 6d. net.
CHARACTER AND THE CONDUCT OF
LIFE   10s. 6d. net.
MODERN MATERIALISM AND EMERG-
ENT EVOLUTION   7s. 6d. net.
ETHICS AND SOME MODERN WORLD
PROBLEMS   7s. 6d. net.

MALLET (Sir C. E.)
A HISTORY OF THE UNIVERSITY OF
OXFORD
In 3 vols.   Each £1 1s. net.

MAETERLINCK (Maurice)
THE BLUE BIRD   6s. net.
Also, illustrated by F. CAYLEY
ROBINSON.   10s. 6d. net.
OUR ETERNITY   6s. net.
THE UNKNOWN GUEST   6s. net.
POEMS   5s. net.
THE WRACK OF THE STORM
6s. net.
THE BURGOMASTER OF STILEMONDE
5s. net.
THE BETROTHAL   6s. net.

MOUNTAIN PATHS   6s. net.
THE GREAT SECRET   7s. 6d. net.
THE CLOUD THAT LIFTED and THE
POWER OF THE DEAD
7s. 6d. net.
MARY MAGDALENE   2s. net.

MARLOWE (Christopher)
THE WORKS. In 6 volumes.
General Editor, R. H. Case.
THE LIFE OF MARLOWE, by C. F.
TUCKER BROOKE, and DIDO.
Edited by the Same. 8s. 6d. net.
TAMBURLAINE, I AND II. Edited by
U. M. Ellis-Fermor.
10s. 6d. net.

MASEFIELD (John)
ON THE SPANISH MAIN
8s. 6d. net.
A SAILOR'S GARLAND   3s. 6d. net.
SEA LIFE IN NELSON'S TIME
7s. 6d. net.

METHUEN (Sir A.)
AN ANTHOLOGY OF MODERN VERSE
195th Thousand.
SHAKESPEARE TO HARDY: An
Anthology of English Lyrics
26th Thousand.
Each, Cloth, 6s. net.
Leather, 7s. 6d. net.

MILNE (A. A.)
BY WAY OF INTRODUCTION
6s. net.
TOAD OF TOAD HALL
A Play founded on Kenneth
Grahame's ' The Wind in the
Willows.'   5s. net.
THOSE WERE THE DAYS: Collected
Stories   7s. 6d. net.
NOT THAT IT MATTERS
IF I MAY
THE SUNNY SIDE
THE RED HOUSE MYSTERY
ONCE A WEEK
THE HOLIDAY ROUND
THE DAY'S PLAY
MR. PIM PASSES BY
Each 3s. 6d. net.
WHEN WE WERE VERY YOUNG
Twentieth Edition. 206th Thousand.
WINNIE-THE-POOH
Tenth Edition. 118th Thousand.
NOW WE ARE SIX
Fifth Edition. 119th Thousand.
THE HOUSE AT POOH CORNER
Third Edition. 105th Thousand.
Each illustrated by E. H. SHEPARD.
7s. 6d. net.
Leather, 10s. 6d net.

MILNE (A. A.)—*continued*

THE CHRISTOPHER ROBIN STORY
BOOK. *Second Edition.*
Illustrated by E. H. SHEPARD.
5s. *net.*
THE CHRISTOPHER ROBIN BIRTH-
DAY BOOK
Illustrated by E. H. SHEPARD.
3s. 6d. *net.*

**MILNE (A. A.) and FRASER-SIM-
SON (H.)**

FOURTEEN SONGS FROM ' WHEN WE
WERE VERY YOUNG '
Twelfth Edition. 7s. 6d. *net.*
TEDDY BEAR AND OTHER SONGS
FROM ' WHEN WE WERE VERY
YOUNG' 7s. 6d. *net.*
THE KING'S BREAKFAST
Third Edition. 3s. 6d. *net.*
SONGS FROM ' NOW WE ARE SIX '
Second Edition. 7s. 6d. *net.*
MORE ' VERY YOUNG ' SONGS
7s. 6d. *net.*
THE HUMS OF POOH 7s. 6d. *net.*
Words by A. A. MILNE.
Music by H. FRASER-SIMSON.
Decorations by E. H. SHEPARD.

MORTON (H. V.)

THE HEART OF LONDON 3s. 6d. *net.*
Also with Scissor Cuts by L.
HUMMEL. 7s. 6d. *net.*
THE SPELL OF LONDON
THE NIGHTS OF LONDON
Each 3s. 6d. *net.*
IN SEARCH OF ENGLAND
THE CALL OF ENGLAND
IN SEARCH OF SCOTLAND
IN SEARCH OF IRELAND
Each illustrated. 7s. 6d. *net.*
THE SOUL OF SCOTLAND 1s. *net.*

NEUBURGER (Albert)

THE TECHNICAL ARTS AND SCIENCES
OF THE ANCIENTS.
Translated by H. L. BROSE.
Illustrated. £2 2s. *net.*

OMAN (Sir Charles)

A HISTORY OF THE ART OF WAR IN
THE MIDDLE AGES, A.D. 378–1485
2 vols. Illustrated. £1 16s. *net.*
STUDIES IN THE NAPOLEONIC WARS
8s. 6d. *net.*

PERRY (W. J.)

THE ORIGIN OF MAGIC AND
RELIGION
THE GROWTH OF CIVILIZATION
Each 6s. *net.*
THE CHILDREN OF THE SUN
£1 1s. *net.*

PETRIE (Sir Flinders)

A HISTORY OF EGYPT
In 6 Volumes.
Vol. I. FROM THE 1ST TO THE
XVITH DYNASTY.
Eleventh Edition, Revised.
12s. *net.*
Vol. II. THE XVIITH AND XVIIITH
DYNASTIES.
Seventh Edition, Revised. 9s. *net.*
Vol. III. XIXTH TO XXXTH
DYNASTIES
Third Edition. 12s. *net.*
Vol. IV. EGYPT UNDER THE
PTOLEMAIC DYNASTY
By EDWYN BEVAN. 15s. *net.*
Vol. V. EGYPT UNDER ROMAN RULE
By J. G. MILNE.
Third Edition, Revised. 12s. *net.*
Vol. VI. EGYPT IN THE MIDDLE
AGES
By STANLEY LANE POOLE.
Fourth Edition. 10s. *net.*

**PONSONBY OF SHULBREDE
(Lord)**

ENGLISH DIARIES £1 1s. *net.*
MORE ENGLISH DIARIES
12s. 6d. *net.*
SCOTTISH AND IRISH DIARIES
10s. 6d. *net.*

RUTTER (Frank)

EL GRECO
Illustrated. £1 16s. *net.*

STEVENSON (R. L.)

THE LETTERS
Edited by Sir SIDNEY COLVIN. 4
Vols. *Each* 6s. *net.*

SURTEES (R. S.)

HANDLEY CROSS
MR. SPONGE'S SPORTING TOUR
ASK MAMMA
MR. FACEY ROMFORD'S HOUNDS
PLAIN OR RINGLETS ?
HILLINGDON HALL
Each illustrated. 7s. 6d. *net.*
JORROCKS'S JAUNTS AND JOLLITIES
HAWBUCK GRANGE
Each illustrated. 6s. *net.*

TAYLOR (A. E.)

PLATO : THE MAN AND HIS WORK
£1 1s. *net.*
PLATO : TIMÆUS AND CRITIAS
6s. *net.*
ELEMENTS OF METAPHYSICS
12s. 6d. *net.*

TILDEN (William T.)
THE ART OF LAWN TENNIS
Revised Edition
SINGLES AND DOUBLES
Each illustrated. 6s. net.
THE COMMON SENSE OF LAWN
TENNIS
MATCH PLAY AND THE SPIN OF THE
BALL
Each illustrated. 5s. net.

TILESTON (Mary W.)
DAILY STRENGTH FOR DAILY NEEDS
Thirty-fourth Edition. 3s. 6d. net.
India Paper. *Leather,* 6s. net.

TRAPP (Oswald Graf)
THE ARMOURY OF THE CASTLE OF
CHURBURG
Translated by J. G. MANN.
Richly illustrated.
Limited to 400 copies.
£4 14s. 6d. net.

UNDERHILL (Evelyn)
MYSTICISM. *Revised Edition.* 15s. net.
THE LIFE OF THE SPIRIT AND THE
LIFE OF TO-DAY   7s. 6d. net.
MAN AND THE SUPERNATURAL
7s. 6d. net.
CONCERNING THE INNER LIFE
2s. net.
THE HOUSE OF THE SOUL 2s. net.

VARDON (Harry)
HOW TO PLAY GOLF
Illustrated. *Nineteenth Edition.*
5s. net.

WAND (J. W. C.)
THE DEVELOPMENT OF SACRA-
MENTALISM 6s. net.
A HISTORY OF THE MODERN CHURCH
8s. 6d. net.

WILDE (Oscar)
THE WORKS
In 16 Vols. *Each* 6s. 6d. net.
I. LORD ARTHUR SAVILE'S CRIME
AND THE PORTRAIT OF MR. W. H.
II. THE DUCHESS OF PADUA
III. POEMS
IV. LADY WINDERMERE'S FAN
V. A WOMAN OF NO IMPORTANCE
VI. AN IDEAL HUSBAND
VII. THE IMPORTANCE OF BEING
EARNEST
VIII. A HOUSE OF POMEGRANATES
IX. INTENTIONS
X. DE PROFUNDIS AND PRISON
LETTERS
XI. ESSAYS
XII. SALOME, A FLORENTINE
TRAGEDY, and LA SAINTE
COURTISANE
XIV. SELECTED PROSE OF OSCAR
WILDE
XV. ART AND DECORATION
XVI. FOR LOVE OF THE KING
5s. net.
XVII. VERA, OR THE NIHILISTS

WILLIAMSON (G. C.)
THE BOOK OF FAMILLE ROSE
Richly Illustrated. £8 8s. net.

Methuen & Co. Ltd., 36 Essex Street, London, W.C.2